Guide to Tax and Financial Planning, 2009

Guide to Tax and Financial Planning, 2009

Including Analysis of the 2008 Tax Law Changes

PricewaterhouseCoopers LLP

John Wiley & Sons, Inc.

NOTE: This guide was prepared and published based on the tax rules and regulations in effect as of September 29, 2008.

Copyright © 2009 by PricewaterhouseCoopers LLP. All rights reserved.
"PricewaterhouseCoopers" refers to PricewaterhouseCoopers LLP (a Delaware limited liability partnership) or, as the context requires, the PricewaterhouseCoopers global network or any other member firms of the network, each of which is a separate and independent legal entity.

This document is provided by PricewaterhouseCoopers LLP for general guidance only, and does not constitute the provision of legal advice, accounting services, investment advice, written tax advice under Circular 230, or professional advice of any kind. The information provided herein was not intended or written to be used, and it cannot be used, for the purpose of avoiding tax penalties that may be imposed on any taxpayer and should not be used as a substitute for consultation with professional tax, accounting, legal, or other competent advisors. Before making any decision or taking any action, you should consult a professional advisor who has been provided with all pertinent facts relevant to your particular situation.

The information is provided "as is" with no assurance or guarantee of completeness, accuracy, or timeliness of the information, and without warranty of any kind, express or implied, including but not limited to warranties of performance, merchantability, and fitness for a particular purpose.

Published by John Wiley & Sons, Inc., Hoboken, New Jersey.

Published simultaneously in Canada.

No part of this publication may be reproduced, stored in a retrieval system, or transmitted in any form or by any means, electronic, mechanical, photocopying, recording, scanning, or otherwise, except as permitted under Section 107 or 108 of the 1976 United States Copyright Act, without either the prior written permission of the Publisher, or authorization through payment of the appropriate per-copy fee to the Copyright Clearance Center, Inc., 222 Rosewood Drive, Danvers, MA 01923, (978) 750-8400, fax (978) 646-8600, or on the web at www.copyright.com. Requests to the Publisher for permission should be addressed to the Permissions Department, John Wiley & Sons, Inc., 111 River Street, Hoboken, NJ 07030, (201) 748-6011, fax (201) 748-6008, or online at http://www.wiley.com/go/permissions.

Limit of Liability/Disclaimer of Warranty: While the publisher and author have used their best efforts in preparing this book, they make no representations or warranties with respect to the accuracy or completeness of the contents of this book and specifically disclaim any implied warranties of merchantability or fitness for a particular purpose. No warranty may be created or extended by sales representatives or written sales materials. The advice and strategies contained herein may not be suitable for your situation. You should consult with a professional where appropriate. Neither the publisher nor author shall be liable for any loss of profit or any other commercial damages, including but not limited to special, incidental, consequential, or other damages.

For general information on our other products and services or for technical support, please contact our Customer Care Department within the United States at (800) 762-2974, outside the United States at (317) 572-3993 or fax (317) 572-4002.

Wiley also publishes its books in a variety of electronic formats. Some content that appears in print may not be available in electronic books. For more information about Wiley products, visit our web site at www.wiley.com.

Library of Congress Cataloging-in-Publication Data:

ISBN 978-0-470-28498-8

Printed in the United States of America

10 9 8 7 6 5 4 3 2 1

Contents

Acknowledgments	xv
Introduction	xvii
About PricewaterhouseCoopers	xviii
How to Use This Book	xix
Let's Get Started	xxii
Tax Law Changes and Financial Planning	**1**
Chapter 1: The Year Ahead	**3**
Recent Legislation	5
The Alternative Minimum Tax	6
Individual Rates on Income, Capital Gains, and Dividends	7
Estate Tax	8
Be Prepared	9
Chapter 2: Getting Ready for 2010	**11**
Income Tax	11
Income Tax Rates	12
Phaseout of Phaseouts for Higher-Income Taxpayers	12
Reduction in Child Tax Credit	13
Reduced Tax Rate on Qualified Dividends	13
Reduced Tax Rate on Long-Term Capital Gains	13

vi   *Contents*

Expensing of Business Property	13
Mortgage Insurance Premiums	14
Mortgage Foreclosure Forgiveness	14
Roth IRA Conversions Available to all Taxpayers	14
Estate Tax	16
Gift Tax	17
Generation-Skipping Tax	18

Chapter 3: Investments and Stock Options — 21

Tax Issues Related to Investing	22
Capital Gains	23
Exceptions to the 15 Percent Rate	25
Collectibles, Qualified Small Business Stock, and Depreciated Real Estate	26
No More Advantage for Five-Year Gains	27
Netting Rules	27
Capital Losses	29
Wash Sale Rule	30
Protecting and Postponing Stock Gains	31
Qualified Small Business Stock	32
Careful Record Keeping: Identification of Securities	33
Dividends	34
Short Sales	35
Foreign Tax Credit	36
Margin Accounts	36
Interest Expense and Investment-Related Expenses	36
Investment Vehicles and Stock Options	39
Mutual Funds	39
Exchange-Traded Funds	41
Real Estate Investment Trusts	41
Preferred Stocks	41
Alternative Investments	42
At-Risk Rules	43
Passive Activity Losses	44
Tax-Exempt and Taxable Bonds	45
Taxable Tax-Exempt Bonds	46
Bond Premium or Discount	47
Nonqualified Stock Options	48
Incentive Stock Options	50

Contents

The "Pension Max" Technique	102
Liquidity for Estate Taxes	103
Whose Life?	103
How Much Coverage Is Enough?	104
For How Long?	105
What Kind of Insurance?	105
Diversification	106
Owner and Beneficiary	106
Policy Owner	106
The Insured as Owner	106
The Spouse as Owner	107
The Children or Grandchildren as Owners	107
A Qualified Plan as Owner	108
An Irrevocable Trust as Owner	108
The Three-Year Rule	110
A Partnership or Limited Liability Company as Owner	110
A Corporation as Owner	110
Policy Beneficiary	110
The Irrevocable Life Insurance Trust	111
Withdrawal Right	112
Contingent Marital Deduction	113
Choice of Trustee and Trustee Powers	113
Generation-Skipping Consideration	113
Survivorship Life Insurance Complications	114
Community Property Complications	114
Life Insurance as an Investment	114
Private Placement Variable Life Insurance	115
Hedge Fund Life Insurance	115
Education Funding	116
Retirement Accumulation, aka the Private Pension	117
Charitable Contributions	118
Donations of Life Insurance	118
Charitable Remainder Trust and Asset Replacement Trust	119
Insuring Businesses and Their Owners	120
Key Person Life Insurance	120
Survivor Income, Estate Taxes, and Inheritances	121
Insurance Funding for Buy-Sell Agreements	121
Insurance Funding for Cross-Purchase Agreements	122
Nonqualified Deferred Compensation	123

Stock Option Exercise Methods	52
Restricted Stock and Other Stock-Based Compensation	54
Putting It All Together: Structuring a Tax-Efficient, Diversified Portfolio	55
Idea Checklist	57

Chapter 4: Retirement Planning — 59

Employer Plans	61
Qualified Retirement Plans	61
Defined Contribution Plans	62
Defined Benefit Pension Plans	67
Nonqualified Deferred Compensation Plans	68
Your Resources	69
Keogh Plans	70
Simplified Employee Pension Plans	71
Traditional and Roth Individual Retirement Accounts	72
Roth 401(k)	73
Higher Contribution Limits	73
Traditional Individual Retirement Accounts	75
Conversions to Roth Individual Retirement Accounts	77
Tax Credit for Retirement Saving	81
Charitable Remainder Trusts	82
Tax-Deferred Annuities	82
Universal Variable Life Insurance	83
Professional Retirement Services	84
Social Security	84
Required Retirement Plan Distributions	86
Idea Checklist	90

Chapter 5: Life Insurance — 93

Types of Life Insurance	93
Term Life Insurance (and Variations)	94
Universal Life Insurance	95
Whole-Life or Ordinary Life Insurance	96
Mixed Whole-Life and Term Insurance	97
Variable Life Insurance	98
Second-to-Die or Survivorship Insurance	98
Insuring the Breadwinner	99
How Much is Enough?	100
For How Long?	101

Split-Dollar Insurance Arrangements	124
Employee Split-Dollar	126
Shareholder Split-Dollar	126
Private Split-Dollar	127
Arrangements before September 13, 2003	127
Income Tax Rules	128
Life Insurance Defined	128
Modified Endowment Contracts: When Life Insurance Is an Annuity	129
Income Tax Advantages	129
Interest on Policy Loans	130
Lapse or Surrender of Policy	130
Foreign Life Insurance	131
Life Insurance Terminology and Illustrations	131
Quick Pay Premiums	131
Minimum Depositing	132
Life Insurance Illustrations	132
Policy Selection and Servicing	133
Idea Checklist	134

Chapter 6: Tax Advantages of Home Ownership   135

Tax Benefits of Owning a Home	136
Mortgage Interest	136
Home Equity Loans	137
Mortgage Insurance Premiums	138
Vacation Homes	138
Rental Properties	140
Home Office Deduction	141
Exclusive and Regular Use	141
Principal Place of Business	142
Personal Residence Trust	143
Home Sales	144
Principal Residence Gains Exclusion	144
Qualifying for the $500,000 Exclusion	145
Partial Exclusion	145
Partial Exclusion Rule for Joint Filers	146
Property Previously Used for Nonresidential Purpose	146

x Contents

Home Purchases	148
Real Estate Taxes	148
Mortgage Points	149
First-Time Homebuyer Tax Credit	151
Reverse Mortgages	152
Idea Checklist	152

Chapter 7: How to Maximize Savings for Education	**155**
Qualified Section 529 Tuition Programs	156
What Expenses Qualify?	158
Gift and Estate Tax Breaks	162
Coverdell Education Savings Accounts	162
Roth IRAs	165
Traditional IRAs	165
HOPE (Helping Outstanding Pupils Educationally) Scholarships and Lifetime Learning Credits	166
U.S. Savings Bonds	167
Home Equity Loans	169
Student Loans	169
Relatives	170
Income Shifting and Capital Gains	170
Employer Education Assistance	172
Idea Checklist	175

Chapter 8: Account-Based Health-Care Arrangements	**177**
Health Savings Accounts	177
Eligibility	179
Contribution Limits	179
Health Reimbursement Arrangements	180
Flexible Spending Accounts	181

Chapter 9: Estate Planning Ideas	**183**
How Estate and Gift Taxes Work	185
Amounts Exempt from Tax	186
Gift and Estate Tax Rates	187
Planning for Phasedown and Repeal of the Estate Tax	190
Draft a Will	192
Review How Your Property Is Owned	193

Consider State Death Taxes	194
Give Gifts	195
Consider Valuation Discounts	197
Consider Trusts	199
Credit Shelter or Family Trust	199
Irrevocable Life Insurance Trust	200
Grantor Retained Annuity Trust	201
Qualified Personal Residence Trust	202
Dynasty Trust	203
Charitable Remainder Trust	203
Charitable Lead Trust	204
Intentionally Defective Trust	206
Qualified Domestic Trust	206
Stock Option Trust	207
Effect of Reduced Tax Rates on Dividends	207
Trustee's Investment Decisions	208
Allocation of Expenses	208
Give a Roth IRA	209
Pay Gift Taxes Now	209
Idea Checklist	210
Chapter 10: Charitable Giving	**213**
Defining Charitable Deductions	213
Making Charitable Contributions	214
Deductible Contributions—Quick Guide	215
Nondeductible Contributions—Quick Guide	216
Valuation Issues	217
Retail Property	218
Stocks and Bonds	219
Closely Held Businesses	220
Notes	221
Life Insurance	221
Real Estate	221
Artwork: Paintings, Antiques, and Other Art Objects	222
Jewelry and Gems	223
Used Cars, Boats, and Aircraft	223
Used Clothing and Household Goods	224
Hobby Collections	224

xii Contents

Appraisals and Substantiation Requirements	225
Penalties for Overvaluation	227
Reduction of Contribution Amount	228
Limitations on Your Deduction	230
The 50 Percent Limitation	232
The 30 Percent Limitation	232
The 20 Percent Limitation	233
Private Foundations	233
Nonoperating Foundations	234
Operating Foundations	234
Pass-Through Private Foundations	234
Tax Compliance and Operating Rules for Private Foundations	235
Alternatives to Private Foundations	235
Donor-Advised Funds	236
Other Alternatives	237

Year-End Tax Savings Strategies   239

Chapter 11: Quick Planning Guide   241

Tax Reduction	242
Tax Deferral	243
Income Shifting	245
Year-End Capital Gains Checkup	246
Year-End Alternative Minimum Tax Diagnosis	248

Chapter 12: Accelerating Deductions   251

State and Local Taxes	254
Real Estate Property Taxes	255
Interest	255
Home Mortgage Interest	255
Business Interest	256
Investment Interest	257
Passive Activity Interest	257
Student Loan Interest	258
Personal Interest	259
Medical Expenses	259
Charitable Contributions	260
Property Donations	262
Substantiation Requirements	264
Deferred Giving	265

Passive Activity Losses	266
Casualty Losses	268
Miscellaneous Itemized Deductions	269
Moving Expenses	271
Idea Checklist	272

Chapter 13: Deferring Income — 275

Year-End Bonuses	277
Deferred Compensation	278
Stock Options or Stock Appreciation Rights	281
Treasury Bills and Bank Certificates	282
Dividends	282
Installment Sales	283
U.S. Savings Bonds	284
Annuities	284
Individual Retirement Accounts	286
Regular 401(k) Plans and Roth 401(k) Plans	286
Shifting Income to Family Members	287

Chapter 14: Alternative Minimum Tax — 293

Understanding the Alternative Minimum Tax	294
Alternative Minimum Tax Computation	296
The More, the Not-So-Merrier	297
Minimum Tax Credit	299
Top Ten Items That May Cause the AMT	300
An Unpleasant Surprise for Many	301
Alternative Minimum Tax-Planning Strategies	302
Taxpayers Subject to the Alternative Minimum Tax for 2008 Only	302
Taxpayers Subject to the Alternative Minimum Tax for 2008 and Beyond	303

Chapter 15: Year-End Planning for Business Owners — 307

Increased Section 179 Expense Election	309
Increased Bonus Depreciation	310
Retirement Plans	311
Bonuses and Deferred Compensation	312
Income Deferral or Acceleration	313

xiv *Contents*

Taxation of C Corporations	314
Alternative Minimum Tax Planning	315
Accounting Method Changes	316
Personal Holding Company Tax	316
Succession Planning	317
Buy-Sell Agreements	318
Deferred Compensation Elections	318
Covenant Not to Compete	319
Earn-Out (Contingent Sale Price)	319
Importance of Early Planning	319
Do Not Wait to Plan	320
International Financial Reporting Standards	321
C Corporation versus S Corporation Comparison	321
A Nuts-and-Bolts Review	**325**
Chapter 16: Fundamental Tax Concepts	**327**
Gross Income	327
Adjusted Gross Income	328
Modified Adjusted Gross Income	329
Itemized or Standard Deductions	329
Personal and Dependent Exemptions	330
Marital Status	331
A Tax Credit or a Deduction	331
Taxable Income	334
Marginal and Effective Tax Rates	334
Social Security Taxes and Benefits	337
Marriage Penalty	338
Accountable Plan	339
Tax Effects of Alimony	340
Social Security Taxes for Domestic Employees	341
Estimated Tax Payments	341
January Tax Strategy Idea Checklist	344
Conclusion	345
About the Authors	**347**
Index	**349**

Acknowledgments

Writing a book, as you might imagine, is a highly collaborative effort. At PricewaterhouseCoopers, we gratefully acknowledge the assistance of key colleagues, including:

    Kent Allison

    Suzie Amer

    Rachel Bormann

    Evelyn Capassakis

    Kathleen Chon

    Sheryl Eighner

    Christopher Essig

    William R. Fleming

    Daniel L. Hall

    Michael A. James

    Ryan Lauridsen

    Robert D. Lyerly

    Christina M. Malek

    James M. Medeiros

Martha Michael
Bernard Palmer
Alfred Peguero
Michael S. Ryan
Allison P. Shipley
Scott A. Torgan
Jason Uetrecht
Vincent Vaccaro
Richard S. Wagman
Becky Weaver
Karl Weger
Karlyn J. Wright
William Zatorski

This book is dedicated to the Private Company Services (PCS) partners and professionals of PricewaterhouseCoopers LLP, who focus on serving the unique needs of private companies and their owners. Working one-on-one with our clients as they grow and evolve to meet the challenges that lie ahead, while helping them manage complex business and personal wealth accumulation issues, is what defines us as a distinct practice.

We hope that you find *Guide to Tax and Financial Planning, 2009* to be a valuable tool that you can use in your personal financial planning endeavors.

RICHARD KOHAN
Principle, Private Company Services
Personal Financial Services Practice

MARK T. NASH
Partner, Private Company Services
Personal Financial Services Practice

BRITTNEY B. SAKS
Partner, Private Company Services
Personal Financial Services Practice

Introduction

Taxes are collected every year—but the manner in which they are collected constantly changes.

Whether there is a major overhaul or some relatively obscure provision, there is always something new to deal with—developments that bring opportunity for some and additional tax burdens for others. Sometimes fairness or tax simplification is the goal behind these changes; at other times, it is special-interest legislation affecting only a small group of taxpayers; occasionally, it is across-the-board relief.

Congress did pass some new tax legislation in 2008. In addition, over the past few years, Congress has made a great number of changes that take effect at different times, or expire at set dates. Layered on this complexity are more than two dozen rules that are adjusted annually for inflation. These varying dates and inflation adjustments make using the new rules and planning for tomorrow extremely confusing and complex. And of course, as we go to press, the country is preparing to elect a new president, on whose agenda tax reform will almost certainly appear.

How can you keep up with all the changes and know which of them can help you save money and plan for your future? The goal of this book is to give you the tools to achieve your financial goals through personal financial planning and proactive tax planning. It identifies the major areas of the tax law that have been or will be changed, including tax rate changes, new deductions and credits, and often-overlooked ways to save tax dollars. It also provides suggestions about how to maximize your current and future financial position. Some examples are: reducing education costs by taking advantage of important tax breaks, utilizing recently expanded tax breaks for company-sponsored retirement plans and individual retirement accounts, and planning strategies around the ever-changing estate and gift tax rules.

This book spells out the most important features of all these changes as well as the impact of important business tax breaks. It clearly identifies and explains new tax-saving advantages and strategies that can benefit you now, and in the coming years.

About PricewaterhouseCoopers

PricewaterhouseCoopers' Private Company Services (PCS) practice is an integrated team of audit, tax, and advisory professionals who focus on the unique needs of private companies and their owners. Within the group, professionals concentrate on the needs of manufacturing, retail, wholesale, distribution, construction, and food and beverage companies, as well as on the needs of law firms and other professional service organizations. Private Company Services professionals are committed to delivering cost-effective, practical solutions and proactive services to their clients.

Our PCS practice includes personal financial services professionals, a national network of experienced personal financial advisors who can help you design strategies to effectively preserve and enhance your wealth. We recognize that you are unique and will require specific services depending on your personal financial goals. Our personal financial services professionals carefully assess our clients' personal financial positions and goals—strategically guiding them through the challenges of financial planning today, including the proliferation of new investment vehicles, insurance products, and retirement plans; changes in tax law and regulations; a volatile economy; and fluctuating interest rates. The result is the execution of a plan based on independent and timely professional financial advice that is designed to manage risk and ensure long-term financial security. For more information about PricewaterhouseCoopers' Private Company Services, visit www.pwc.com/pcs.

PricewaterhouseCoopers (www.pwc.com) provides industry-focused assurance, tax, and advisory services to build public trust and enhance value for its clients and their stakeholders. More than 140,000 people in 149 countries across our network share their thinking, experience, and solutions to develop fresh perspectives and practical advice.

How to Use This Book

In each chapter, we highlight and explain the vital sections of new tax rules, with concrete examples that tell taxpayers what they need to know to build a solid base for planning and to begin mapping their own financial planning strategies. However, oversimplification is dangerous. We strongly recommend that taxpayers understand at least the basic provisions of the law before taking any action—that is why we wrote this book. Here is what lies ahead:

- **Chapter 1** looks ahead at the uncertain landscape taxpayers face as many existing tax code provisions approach expiration and as a new president takes office.
- The year 2010 figures prominently in a variety of tax legislation. **Chapter 2** identifies the several key tax provisions scheduled to sunset in 2010 and what that will mean to taxpayers.
- The tax issues related to investments and stock options are the subject of **Chapter 3**. The tax consequences of many investment vehicles vary widely and change annually; a clear and current understanding of these consequences is critical to the development of a sound investment strategy.
- Retirement planning should be part of each taxpayer's strategy from the beginning of employment. **Chapter 4** discusses how to make planning for retirement a reality.
- **Chapter 5** discusses the different types of life insurance policies as well as their various features and tax implications.
- For many, their home is the biggest item on their balance sheet and in their budget. **Chapter 6** explores the tax advantages and subtleties of home ownership.
- The escalating costs of higher education can make paying tuition and other expenses difficult. Fortunately, the tax law provides incentives for both saving for education in the future and paying for education now. **Chapter 7** covers how to maximize tax law opportunities to save and pay for education.
- The high costs of medical care have become more challenging as health-care-related expenses continue to rise. Account-based health-care arrangements, explained in **Chapter 8**, provide some important options for paying health-care costs on a tax-advantaged basis.
- How can you structure your estate for a time when the estate tax is gradually phasing out, only to reappear after 2010?

- **Chapter 9** offers estate planning ideas that help in planning through uncertainty.
- **Chapter 10** gives detailed guidance on the rules for deducting charitable contributions.
- **Chapter 11** sums up important strategies for year-end tax planning in a quick planning guide.
- When planning to reduce your taxes, moving deductions into the current tax year can save significant dollars. **Chapter 12** describes those deductions that may be best to accelerate.
- **Chapter 13** applies the same year-end tax-saving principles to deferring income from one year to the next.
- **Chapter 14** describes the alternative minimum tax (AMT), discusses who may be subject to it, and explains tax-planning implications to avoid or minimize it.
- Year-end planning for a business owner involves all of the personal strategies previously discussed, but does not end there. Many additional considerations that can generate tax savings for business owners and for their companies can be found in **Chapter 15**.
- **Chapter 16** provides a nuts-and-bolts review of basic tax concepts as they have evolved in the Internal Revenue Code and puts recent changes into context.

Throughout each chapter are a number of special features. Most of these are *Observations*—brief, clear explanations of specific features of the new law and how they will be applied. Many *Examples* are provided. There are also occasional passages labeled *Caution*, warning of a possible blunder taxpayers might make based on a misinterpretation of the law. A *Legislative Alert* is highlighted to warn you of possible changes to come. Congress may enact these changes after this book has been completed. In addition, most chapters contain an *Idea Checklist*, offering you a quick summary of concepts to be used for taking advantage of today's favorable tax rules.

Let's Get Started

If you are like most people, taking responsibility for your financial planning, particularly tax planning, is an intimidating and daunting task. Most of us do not look forward to the day when we get to deal closely with the Internal Revenue Service, but we can benefit greatly if we take the initiative, educate ourselves, and make the effort to overcome our fears. Financial planning empowers you to take charge of your financial future, and tax planning is a large part of that process. The best way to achieve your financial goals is to invest the time and effort, form a strategy, and then act on it. You will be glad you did.

Tax Law Changes and Financial Planning

Chapter 1
The Year Ahead

Looking back at the past year and ahead at 2009, one constant appears immediately: change.

After four years of robust growth and moderate inflation, the global economy switched gears. The first half of 2008 brought slowed growth amid rising inflationary pressures and continued dislocations in financial markets. As the year progressed, emerging markets enjoyed continued growth despite rising commodity prices, while elsewhere the fallout from the credit crunch that struck in 2007 continued to be felt in weak housing markets.

Domestically, record oil prices and rising food prices, along with the continued weakness of the dollar, continue to drive inflation. In response, the Federal Reserve lowered interest rates throughout much of 2008. Declining home values in many parts of the country and falling U.S. stock prices are increasing the financial pressure on households already saddled with record amounts of debt.

Looking ahead, economists expect the economic slowdown to continue well into 2009. And while domestic spending will likely remain restrained for the foreseeable future, U.S. growth may be supported by a reasonably strong global economy and a weak dollar.

In September, the financial system entered an unprecedented crisis marked by the failure and sale of prominent Wall Street firms and the government bailout of several large financial institutions. As this book went to press, the U.S. government began discussions on what is considered to be the biggest government intervention in financial markets in U.S. history—and which could require a significant commitment of taxpayer funds. Thoughtful investors continue to evaluate how these shifts in the financial markets could or should impact their investment strategies. In addition, those who follow tax legislation posit that any government intervention to stabilize the financial markets may only exacerbate a federal budget already in the red from a war on terrorism and domestic spending priorities. Is it possible to meet all of these Congressional objectives without increasing tax revenue? And, if not, upon whose shoulders should the added tax burden fall?

In the midst of these tremendous economic shifts, U.S. taxpayers are preparing for more ambiguity. In the run-up to the presidential election, both candidates have promised big change. And it is relatively certain that, regardless of who wins in November, at least some of that change will arrive by way of the tax code. New presidents almost always propose some sort of adjustment to the tax system within their first year in office, and 2009 should be no different, due to a number of tax code sunsets scheduled for midnight, December 31, 2010.

The Economic Growth and Tax Relief Reconciliation Act of 2001 and the Jobs and Growth Tax Relief Reconciliation Act of 2003 enacted a number of tax cuts that are set to expire after 2010. If that happens, tax rates on wages, dividends, and capital gains will rise; and the estate tax, which has been on a gradual course toward a full one-year elimination in 2010, would return to its highest levels in a decade. Several other provisions, including increased tax benefits relating to children, marriage penalty relief, and education, will also expire. All told, this would cause a tax increase for individuals of $250 billion or more—overnight.

At the same time, as legislators work to find a way to fund individual tax relief, given the size of the federal budget deficit and concern over the competitiveness of the U.S. tax system, substantial corporate tax reform could come into play in 2009.

The combination of the economic slowdown and the increased likelihood of tax reform may drive individuals to reevaluate their tax and financial plans. The chapters ahead are designed to assist those individuals in recharting their courses.

Recent Legislation

In the past year, we've seen relatively little major tax-related legislation, but some bills have been passed that will impact filings.

In addition to the recovery rebates, or stimulus payments, paid to qualifying individuals, the Economic Stimulus Act of 2008 contains certain tax benefits for businesses. Two provisions, addressing expensing and bonus depreciation of property, accelerate tax benefits for businesses that purchase qualifying property this year. The Act increases the maximum amount of annual property purchases that can be expensed to $250,000 in 2008. Under the new provision, the total amount of qualifying property that can be purchased before the expensing limit reduces is increased; the previous total of $510,000 is now $800,000 for 2008. The Economic Stimulus Act also provides a 50 percent special depreciation allowance for qualifying property purchased in 2008. Additionally, the Act increases the total depreciation amount a business can deduct for certain passenger automobiles used in business.

Chapter 15 contains a more detailed discussion of the business provisions of the Economic Stimulus Act of 2008 as well as year-end planning advice for business owners.

The Heroes Earnings Assistance and Relief Tax (HEART) Act, passed in May 2008, includes a variety of tax cuts for military personnel and veterans, as well as incentives for civilian employers who hold jobs for or continue paying some salary to troops called to duty. The total tax relief provided by the HEART Act is estimated to exceed $1.2 billion. The revenue loss associated with this legislation was offset in part by a new mark-to-market exit tax on certain individuals giving up their U.S. citizenship or long-term foreign resident status.

Finally, the Housing Assistance Tax Act of 2008, enacted in July, includes several provisions for housing-related tax relief, including special provisions for future and current homeowners. Among these, first-time homebuyers with qualifying incomes who complete the purchase transaction between April 9, 2008, and June 30, 2009, will receive a tax credit of $7,500 or 10 percent of the purchase price (whichever is the lesser amount).

For 2008 only, current homeowners who take the standard, nonitemized federal income tax deduction are eligible for an additional deduction of up to $1,000. The Housing Assistance Tax Act also includes a low-income housing credit and a real estate investment trust (REIT) tax simplification package. Revenue offsets associated with this legislation include a new limit on the capital gains exclusion on sale of a principal residence.

For a more detailed discussion of the Housing Assistance Tax Act of 2008 and of the more general tax implications of home ownership, refer to Chapter 6.

In addition to the new provisions contained in these bills, individuals may want to pay close attention to three key areas that will have the most impact on their next filings and therefore warrant careful consideration.

The Alternative Minimum Tax

The alternative minimum tax (AMT) was originally intended to make sure that high-income taxpayers with a variety of deductions, credits, and exemptions could not avoid paying at least some federal income tax. But because the AMT exemption is not indexed for inflation, unlike the regular tax system, it has over time begun to affect an increasing number of middle-income taxpayers. In 1990, for example, only 200,000 taxpayers were subject to the AMT; by 2006, 4.2 million taxpayers were. And far more would have been affected by the AMT annually if not for the series of patches—or temporary increases in the AMT exemption limit—that have been enacted since then.

To prevent an additional 21 million taxpayers from paying the AMT in 2007, Congress increased the AMT exemption to $66,250 for joint filers and $44,350 for single filers, and extended and increased certain other tax credits, such as education credits, against the AMT. If those temporary provisions are not extended again, more than 25 million taxpayers will be subject to the AMT in 2008.

The problem of the AMT is so complicated—and expensive—that most agree it can only be resolved as part of larger tax reform legislation. As a result, lawmakers are expected to enact another temporary one-year AMT patch by the end of this year, before the real debate over long-term solutions begins in 2009.

Chapter 14 discusses the AMT in detail and explores some approaches to the careful preparation needed to protect your assets and long-term financial plans.

Individual Rates on Income, Capital Gains, and Dividends

If the current tax rules are allowed to expire and no new legislation is enacted, the individual tax code would largely revert to its pre-2001 status. For most taxpayers, that would mean higher taxes:

- The 10 percent bracket for low-income taxpayers would revert to 15 percent; a portion of the 15 percent bracket for married filers would be taxed at 28 percent; and other brackets would increase, with the top marginal rate reaching 39.6 percent,

- The capital gains rates, currently 0 percent and 15 percent, would revert to 10 percent and 20 percent, respectively. Dividends, currently taxed at 0 percent and 15 percent, would be taxed as ordinary income and, as such, would be subject to a top rate of 39.6 percent.
- The increased $1,000 child tax credit would be halved, the increased standard deduction providing tax relief for married filers would decline by more than 15 percent, and many education incentives would also expire after 2010.*

Chapter 2 focuses on all of the expiring provisions in 2010 and discusses planning considerations to prepare for upcoming changes.

Estate Tax

The Economic Growth and Tax Relief Reconciliation Act of 2001 set into motion the phaseout and eventual repeal of the federal estate tax, to be completely eliminated for one year in 2010. In 2009, estates will be taxed at a rate of 45 percent, with an estate tax exemption of $3.5 million. If the law is left as it is today, the estate tax will return in 2011 to its 2001 levels—a 55 percent tax rate and a $1 million exemption.

With the Democrats heading into the 2008 presidential election with a slight Senate majority that is expected to increase, it is unlikely that a full repeal of the estate tax will take effect in 2010. So far, the divisions on this issue have fallen mostly along party lines, with neither party having been able to secure the votes to enact any new legislation.

The future level of the estate tax depends largely on the ability of the next president and Congress to reach a consensus on

---

*PricewaterhouseCoopers, *What You Need to Know about the Coming Debate on Tax Reform* (New York: PricewaterhouseCoopers, 2008).

this issue. Both presidential candidates have proposed to retain an estate tax instead of seeking to repeal it fully. Senator John McCain (R-AZ) has proposed a top estate tax rate of 15 percent and a $5 million exemption. Senator Barack Obama (D-IL) has proposed a top estate tax rate of 45 percent and a $3.5 million exemption.

In any case, individuals should make sure they have current and updated estate plans that take advantage of a coordinated, systematic approach to lifetime and testamentary transfers, and include the flexibility to adapt to the possible changes in tax law that may occur.

Chapter 9 explores several strategies for estate planning that, given the uncertainty around the tax law, are worth considering.

Be Prepared

Preparation is the best tonic for uncertainty, and between slowed economic growth at home and the coming tax reform, uncertainty seems plentiful. But opportunity is inherent in times of change. Individuals who take the time now to develop and fine-tune a proactive tax and financial plan will be best positioned to take advantage of those opportunities as they arise.

The next chapter focuses on the income, estate, gift and generation-skipping tax law changes that are scheduled to occur beginning in 2010 and could significantly impact taxpayers. In order to be prepared and consider long-term planning strategies, read on to see how to protect yourself and take advantage of this information.

Chapter 2
Getting Ready for 2010

For political and congressional budgetary reasons, many provisions of the tax code have preprogrammed start and end dates. That is, the tax benefits from these provisions are in force for only a set period of time unless Congress acts to extend them. The year 2010 features prominently in a variety of tax legislation stretching back to the turn of the century (2001).

In order to do long-range tax planning, taxpayers must be aware of the changes anticipated in 2010. The purpose of this chapter is to identify several key changes, discuss their impact, and comment on them. In some cases the benefits begin in 2010 and in some cases the benefits end after 2010. The material is divided into income tax, estate tax, gift tax, and generation-skipping tax sections.

Income Tax

There are a wide variety of income tax changes that take place for 2010 and after. Most involve rate changes. The most exciting opportunity is associated with Roth IRA (individual retirement account) conversions.

Income Tax Rates

The year 2010 is scheduled to be the last year of reduced income tax rates enacted in 2001 and thereafter. Beginning in 2011, the maximum income tax rate reverts to 39.6 percent (from the current 35 percent). Further, the 10 percent tax bracket will disappear.

> **Observation**
>
> These rate changes provide a built-in income tax increase, regardless of changes in the president and Congress. However, many expect that the new president and new Congress will propose changes to income tax rates before 2010.

Phaseout of Phaseouts for Higher-Income Taxpayers

Currently itemized deductions and personal exemptions are phased out for higher-income taxpayers. This phaseout has been at a steadily reduced rate from 2007 to 2009.

Beginning in 2010, the full phaseout of itemized deductions and personal exemptions again takes place. Higher-income taxpayers will lose 3 percent of their deductions (subject to certain limits and exclusions) and all of their personal exemptions if their income exceeds certain thresholds.

> **Observation**
>
> The combination of higher tax rates and increased phaseout of deductions and exemptions means that the alternative minimum tax (AMT) will affect fewer higher-income taxpayers. However, the impact of the AMT on millions of middle-class Americans will still drive the need for comprehensive AMT reform.

Reduction in Child Tax Credit

The maximum child tax credit will drop from $1,000 to $500. This credit is phased out for higher-income taxpayers.

Reduced Tax Rate on Qualified Dividends

Currently, qualified dividends are subject to a favorable 15 percent maximum tax rate. This favorable rate was extended through 2010. Beginning in 2011, all dividends will once again be taxed at ordinary income tax rates (maximum 35 percent marginal rate, although potentially 39.6 percent as mentioned earlier). This change, coupled with increased ordinary income tax rates, could make dividend-paying stocks less attractive in some portfolios.

Reduced Tax Rate on Long-Term Capital Gains

The year 2010 is the last year for the 15 percent maximum tax rate on long-term capital gains. Also ending is the special 0 percent tax rate for those in the lowest income tax brackets. Beginning in 2011, the long-term capital gains rate goes back to 20 percent. The special tax rates for collectibles (28 percent) and real estate depreciation recapture (25 percent) do not change. The maximum capital gains rate for those in the lowest tax brackets increases to 10 percent.

Reappearing in 2011 is the special reduced long-term capital gains rate for special five-year long-term gains. You must have purchased the asset after 2000 and held the asset for more than five years to qualify for a reduced rate of 18 percent. The reduced rate is 8 percent for taxpayers in the lowest tax brackets, and applies to assets held for more than five years regardless of the purchase date.

Expensing of Business Property

The expanded ability allowing taxpayers to expense 100 percent of property purchased for business purposes drops after 2010.

Beginning in 2011, the maximum immediate expensing deduction for business property reverts to $25,000.

Mortgage Insurance Premiums

Private mortgage insurance (PMI) premiums refer to the additional charges applied to mortgages where the down payment on the property does not meet certain criteria. This is essentially an additional interest charge for a slightly higher-risk loan. The additional PMI charges are deductible as mortgage interest through 2010 (for mortgages issued after 2006). Beginning in 2011, the PMI charges will no longer be deductible.

Mortgage Foreclosure Forgiveness

Beginning in 2010, any mortgage debt forgiven in connection with a foreclosure of a principal residence will again be considered taxable income (unless certain other exceptions apply). Currently debt forgiveness on a residence foreclosure is not taxable in some circumstances.

Roth IRA Conversions Available to all Taxpayers

This is probably the most exciting income tax change for 2010. Currently, high-income taxpayers—that is, taxpayers with adjusted gross income (AGI) over $100,000—are not permitted to convert existing IRAs into Roth IRAs. The income limitation goes away, but only for 2010. Thus, all taxpayers will be able to convert IRAs to Roth IRAs during that year.

The Roth IRA has several advantages. First, all investment earnings are free of income tax as long as distributions take place after age 59½ (and the account has been established for at least five years). Second, the required minimum distributions rules that apply to traditional IRAs do not apply to Roth IRAs, which means that they can continue to grow tax free after age 70½. The Roth IRA is a fabulous asset to leave to children or grandchildren.

The disadvantage of the Roth IRA conversion is that you must pay income tax on the taxable portion of the IRA. This can be a significant cost.

Example
Jill has an IRA worth $490,000. The entire amount is taxable when withdrawn (no nondeductible contributions were ever made). Jill elects to convert her IRA to a Roth IRA in 2010. She must pay federal and state income tax on the entire $490,000 (a tax of about $180,000). Once she makes the election and pays the tax, future distributions from the Roth IRA will be free of income tax.

Normally, the tax related to the conversion must be paid in the year of the conversion. However, another 2010 feature is the ability to pay the income tax associated with the Roth conversion over two years (in 2011 and 2012).

Observation
Many people have been making IRA contributions (even nondeductible contributions) in anticipation of this change.

Caution
There is a proportional rule that affects the conversion calculation. This rule applies when IRAs contain after-tax contributions (normally reported on Form 8606). All IRAs are aggregated in determining the ratio of taxable to nontaxable distributions and conversions. Thus, it is not possible to isolate nondeductible contributions in a single IRA and convert just that IRA. Instead, all IRAs (including rollover IRAs) are part of the overall ratio.

(Continued)

Continued

EXAMPLE

Bob has three IRAs. One is a rollover of an employer 401(k) plan when he switched jobs in 1999. That IRA has $50,900 in it and is with his broker. Bob also has a nondeductible IRA with a mutual fund that has $35,000 in it (his contributions were $34,000). Finally, he has a bank certificate of deposit (CD) IRA for $5,400 that he created after getting his first job. His IRA accounts total $91,300, consisting of $34,000 of after-tax contributions and $57,300 that is taxable. Thus, 62.76 percent of any distribution/conversion is taxable ($57,300 ÷ $91,300). Bob converts his mutual fund IRA expecting that only $1,000 is taxable ($35,000 value less $34,000 contributions). However, the correct result is that $21,966 of the account (62.76 percent of $35,000) is taxable.

Estate Tax

The estate tax is scheduled for elimination for 2010 only. As discussed in Chapter 1 and Chapter 9, few expect this to be a permanent repeal given the current political and economic climate. The uncertainty surrounding the future of the estate tax has created major issues for estate planning over the past several years.

As discussed in detail in Chapter 9, currently a federal estate tax is imposed on all assets owned at death. There is a $2 million estate tax exemption per person (scheduled to increase to $3.5 million in 2009) and a maximum estate tax rate of 45 percent. Assets owned at death receive a step-up in basis equal to the fair market value on the date of death (or alternate valuation date). Some assets (annuities, IRAs, and retirement plans) do not get a step-up.

Current law calls for the federal estate tax to be totally repealed for individuals who die in 2010. (The generation-skipping tax is also totally repealed. See discussion later in the chapter.) Part of the revenue offset from the repeal of the estate and generation-skipping taxes comes from a curtailment of the step-up in basis provisions.

For taxpayers dying in 2010, the basis step-up will be limited to a $1.3 million allowance that can be applied to assets held at death. Assets passing to the surviving spouse are eligible for an additional $3 million step-up in basis allowance. The executor of the estate makes the decision as to what assets receive the step-up allowance. This means that all inherited assets that do not receive an allocation of these step-up allowances will have a carryover basis from the decedent to the heirs.

> ### Observation
> Carryover basis was the rule between 1976 and 1978. That carryover basis legislation was repealed retroactively in 1978 due to an inability to track cost basis.

In 2011, the federal estate tax and generation-skipping tax revert to the 2001 rules with a $1 million unified estate and gift tax exemption (as indexed for inflation) and a top rate of 55 percent. Further, a 5 percent surtax is reinstated for large estates to recapture the benefit of lower rate brackets, resulting in the largest estates essentially paying a flat tax of 55 percent.

Gift Tax

Although the federal estate tax is scheduled for repeal for 2010, the gift tax is scheduled to remain in effect without repeal.

Currently, gifts of less than $12,000 per person are excluded from the gift tax (the annual exclusion). It is expected that this annual exclusion will rise to $13,000 for 2009. There is a further $1 million lifetime gift tax exemption (this is the part of the $2 million estate tax exemption that can be used during one's lifetime). Gifts in excess of the annual exclusion and lifetime exemption are subject to gift tax rates up to 45 percent.

In 2010, the annual exclusion of $13,000 (as expected in 2009) and lifetime exemption of $1 million remain in effect. The maximum gift tax rate is reduced to 35 percent in 2010.

For 2011 and thereafter, the gift tax exemption and the gift tax rates revert to 2001 levels (maximum gift tax rate of 55 percent). For 2011 and thereafter, the unified estate and gift tax exemption will return to its 2001 level of $1 million (as indexed for inflation).

Generation-Skipping Tax

The generation-skipping transfer (GST) tax is imposed on transfers to those in a generation more than one level below you (such as grandchildren). This is a flat tax equal to the maximum estate tax rate (currently 45 percent).

The generation-skipping tax is repealed for 2010. This suggests that 2010 could provide an excellent opportunity to consider gifts to grandchildren or to dynasty trusts. Gifts in excess of the $1 million gift tax exemption would generate a current gift tax liability in 2010, but could remove those assets and their future growth from the estates of multiple future generations.

The generation-skipping tax is reinstated in 2011 along with the federal estate tax. Because the highest estate tax rate increases to 55 percent in 2011, the GST will increase from 45 percent to 55 percent in that year as well.

■ ■ ■

As the tax code is currently structured, 2010 promises to be a transitional year. We have not presented in this chapter an exhaustive discussion of the changes that are scheduled to occur, but have tried to highlight major changes that must factor into your tax planning. As noted in Chapter 1, the next president and Congress are likely to address tax reform before many of these changes are scheduled to take effect.

We now move to discuss, in detail, how taxpayers should handle their personal, estate, business, and financial affairs to take advantage of new opportunities in light of the current tax laws. We will start with a review of investments and stock options.

Chapter 3
Investments and Stock Options

Many believe that we have entered into one of the most unusual and potentially destabilizing financial environments in our nation's history. Financial problems that had started with the credit problems caused by the subprime mortgage loan crisis have spread across the full scope of our financial system. Brokerage firms have failed, others have elected to convert to banks to access capital to prevent their own failure, and other financial institutions have received financial bailout deals to prevent their demise which would further exacerbate a very financially dangerous situation. As of the printing of this book, the Treasury Department has proposed a $700 billion bailout plan with the hope that it will go a long way toward curbing the panic in the markets. There are proposals for increased regulation of financial institutions, but we cannot be sure what that will eventually entail. Without any investment banks remaining, what institutions and business practices will be the target of these regulations?

As we have seen recently, the stock markets can be very volatile. Many people have watched their investment portfolios capture extraordinary gains, which quickly gave way to substantial losses. Most likely, this market volatility will continue for some time, so investors must keep themselves informed and take care not to accept more financial risk than they can manage within their personal financial situation.

For the past several years, investors have been rewarded with reduced regular income tax rates for interest and short-term capital gains, and even lower tax rates for long-term capital gains and qualified dividends. These lower tax rates should attract the attention of all investors, whether they invest in stocks, bonds, sophisticated hedge funds, or simple certificates of deposit (CDs). However, the lower tax rates are not permanent. The reduced regular income tax rates are scheduled to apply only through 2010, and the reduced tax rates on long-term capital gains and qualified dividends are now set to expire at the end of 2010 as well. It is imperative for investors to continuously monitor their portfolios in light of the ever-changing tax environment to maximize their after-tax investment rate of return.

In this chapter, we first explore the tax issues related to investing and then provide an analysis of various types of investment vehicles and stock-based compensation. When putting all of this together, the goal is to maximize your real rate of return (your return after taxes and inflation) and reduce risk. In today's economy, managing risk is particularly important. At the end of the chapter, you'll find a checklist of ideas to consider as you plan investment strategies for the decade to come.

Tax Issues Related to Investing

When implementing an investment strategy, it is important to consider your risk profile, time horizon, and goals and objectives before finalizing your investment plan. It is suggested that you evaluate whether tax-efficient implementation solutions would be a good fit for your portfolio. It is important, however, to make sure the tax considerations are secondary to investment fundamentals.

Capital Gains

Long-term capital gain income or loss results when a taxpayer sells or exchanges a capital asset that is held for longer than one year. Examples of capital assets include shares of corporate stock or securities, a personal residence, or a parcel of undeveloped land.

The tax rate on long-term capital gains (gains from assets held for more than one year) is currently only 15 percent.

Example

In April 2008, an individual in the top ordinary income tax bracket (35 percent in 2008) sells stock that he purchased over a year earlier, recognizing a gain of $10,000. The long-term capital gains tax attributable to this sale is $1,500 (15 percent of $10,000).

Observation

The reduced tax rates on long-term capital gains make stock investments more advantageous and reduce the attractiveness of alternative strategies like contributing to regular IRAs (but not Roth IRAs), tax-deferred annuities, and taxable fixed income investments. Distributions from IRAs and tax-deferred annuities, as well as interest from taxable bonds, are taxed at the higher ordinary income tax rates. However, like all investment decisions, it is not just the tax implications that matter in the decision process. For example, you still must consider the volatility of investment returns, the investment period, the distribution period from the tax-deferred accounts, and the tax rates in the future.

Observation

The capital gains rate is effectively increased for taxpayers in high tax brackets through the itemized deduction cutback and the personal exemption phaseout. The loss of personal exemptions and the phaseout of itemized deductions have been lessened because the phaseouts of these write-offs are gradually being reduced, and are scheduled to be eliminated in 2010.

Observation

The 15 percent tax rate on long-term capital gains and qualified dividends is extended to run through 2010, so investors with unrecognized gains may want to evaluate selling assets now to take advantage of the current low tax rate. Investors will want to compare the prospective tax savings to the future appreciation potential for the investment before making any decision. In addition, an investor who believes tax rates will increase in the near future and that an investment will continue to appreciate may choose to sell the asset, pay tax at the 15 percent rate, and then repurchase the asset.

Observation

Investors should also take note that the phaseout of the estate tax has a catch-22 clause that should impact their investment decisions: In 2010, not all securities and other capital assets held in an estate at death will escape capital gains tax when passed on to heirs. Under current law, in 2010 the heirs' tax-free gains on inherited property will be limited to a total of $1.3 million. An additional $3 million of gains on property received by a surviving spouse will also escape capital gains tax. Until now, many investors have assumed that securities with very large gains should be retained until death for heirs to receive a tax-free step-up in tax basis. In some instances, that strategy may not be appropriate because of the limit on capital gains that can pass to heirs tax-free in 2010. However, stay tuned, because this is a tax provision that may be altered with the change in the presidency. For more information, please refer to the discussion on estate taxes in Chapter 9.

Exceptions to the 15 Percent Rate

Beginning in 2008, individuals in the 10 percent or 15 percent ordinary income tax bracket have a long-term capital gains tax rate of 0 percent. This rate is applicable through 2010.

Example

Assuming your daughter is older than 18 (or if a full-time dependent student, older than 23) and her regular income (from wages and interest) is taxed at no more than 15 percent, if she sells stock that she purchased more than a year ago for a gain of $10,000, she will not pay any capital gains tax on this sale.

Observation

The availability of the 0 percent tax rate for those in the lowest two tax rate brackets previously presented a great family income-splitting opportunity. However, with the implementation of the 2007 Small Business Act, the so-called kiddie tax rules apply to older children. These rules once applied to children under the age of 14, then to those under the age of 18 (the age limit in effect for 2007). Beginning in 2008, these rules apply to children under the age of 19 or, if a dependent full-time student, under the age of 24. The kiddie tax subjects children's unearned income (typically investment income) to their parents' higher rates.

Higher income tax bracket parents can transfer stock or other capital assets to their lower income tax bracket children or grandchildren. The children or grandchildren can, in turn, sell the assets and qualify for the 0 percent tax rate to the extent that the gains do not push their income above the 15 percent bracket. Of course, this assumes the kiddie tax (as described earlier) does not apply. The holding period for the asset transferred carries over to recipients of the property when the gift is made. As a result, the transfer can result in a tax savings of 10 percent.

Example

An individual in the top tax bracket (35 percent in 2008) owns stock purchased more than one year ago on which he has a $10,000 gain. If he sells the stock in 2008, for example, his long-term capital gains tax would be $1,500, or 15 percent of $10,000. If he gifts the stock to his 23-year-old grandson, who has only a few thousand dollars of taxable income this year, there would be no tax incurred by the grandson's sale of the stock, saving $1,500.

Collectibles, Qualified Small Business Stock, and Depreciated Real Estate

A higher maximum tax rate of 28 percent applies to long-term capital gains from the sale of collectibles (such as art or antiques) and to one-half of the long-term capital gains from the sale of qualified small business stock (the other half of the gain on the sale of such stock, up to certain limits, is tax-free) if the taxpayer is in the 28 percent, or higher, tax bracket. Furthermore, there is a 25 percent tax rate on part of the gain resulting from the sale of real estate where depreciation deductions were previously taken.

Example

An individual who is not an art dealer sells an oil painting from her personal collection, which she has owned for many years, for $100,000 more than she paid for it. Her capital gains tax liability is $28,000 or 28 percent of $100,000.

No More Advantage for Five-Year Gains

There has always been a required minimum holding period to qualify for long-term capital gains tax rates. Over the years, it has varied from more than six months to more than two years. Before May 7, 2003, there was a separate holding period for special capital gains rates. The rate was an 18 percent tax rate (or 8 percent for those in the two lowest tax brackets) for certain capital assets held more than five years:

- An *18 percent rate* would have applied to sales of property held for more than five years if the holding period for the property began in 2001 or later.

> ### Observation
> Investors had the opportunity to qualify assets purchased before 2001 for the 18 percent tax rate by electing to treat any or all of the assets as having been sold and repurchased at the beginning of 2001.

- An *8 percent rate* would have applied to sales of property held for more than five years and sold in 2001 or later. There was no requirement for the holding period to have begun after 2001 to qualify for this low tax rate.

These special tax rates have been repealed for now. However, they should not be completely forgotten since they are scheduled to return after 2010, when the current low capital gains tax rates expire. In the meantime, a 0 percent tax rate will be available for long-term capital gains and qualified dividends for those in the 10 percent or 15 percent tax bracket for tax years 2008 through 2010.

Netting Rules

Favorable capital gains tax rates and the long-term capital gains holding period requirements may influence the decision as to when a property is sold, which in turn affects the tax that is ultimately paid. When calculating capital gains income, keep in mind that the following ordering rules apply to netting capital gains and losses. The rules are fairly complicated, but they generally produce the lowest overall tax.

Long-term (for this purpose, a holding period of more than one year) capital gains and losses are divided into three groups determined by tax rates:

1. A *28 percent group* (for long-term capital gains from the sale of collectibles such as art or antiques, and half of the long-term capital gains from the sale of qualified small business stock, or QSBS).
2. A *25 percent group* (for some or all of the gain from the sale of depreciable real estate).
3. A *15 percent group* (for all other capital assets).

For those in the two lowest ordinary income tax brackets, gains and losses in the 0 percent, 8 percent, and 10 percent groups also must be netted. Long-term gains and losses within a tax rate group are first netted against one another. Net losses within a long-term tax rate group are then used to offset net gains from the long-term tax rate group with the highest tax rate. If there are net losses remaining, they offset gains from the next-highest tax rate group.

> ### Example
>
> Assume that for 2008 there will be net losses in the 15 percent tax rate group. The net losses first offset any net gains in the 28 percent tax rate group; the losses then offset net gains in the 25 percent tax rate group. This automatically produces maximum tax savings from the losses. Similarly, long-term capital loss carryovers offset net gains for the highest long-term tax rate group first, then the other long-term tax rate groups in descending order.

A net long-term capital loss carryover from 2007 first offsets 2008 net 28 percent capital gains, then net 25 percent capital gains, and finally net 15 percent gains.

Net short-term capital losses offset net long-term capital gains, beginning with the highest tax rate group.

A net short-term capital loss first offsets net 28 percent capital gains, then net 25 percent capital gains, and finally net 15 percent capital gains.

Net long-term capital losses can offset short-term capital gains.

Capital Losses

Capital losses are deductible dollar for dollar against capital gains. In addition, married filing jointly and single taxpayers may deduct up to $3,000 ($1,500 if married filing separately) in net capital losses (either short- or long-term) each year against ordinary income (such as wages or interest income). Net capital loss amounts in excess of $3,000 may be carried forward indefinitely.

Observation

It is always helpful to review your realized and unrealized capital gains and losses as well as loss carryovers on a periodic basis. This is especially important for future-year tax planning. If you have unrealized capital losses, consider recognizing losses to the extent of realized capital gains if it is also prudent to do so from an investment perspective. Also, you may wish to realize an additional $3,000 in losses since the incremental amount can be used to offset taxable ordinary income.

Wash Sale Rule

If securities or mutual funds held have significantly declined in value and a recovery in price is not anticipated in the near future, consideration should be given to selling the securities or funds currently to take advantage of the loss. For investment reasons, there may be an ongoing desire to maintain a similar type of investment. The repurchase must be made carefully, however, so as not to immediately repurchase the same or *substantially identical* assets (the Internal Revenue Service uses this term to broaden the prohibited repurchase of securities and/or mutual funds that are not identical to what you had sold but are essentially the same). Tax wash sale rules prevent a taxpayer from recognizing the tax loss if the repurchase occurs within 30 days before or after the sale of the same, or a substantially identical, security.

If the wash sale rule is triggered, the resulting loss is suspended and added to the cost basis of the new securities purchased (the amount you pay for the security plus other acquisition costs, such as brokerage commissions). When the replacement security is sold, the suspended loss amount reduces the taxable gain or increases the taxable loss.

To avoid the wash sale rule, you must either avoid purchasing the same or substantially identical assets within the 61-day period, or buy the same or substantially identical assets at least 31 days before or after the sale of the securities or mutual funds. The latter alternative involves substantial investment risk, as the market can move against the targeted strategy in the 31-day waiting period.

> **Caution**
> Be careful not to trigger the wash sale rule unwittingly. A wash sale will happen, for example, if you sell part of your investment in a security or fund at a loss, and a dividend paid on the remaining shares is automatically reinvested in the same shares within the restricted 30-day (before or after) period.

Protecting and Postponing Stock Gains

Current tax law prevents the use of the *short sale against the box* technique to safely lock in gains while postponing the taxable recognition that would occur upon the sale. A short sale is the process of selling shares that you do not own and later purchasing the shares back (sell high/buy low). A short sale against the box takes place when you own shares in a company that you do not wish to dispose of currently, but that you want to protect against price declines. You are willing to give up some of the potential price appreciation in doing so by short selling the same company using shares you do not own. At a later date, you tender your shares as repayment of the short sale or you purchase the shares in the market. Two other viable strategies remain:

1. *Buying put options covering stock you own:* A put option entitles the holder to sell a number of shares (usually in lots of 100 shares) of the underlying security at a stated price on, or before, a fixed expiration date. By purchasing an option to sell a security at a fixed price, you ensure that any decline in the price of the security is likely to be offset, at least in part, by an increase in the price of the put option purchased.

2. *Writing covered call options:* A call option entitles the holder to purchase a number of shares of the underlying security at a stated price on, or before, a fixed expiration date. When a call is written, the seller of the call option receives money today in exchange for agreeing to sell the security at the call price in the future. As a result, the holders of a security who write a call option on the security give up the upside potential on the stock above the call price in order to protect their position to some extent by the proceeds from the sale of the option.

Strategies that are more complex also exist, including collars and variable prepaid forwards. Additionally, by using a charitable remainder trust (CRT), capital gains can also be deferred or possibly eliminated (see the discussion of CRTs in Chapter 9).

> ### *Observation*
> The lower tax rate on long-term capital gains should cause taxpayers to review their stock-hedging strategies. Carrying costs associated with hedging strategies that were acceptable with a 20 percent capital gains tax rate may be excessive with a 15 percent capital gains tax rate. At some point, it may make sense for taxpayers to simply pay the capital gains tax and unwind the hedging strategy. This could be particularly true for grandfathered short-against-the-box transactions where the underlying security has continued to appreciate.

Qualified Small Business Stock

A little-known and largely unused gain deferral provision is available to defer the tax on gain from the sale of qualified small business stock (QSBS). This provision only applies to taxpayers, other than a corporation, if the QSBS has been held for more than six months before it is sold. In addition, tax deferral is available only if the proceeds from the sale of QSBS are used to purchase other QSBS within 60 days after the sale. There is no requirement that taxpayers purchase QSBS in just one company, allowing investors to diversify their holdings. The tax deferral is achieved by reducing your tax cost basis in the purchased QSBS by the amount of gain deferred on the sale (a QSBS rollover provision). For this purpose, the definition of QSBS generally means C corporation stock that is purchased at original issue (directly from the corporation, not from another seller), and the purchase must occur after August 10, 1993. In addition, there are other requirements to meet the definition of QSBS and qualify for gain deferral.

Careful Record Keeping: Identification of Securities

If you hold many securities, it is imperative to keep accurate records of your purchase history to maximize the tax savings at the time of sale. Because of differences in holding periods and the tax basis of individual lots, a sale can trigger a short-term or long-term gain or loss, depending on which securities are sold or deemed to have been sold. If you redeem an actual security certificate at the time of sale, the securities sold will be those identified on the certificate. If one certificate represents securities acquired on different dates or at different prices, the specific securities to be sold can be identified to the executing broker in writing. If you do not identify specific securities, you will generally be deemed to have sold the first securities acquired, which would have the longest holding period (and therefore might be taxed at a lower rate), but may also have the largest taxable gain.

> ### Observation
> Mutual fund shares, discussed in more detail later in this chapter, are usually treated in the same way as other securities, or you can use their average cost when determining basis. Once you apply either the earliest-cost or average-cost method to a particular security, you must continue to use that method in future years.

> ### Observation
> When selling stock that has risen in value, you can reduce taxes by identifying the securities with the highest tax basis as the ones that are being sold. However, if the securities have been held for one year or less, any gain will be short-term and subject to tax at ordinary income tax rates.

Dividends

Dividends received by an individual shareholder from domestic and many foreign corporations, including American depositary receipts (ADRs), that meet the definition of *qualified dividend income* are taxed at the same low rates that apply to long-term capital gains. This treatment applies for purposes of both the regular tax and the alternative minimum tax (AMT). Thus, qualified dividends are taxed at rates of 0 percent for taxpayers in the two lowest tax brackets, and at 15 percent for those whose income is taxed above the 15 percent tax bracket. Qualified dividend income passed through to individuals from partnerships, S corporations, limited liability companies, and trusts maintains its character as qualified dividend income and thus is taxed to individuals at the reduced tax rates.

Caution

Even though the reduced tax rates on long-term capital gains and qualified dividends apply for both AMT and regular income tax purposes, these types of income can nonetheless help trigger the AMT. Taxpayers in the 28 percent, 33 percent, and 35 percent marginal tax-rate brackets who receive dividend income may find themselves subject to the AMT due to the disparity in the tax rates between the AMT and the regular tax. For example, a taxpayer in the 35 percent tax rate bracket with $1 of qualified dividend income would save $0.20 for regular tax purposes (35 percent versus 15 percent tax rate), but only $0.13 for AMT purposes (28 percent versus 15 percent tax rate). In addition, the phaseout of the AMT exemption results in AMT income effectively being taxed at 125 percent of the applicable AMT rate. Thus, it is possible that a taxpayer in the AMT phaseout range will pay an effective tax rate of 22 percent (15 percent plus 25 percent of 28 percent) on long-term capital gains and qualified dividends rather than the stated AMT rate of 15 percent.

A share owner must hold dividend-paying stock for more than 60 days during the 121-day period beginning 60 days before the ex-dividend date for the dividends received on the stock to be eligible for the reduced tax rates. For dividends received on certain preferred stock (generally dividends that represent an earnings period of more than one year), shareholders must hold the stock for more than 90 days during the 181-day period beginning 90 days before the ex-dividend date. These required holding periods do not include any days on which the taxpayer has reduced the risk of loss on the stock by purchasing a put, selling a call (other than a qualified covered call), executing a short sale of the stock, or having entered into a cashless collar or prepaid variable forward contract. Additionally, a taxpayer who is under an obligation to pay the dividend to another party will not receive qualified dividend income. Thus, a person with a short-against-the-box position will pay tax at ordinary tax rates on dividends received.

If an individual receives an extraordinary dividend eligible for the reduced tax rates, any loss on the sale of the dividend-paying stock is treated as a long-term capital loss to the extent of the dividend. (A dividend on preferred stock is treated as extraordinary if it equals 5 percent or more of the shareholder's adjusted tax basis in the preferred stock; a dividend on common stock is treated as extraordinary if it equals 10 percent or more of the shareholder's adjusted tax basis in the common stock.) These rules make it more difficult for taxpayers to convert short-term capital gains into dividend income taxed at lower tax rates. However, taxpayers who have short-term capital gains and no potential long-term capital gains or losses could use extraordinary dividends to avoid the higher tax on short-term capital gains. The taxpayers would still have to meet the holding period requirements described earlier.

Short Sales

A short sale is the sale of a security that is not currently owned. When a dividend is paid on stock that has been shorted before the date the short sale is closed, the short seller must pay the lender of the shares an equivalent amount in lieu of that dividend. In general, these *in lieu of dividend* payments are treated as interest paid for the use of the property borrowed for the short sale.

Once the borrowed shares or securities have been sold pursuant to a short sale, neither the short seller nor the lender retains any ownership interest in the stock; therefore, the in lieu of dividend payment made to the lender of the stock by the seller is not a dividend in the sense of being a distribution made by the corporation with respect to its stock. As such, in lieu of dividend payments do not qualify for the reduced tax rates.

Foreign Tax Credit

Special rules apply in determining a taxpayer's foreign tax credit limitation for qualified dividend income. Because qualified dividends receive preferential tax treatment in the United States, dividends taxed overseas will need to be adjusted accordingly when the foreign tax credit is computed.

Margin Accounts

In the past, investors may not have known or cared whether their stock was borrowed and they were receiving in lieu of dividend payments rather than actual dividends. Now, however, if a dividend is considered an in lieu of dividend payment, the lower dividend tax rates will not be available. As a result, margin accounts have a potential tax disadvantage, since most agreements governing margin accounts specifically allow for the borrowing of shares held in a margin account.

Interest Expense and Investment-Related Expenses

Taxpayers incur the following types of expenses related to their investment activities: portfolio management fees, trading fees, and interest expense.

Portfolio management fees are deductible as a miscellaneous itemized deduction subject to the 2 percent floor. This means that the total portfolio management fees, when added to other miscellaneous itemized deductions such as tax preparation fees, employee expenses, and safe-deposit box fees, must exceed 2 percent of your adjusted gross income (AGI) in order to receive any benefit.

> **Observation**
>
> The deductible portion of the miscellaneous itemized deductions is an add back for AMT. Thus, taxpayers subject to AMT, or close to being subject to AMT, may not receive a benefit for these expenses.

> **Observation**
>
> As a result of recent guidance from the Internal Revenue Service (IRS) and the U.S. Supreme Court relating to miscellaneous deductions for trusts, portfolio management fees incurred in a trust will generally be subject to the 2 percent floor.

Trading fees and other costs incurred to purchase, sell, or hold a security are not deductible; instead the basis or sales price is adjusted. For instance, a fee for purchasing the stock would be an addition to basis, where the fee to sell the security would reduce the sales price. Thus, these fees reduce the capital gain realized.

Interest expense is the interest paid on borrowed funds. Funds can be borrowed for many different purposes: to purchase a house or car or to purchase securities. Mortgage interest is discussed in Chapter 6, along with home equity interest. Personal interest is not deductible.

Investment interest expense is the interest paid on funds borrowed to invest. The interest paid is an itemized deduction, which is deductible to the extent of investment income.

Example

Sally takes out a margin loan, the proceeds of which are used to invest in a diversified portfolio. She pays $100 of interest expense in 2008. Sally has $80 of investment income in 2008. Thus, she can deduct $80 as investment interest expense; the other $20 is carried forward to future years, and is used when sufficient investment income exists.

Observation

It is important to note that it needn't be a margin loan; the interest paid on any loan taken out where the proceeds are used to invest is considered investment interest expense. When determining what type of interest expense you paid, you trace the interest back to the purpose of the loan. For example, if you take out a margin loan and use the proceeds in your business, this would be treated as business interest expense, not investment interest expense.

Observation

The deduction for investment interest expense is limited to investment income, which is defined as interest income and other portfolio income taxed at your marginal rate. Thus, qualified dividends and long-term capital gains are not considered investment income. However, you can make an election to include this income as investment income. This election taxes the income at your marginal rates, instead of the lower 15 percent rate, but will allow a larger investment interest expense deduction.

Investment Vehicles and Stock Options

Now that we have discussed the basics of the taxation of investments, one should understand how these rules apply to the different investment vehicles available in today's market.

Mutual Funds

One of the most popular investment vehicles today is the mutual fund. Mutual funds are financial instruments that collect assets from multiple investors and invest those assets on the investors' behalf according to a predetermined investment strategy. Mutual funds can serve as a cost-efficient way for investors to diversify their assets, as the pooling of many different investors' money allows each investor to hold shares of many different companies. Additionally, mutual funds afford small investors the ability to access sophisticated investment management skills that normally would not be available to them.

Generally, there are two types of funds: open-end funds and closed-end funds. Open-end funds issue and redeem shares at a net asset value (NAV) that is determined by the total assets held by the fund divided by the total shares outstanding. Closed-end funds have shares that cannot be redeemed at NAV but instead are listed and traded on a stock exchange.

Mutual funds generally are able to pass through qualified dividend income received to the fund's shareholders where the qualified dividend will be taxed at the reduced rates. However, other types of income received by a mutual fund, such as interest received on notes or bonds, or short-term capital gains, are not qualified dividend income, even though the payments are made to mutual fund shareholders in the form of a dividend. Therefore, money market fund dividends, which represent interest earned by the money market fund, are not qualified dividend income.

When selecting a mutual fund, there are several criteria to evaluate. First, you should consider the type of investments within the mutual fund (e.g., large-cap value stocks or tax-exempt municipal bonds). In addition, consideration should be given to the fund performance (as compared to a benchmark) over the life of the fund, the manager tenure/turnover, and finally the expense ratio. Investing in lower-cost funds, such as index funds and no-load funds, means you will have more money to invest and appreciate, and less going toward fees.

> ### *Observation*
> Some mutual funds are more tax efficient than others. For example, index funds, which are mutual funds that are designed to track a specific index such as the Standard & Poor's 500 or Morgan Stanley Capital International (MSCI) Europe, Australasia, Far East (EAFE) index, are more tax efficient than mutual funds that are more actively managed. This is because there is less turnover of the portfolio, which results in less taxable income flowing out to investors.

> ### *Observation*
> Recently, life cycle funds have surged in popularity, especially within 401(k) plans. Life cycle funds are balanced mutual funds, investing in several different asset classes, based on the investor's time horizon. For example, if your retirement goal is the year 2020, purchasing a life cycle 2020 fund would provide the appropriate asset allocation for this time horizon (assuming a moderate risk tolerance). These funds are able to provide not only an age-appropriate asset allocation, but also constant portfolio rebalancing.

Exchange-Traded Funds

The popularity of exchange-traded funds (ETFs) has grown enormously over the past five years due to the flexibility they offer. They are essentially investment portfolios, similar to index mutual funds, which trade like stocks on an exchange. An owner of an ETF has the legal right to ownership over a portion of a basket of securities. ETFs provide diversification at a lower cost, as expense ratios in ETFs are much lower than those of mutual funds (however, ETF investors typically must pay commissions). ETFs are more tax efficient as well, as there is less turnover of the shares in the portfolio. In addition, equity ETFs hold securities that are eligible for the qualified dividend lower tax rate. If fixed income ETFs are purchased, however, most of the income would be considered nonqualified and taxed at the higher marginal rates, similar to a comparable mutual fund.

Real Estate Investment Trusts

Real estate investment trusts (REITs) are similar to closed-end funds in their structure; however, instead of having broad investment mandates, they primarily invest in physical real estate or loans secured by real estate. Generally, REITs are not eligible for the reduced dividend rates. However, dividends received by a REIT shareholder will be considered qualified dividend income to the extent that the REIT had net taxable income in the preceding year.

It is not news to anyone that the real estate market has suffered during the past year. However, if you want to own REITs for the diversification benefits they can add to your portfolio (as a hedge for stocks), consider investing even in down markets. The prices on REITs are lower than in recent years, and the lower price tends to increase the dividend yield.

Preferred Stocks

Preferred stocks possess the characteristics of both bonds and stocks. Like bonds, they pay out a fixed income stream in the form of a dividend each year. However, like a stock, the company issuing the preferred stock has no contractual obligation to pay out its dividend each year. It is at the discretion of the company whether to pay the dividend in a given year. If the dividend is not paid out, the dividends of preferred stocks are usually cumulative and all dividends owed to preferred shareholders from prior years must be paid out before any dividends are paid to common stockholders.

From an asset allocation standpoint, it is not unusual for preferred stock to be considered part of an allocation to fixed income since the volatility in the stock price is usually muted relative to common stock, and because the payment of the dividend is typically a large component of the long-term return derived from preferred stock.

Whether dividends on preferred stock qualify for the reduced dividend tax rate depends on the classification of the preferred stock. If the preferred stock pays a dividend from corporate earnings and profits and the preferred stock is considered a stock, then the dividend will be taxed at no more than 15 percent. If, however, the preferred stock is considered a debt instrument, its dividend will continue to be taxed at ordinary income tax rates. Since many preferred stocks are bonds in disguise, their dividends will not be eligible for the 15 percent tax rate.

Alternative Investments

Over the past few years the popularity of alternative investments has soared. Investors looking for noncorrelated, high-return investments are seeking out investments in hedge funds, private equity, and publicly traded partnerships. These investments bring unique tax implications of which investors should be aware.

Investors in hedge funds, private equity, and publicly traded partnerships are treated as partners for tax purposes. Thus, the investor must report his or her allocable share of the income and expenses for the activity. This adds complexity to the tax return, especially if the activity has multistate or cross-border assets. In addition, the passive activity loss rules and at-risk rules (discussed next) apply in determining if net losses, credits, and expenses flowing through the activity are deductible.

In addition to adding complex tax issues, hedge funds and private equity investments are also not as liquid as other traditional types of investments such as stocks and bonds. Typically there are only one or two times during the year that an investor may be able to buy or sell the investment.

> **Observation**
>
> Alternative investments can be used to diversify your portfolio to help manage risk and potentially increase your return. However the investor should consider his or her liquidity needs and the tax ramifications of buying these investments before adding them to their portfolio.

At-Risk Rules

The at-risk rules are in place to curb abusive use of tax shelters caused by nonrecourse financing. The taxpayer may deduct a loss from an activity only to the extent the taxpayer is considered at risk for the activity. Generally, the amount at risk includes the amount of money and the basis of other property contributed to the activity, as well as amounts borrowed related to the activity for which the taxpayer bears an economic risk of loss. Thus, the taxpayer must be personally liable for repayment or must have pledged property as security for the borrowed amount. Nonrecourse debt does not qualify as an amount at risk. Unlike the passive activity loss rules discussed next, the at-risk rules are applied on an activity-by-activity basis. Any loss that is limited is carried forward to future years.

> **Observation**
>
> Making additional equity contributions or lending additional recourse amounts can increase at-risk basis and free up suspended losses.

> **Observation**
>
> When holding an interest in a flow-through entity such as a partnership or an S corporation, it is important to track your tax basis and at-risk basis yearly.

Passive Activity Losses

Investment losses from business and rental activities are limited by a complex set of provisions known as the passive activity loss rules. In general, losses and credits from passive activities can offset only passive income and may not be used against earned income (such as salaries) or portfolio income (such as dividends or interest). Passive activities generally include any business or rental activity in which you do not materially participate. For example, renting a residence or commercial property is usually considered a passive activity.

> **Observation**
>
> Real estate professionals may deduct losses and credits from rental real estate activities in which they materially participate without limitation from the passive loss rules.

> **Observation**
>
> Taxpayers who manage a few different activities or businesses may be able to group these activities into one business for the purpose of the material participation test.

Consider these strategies if you have unused passive activity losses:

- Purchase investments that generate passive income, to the extent that the purchase is consistent with your overall investment strategy.
- Become a material participant in the activity, if feasible, by increasing your level of involvement.
- Sell or dispose of your entire interest in the passive activity to free up the losses.

> **Observation**
>
> Rules that are even more restrictive apply to certain types of passive activities such as publicly traded partnerships. Publicly traded partnership losses can offset only publicly traded partnership income from the same partnership, not income from other types of passive activities.

Tax-Exempt and Taxable Bonds

Most interest earned on bonds is subject to tax at ordinary income tax rates. Generally, tax-exempt bonds are issued by municipalities and are often referred to as muni bonds. In most interest rate environments, bonds paying tax-exempt interest are appropriate only for investors in higher income tax brackets (federal and state), although the actual income tax rate where municipal bonds become more favorable is not static and will move over time depending on market dynamics.

Depending on the date on which the bond matures and the current market conditions, some long-term municipal bonds may produce a higher after-tax yield even in the 15 percent tax bracket (see Chapter 11). The decision is driven by the interest rate differential between taxable (most commonly Treasury and corporate bonds) and tax-free bonds, assuming similar maturity and credit quality. It is also important to take into account the state tax implications. Most investments in tax-exempt securities issued by a political subdivision in a state other than the taxpayer's state of residence subjects the taxpayer to state income tax even though the interest is free from federal income tax.

Observation

Lower tax rates impact the relationship between tax-exempt and taxable bonds and will reduce the attractiveness of tax-exempt bonds, everything else being equal. Recently, since the federal tax rates have declined and tax brackets have been adjusted upward for inflation, allowing more income to be earned without pushing a taxpayer into a higher tax rate bracket, tax-exempt bond issuers are being forced to raise the interest rates on their bonds to remain competitive with similar-quality taxable bonds.

Taxable Tax-Exempt Bonds

Certain municipal bonds (e.g., private activity bonds) are tax-exempt for regular income tax purposes but are taxable for the AMT. As a result, private activity bonds typically carry a slightly higher interest rate than bonds that are exempt from both regular tax and the AMT.

Observation

The demand for private activity municipal bonds should decrease going forward, since many more taxpayers are now subject to the AMT.

> **Caution**
>
> Just because a taxpayer may not have been subject to the AMT in the past does not mean that the taxpayer will not be subject to the AMT in the future. Unlike regular income tax rates, the AMT rate brackets and exemption amounts are not indexed annually for inflation. This AMT liability, therefore, has been affecting more and more taxpayers, many of whom consider themselves in the middle class and have thought the AMT was a tax that only the wealthy paid.

Taxpayers who are paying the AMT, or whose tax situations place them close to the AMT, should carefully consider whether investing in private activity bonds makes sense for them. In effect, this interest is taxable to them as AMT taxpayers, and thus the after-tax yield of the bond is probably less than the after-tax yield would have been on fully taxable bonds. Conversely, taxpayers who are not in an AMT situation (and do not predict being so in the future) and who have determined that tax-exempt bonds are suitable for their investment portfolios should seek out private activity bonds to take advantage of the slightly higher interest rate that they carry over other tax-exempt bonds.

Bond Premium or Discount

Investors who pay more than face value to purchase a bond are said to have purchased the bond at a premium. Bonds purchased at a premium usually carry a higher rate of interest than the prevailing rate for newly issued comparable bonds at the time of purchase. Taxpayers who own bonds purchased at a premium must amortize the premium of a tax-exempt bond by reducing its basis over time, although for taxable bonds, a taxpayer can elect to amortize the premium by offsetting the premium against the bond's interest. If taxpayers elect to amortize the bond premium, they must do so for all bonds owned currently and later acquired.

If the premium is not amortized over the bond's life, a loss will typically result when you sell or redeem the bond.

If a bond is purchased at a discount from its original issuer, the difference between the issue price and the redemption price—called original issue discount (OID)—is considered interest income. In almost all cases, a portion of this interest must be included in income each year even though the income is not received until the bond is redeemed. Taxable OID bonds, therefore, are better suited for purchase in tax-deferred accounts, such as individual retirement accounts (IRAs) or 401(k) accounts, or tax-exempt accounts such as Roth IRAs.

The OID rules do not apply to U.S. savings bonds, notes that mature in one year or less, or tax-exempt bonds (unless the bonds have been stripped of their coupons). If a taxable bond is purchased with a market discount—that is, it is a bond that has lost value since its issue date (usually because interest rates have risen since the time of issuance)—the resulting gain on sale will, in most cases, be considered interest income to the extent of the accrued market discount. The market discount must be accrued and recognized as ordinary income upon sale. If the bond is sold at a price in excess of the accrued discount, the excess is capital gain. Unlike the rule for taxable bonds, the entire market discount on municipal bonds is treated as ordinary income to the extent of the gain on the disposition of the municipal bond.

Nonqualified Stock Options

Nonqualified stock options generate compensation income at the time the options are exercised. The compensation income equals the difference between the fair market value of the stock at the time of exercise and the exercise price. Subsequent appreciation in the value of the stock is taxed at capital gains tax rates. Most individuals benefit by exercising nonqualified stock options shortly before the options expire, subject to the normal market risk associated with any investment decision. Early exercise, at or near the strike price, eliminates the downside protection afforded by stock options. By holding off on exercising the option until the latest point possible, a taxpayer will benefit from the presumably increased stock value without actually making a cash investment in the stock.

However, if the appreciation potential of the stock is expected to be great, early exercise can be advantageous because it minimizes the portion of the gain that will be taxed as compensation (at ordinary income tax rates) and maximizes the amount that will qualify for capital gains tax rates. This is called an exercise-and-hold strategy. The decision about when to exercise options is more complex than just considering the time remaining on the option grant and the related income tax consequences. The option holder should also take into account the amount of appreciation to date, the future prospects of the company, the dividends forgone by delaying exercise, and his or her particular tax and investment position as well as personal cash flow needs.

Withholding of federal income tax, Social Security, Medicare, and state and local taxes are all due when the options are exercised. If the stock option is exercised and then sold quickly, the cash generated from the sale can be used to help satisfy these tax-withholding obligations.

> ### *Observation*
> If a taxpayer intends to retain all of the stock obtained via the exercise of stock options, it is important to plan how to satisfy these withholding obligations properly. Some plans allow the use of shares to cover withholding taxes. Some employers grant phantom stock in connection with nonqualified options, which can help cover withholding taxes.

Incentive Stock Options

The lower long-term capital gains tax rates make incentive stock options (ISOs) more attractive. However, careful planning is needed to maximize the benefits of ISOs if the AMT is a concern.

For regular tax purposes, an ISO exercise is not a taxable event (state and local tax treatments may differ). However, at exercise, the difference between the fair market value of the stock on the date of the exercise and the exercise price is added to an individual's AMT income for the purpose of computing the AMT. Additionally, unlike nonqualified stock options, ISOs are not subject to federal payroll taxes or withholdings at the time of exercise, even if there is a disqualified disposition.

The Small Business and Work Opportunity Tax Act, signed into law by President George Bush on May 28, 2007, included a provision that will impact the ability to use the AMT credit created from previous tax return filings when the AMT was the actual tax paid.

The individual AMT attributable to deferral adjustments related to ISOs generates a minimum tax credit that is allowable to the extent the regular tax (reduced by other nonrefundable credits) exceeds the tentative minimum tax in a future taxable year. Unused minimum tax credits are carried forward indefinitely. This legislation allows individuals who have unused minimum tax credits to claim a refundable credit equal to 20 percent of the long-term unused minimum tax credits per year (a minimum of $5,000) for the next five years. The AMT refundable credit is phased out for higher-income taxpayers. The provision is effective for taxable years beginning after the date of enactment and before 2013.

An ISO is subject to a number of requirements imposed by the tax code that do not apply to nonqualified stock options, including the following:

- Incentive stock options cannot be:
  - Issued with an exercise price that is lower than the value of the stock on the date the options are granted.
  - Exercised more than 10 years after the options are granted.
  - Transferred except at death, and during the grantee's lifetime may be exercised only by the grantee.
- Incentive stock options must be exercised within 90 days of termination of employment to retain the ISO status.
- Incentive stock option grants have an annual limit of $100,000.
- Incentive stock option stock cannot be sold within a year of the option exercise date or within two years of the option grant date to obtain favorable ISO tax treatment. If option stock is sold before either of these two periods has expired, the option is taxed as a nonqualified stock option, usually resulting in compensation income to the option holder.

Observation

For taxpayers not otherwise subject to the AMT, ISO exercises should generally be timed to occur over the life of the option (usually 10 years) to minimize the AMT impact and to commence the one-year holding period needed to qualify for the 15 percent capital gains tax rate. If little or no planning goes into an ISO exercise, a taxpayer may be required to pay taxes earlier or in larger amounts than necessary.

Caution

Care should also be taken not to sell or otherwise dispose of the stock received from an ISO exercise before one year from the exercise date or two years from the grant date, whichever is later. If a sale or disposition occurs prior to one year from the exercise date or two years from the date of grant, the sale will be taxed at ordinary income tax rates. Dispositions can also occur if the stock is gifted.

Observation

Generally, it is best to exercise ISOs early in the year if the AMT is likely to be paid. The early exercise provides flexibility to sell the shares before year-end and avoid the AMT if the stock drops in value. In this case, the taxpayer will only pay ordinary income tax on the actual gain, rather than the AMT on the spread between the fair market value at exercise and the exercise price.

Observation

Generally, the more ordinary income you have in any given year, the less likely you are to be subject to the AMT. Thus, many executives exercise nonqualified stock options and ISOs in the same year; the former increase their taxable income so that they are less likely to pay AMT on the spread from the ISOs. In addition, if bonuses vary significantly from year to year, it may make sense to exercise the ISOs in the year in which your bonus is higher. If you are likely to be subject to AMT indefinitely (absent a law change), you may consider a disqualifying disposition of the ISO.

Stock Option Exercise Methods

There are several methods used to fund the purchase price of the option at exercise, including cash, margin loan, cashless, and stock swaps. Cash and margin loan funding are straightforward transactions and the most popular when exercising ISOs, as ISOs require you to purchase the stock and hold it for at least one year. These are also called "exercise and hold" transactions.

The most common form of a cashless exercise is the sale of the shares upon exercise, which funds the exercise price and tax liability withholding. The employee is then distributed the remaining cash. These transactions, called "exercise and sell" transactions, are the most common form of exercise for nonqualified stock options for executives wishing to diversify holdings.

> ### Observation
> Even though federal tax is withheld on the exercise of the nonqualified stock option, it is withheld at only the statutory rate of 25 percent (or 35 percent if over $1 million). Thus, there may be additional tax that is due if your marginal tax rate is higher than 25 percent. This should be taken into consideration when investing excess cash from an "exercise and sell" transaction or funding a cash or margin loan exercise.

Some option plans permit a taxpayer to pay the exercise price in the form of existing shares (i.e., a stock swap), thereby eliminating the need to fund the exercise with cash. Using stock to pay for the exercise of stock options is also a way to help reduce the investment concentration in employer stock, a common issue for executives who have employer stock options as part of their compensation package.

> ### Observation
> Overall, many factors determine when to exercise an option and what method of exercise to use. One should consider factors such as: company requirements for stock ownership, age of the options, overall asset allocation, anticipated growth in company stock, general stock market conditions, cash flow situation, and of course your tax (regular and AMT) situation. There is no one size that fits all situations.

Restricted Stock and Other Stock-Based Compensation

Stock options are not the only types of equity-based compensation that employers use when designing a compensation program for their executives. Other types of equity-based compensation include performance stock, stock appreciation rights, restricted stock, and restricted stock units (RSUs).

Performance stock is an award whose value is based on the value of the company's actual stock and depends on the achievement of a predetermined set of objectives or the passage of time. Performance stock awards are taxable when they are available. Stock appreciation rights are the right to receive an amount of compensation equal to the appreciation of the company stock over a period of time. Stock appreciation rights are taxable when the right vests.

The most commonly used forms of equity-based compensation are restricted stock and restricted stock units. Restricted stock is the award of company shares that contain restrictions. The employee actually has his or her name on the stock certificate, and has voting and dividend rights. This is not the case with RSUs, which are the promise to deliver company shares after restrictions lapse. For both of these, the taxable event occurs when the restrictions lapse. The employee's compensation will equal the fair market value of the stock (less price paid, if any). The company is required to withhold (at the statutory rate of 25 percent, or 35 percent if over $1 million).

Observation

If you wish to diversify and reduce your concentration in your employer securities, consider selling your stock as soon as the restrictions lapse.

An 83(b) election can be made (if applicable) to be taxed in the year the restricted stock is granted, instead of the year in which the restrictions lapse. This election must be made in the year in which the restricted stock is granted to the employee, filed with the tax authorities within 30 days of the receipt of the grant, and attached to the tax return for that year. It is important to note that this is available only for restricted stock, not RSUs.

> ### Observation
>
> The 83(b) election must be considered very carefully before it is made. It can be a significant tax saver when the election is made and the stock value is low, resulting in very little taxable income. If over time the stock significantly appreciates, all that value will be taxed at the favorable capital gains tax rate. Alternatively, if the stock value does not appreciate (or even declines), you will have paid tax on the compensation value at the time of election, resulting in at least the loss of the use of the money (if the stock value remained constant) or the lost cash paid in taxes if the stock price declined.

Putting It All Together: Structuring a Tax-Efficient, Diversified Portfolio

In today's uncertain economic environment, managing risk and ensuring portfolio efficiency have become particularly important. A proven way to minimize risk is to structure a diversified portfolio that is based on your ability to tolerate risk. Diversification among the asset classes (stocks, bonds, etc.) is important, but diversification within an asset class (e.g., into large-cap stocks, small-cap stocks, and industry-specific investments) is equally important.

The most efficient portfolio is one that maximizes the real rate of return, or your return after inflation and taxes. Each investor should conduct an asset allocation analysis to ensure that the portfolio is as tax efficient as possible. Tax efficiency can be maximized by determining where an investor should hold which asset (i.e., in either a taxable or a tax-deferred account). There is no simple answer to the question of which investment is the most beneficial in each type of account. Consideration should be given to the character of the expected investment return produced by the investment, short- or long-term capital gain, nontaxable or taxable ordinary income, the expected portfolio turnover, the expected return volatility, and the time period of tax deferral.

Historically, investments producing significant amounts of taxable income each year (taxable interest or dividends, short-term capital gains, or ordinary income) most likely would have been allocated first to tax-deferred or tax-free accounts. So, too, would investment styles with significant portfolio turnover. Additionally, investments producing long-term capital gains with little portfolio turnover most likely would have been allocated to taxable accounts.

Now, taxpayers with long-term tax-deferral opportunities may be well advised to put their potentially highest-earning assets in tax-deferred accounts even if the withdrawal will be taxed at a rate much higher than the 15 percent current tax rate. Tax-deferred compounding on high-growth-rate assets for long periods of time can more than offset the benefits of low current tax rates.

Likewise, with the taxation of qualified dividends at the low 15 percent tax rate, it may make sense to not put high-dividend-paying stocks in tax-deferral accounts and instead pay the tax currently.

Taxpayers with shorter-term tax-deferral opportunities generally should place more emphasis on the current tax rates (and tax efficiencies) when making asset allocation decisions. Shorter periods of tax deferral may not justify the loss of lower-tax-rate earnings, or the risk of increased tax rates after the presidential election.

Idea Checklist

- ☑ As part of your ongoing and regular review of your asset allocation, reevaluate whether higher-return, tax-efficient assets should be placed in taxable or tax-deferred accounts. However, keep tax considerations secondary to investment fundamentals.

- ☑ Consider how reduced long-term capital gains and qualified dividend tax rates affect investment allocations among your taxable and tax-deferred accounts.

- ☑ Make gifts of capital assets to your low income tax bracket children or grandchildren (but watch out for the kiddie tax) to take advantage of capital gains having a 0 percent rate.

- ☑ Review your capital gains and capital loss positions over the course of the year; do not wait until just before year-end. Try to offset capital gains with capital losses. Keep in mind the 30-day (before and after) wash sale rule.

- ☑ Consider reallocating some of your bond portfolio to dividend-paying stocks now that qualified dividends are taxed at no more than 15 percent. But again, keep the tax considerations secondary to investment fundamentals.

- ☑ Make full use of the $3,000 capital loss deduction that can be used to offset your ordinary income.

- ☑ Determine whether tax-exempt bonds are an appropriate investment. If so, consider whether investing in private activity bonds (taxable tax-exempt bonds) will improve your yield.

- ☑ Executives with ISOs should consider, if possible, how to minimize the AMT on their ISO exercise and should hold the shares for more than one year from exercise (and two years from option grant) to ensure qualifying their gain for the 15 percent capital gains tax rate.

- ☑ Consider whether alternative investments, such as hedge funds, are appropriate additions to your portfolio in your attempt to manage risk while producing a reasonable return. However, consideration should be given to the tax implications and liquidity restrictions of these investments before making the investment.

- ☑ Consider the potential wealth opportunities of your stock-based compensation and how the concentration in one stock could affect your overall portfolio risk. Consider what will help maximize the wealth opportunities, while taking into account the effect on your overall portfolio and the objective of minimizing taxes.

A key goal for most taxpayers' investment strategies is to accumulate funds for retirement. Chapter 4 assesses the many ways in which the tax law provides incentives for retirement savings.

Chapter 4
Retirement Planning

Today, most workers have much greater tax incentives to save for retirement than ever before because of more favorable rules for traditional individual retirement accounts (IRAs), Roth IRAs, Keogh plans, and corporate retirement plans. Those who can take advantage of these opportunities can lower their taxes now, while helping to ensure their comfort and financial security during retirement. The improvements are particularly welcome now, because individual retirement planning is more important than ever. With employer-paid pensions becoming increasingly rare every year and more businesses downsizing, wage earners face the prospect of financing more of their retirement with their own resources. For most people, retirement income is likely to come from three sources:

1. Tax-favored retirement plans, perhaps including defined benefit pension plans, but more likely profit-sharing, stock bonus, IRA and Roth IRA, and employer-sponsored savings plans. These plans include the 401(k) and Roth 401(k); 403(b) (for teachers and employees of tax-exempt organizations); simplified employee pension (SEP) plan and Keogh plan (for the self-employed); savings incentive match plan for employees (SIMPLE—for workers in firms with fewer than 100 employees); and 457 plan for government employees.

2. Investments outside of tax-favored retirement plans.
3. Social Security.

Tax legislation over the past few years has allowed taxpayers to increase their contributions to qualified savings plans, with workers age 50 and over permitted to make generous catch-up contributions. High-income employees, who do not qualify for Roth IRAs, may be able to enroll in an employer-sponsored Roth incentive savings plan. In this type of plan, employees contribute after-tax funds, but they are allowed to withdraw the money and appreciation tax-free with no fixed schedule of required lifetime distributions. Roth funds can even be left free of income tax to an heir. Some lower-income workers can get a tax credit of as much as 50 percent of the money they contribute to qualified retirement plans and IRAs, which directly offsets their taxes for the year of the contribution.

Because capital gains tax rates are only 15 percent through 2010, taxpayers must keep in mind the benefits of capital gains tax breaks when planning for retirement. Retirement plans allow tax-free compounding of profits, but most payouts are taxed at ordinary income tax rates in the year they are received. Those who expect relatively high income in retirement should weigh the merits of forgoing the tax deferral, investing after-tax funds for retirement, and being taxed on sale at lower capital gains tax rates. However, they should not forget that the alternative minimum tax (AMT) could void much of the advantage. Capital gains, while not subject to the AMT, can push total income into the AMT range, subjecting other income and deductions to the AMT.

Observation

Some studies have shown that lower-income individuals may actually pay more tax and have less money available to spend in retirement by contributing to 401(k) or other retirement plans. Part of the reason for this is the high marginal tax rate on Social Security income for some taxpayers. (See the Social Security section later in this chapter.)

Moderate-income taxpayers should use retirement plans and/or IRAs to save for retirement for these reasons:

- Putting money aside in a retirement plan clearly segregates and identifies the funds for retirement, thus reducing the temptation to spend the funds for other purposes. Indeed, the penalties for early withdrawal and, in some cases, the unavailability of the funds make it more difficult to use the funds prematurely.
- Many 401(k) plans have some portion of the employee contribution matched by the employer. The match is not available for savings outside of the plan.
- While current tax law may, under some circumstances, result in higher taxes at retirement for tax-deferred plan proceeds, it is difficult to predict personal circumstances many years in the future and even more difficult to predict the applicable tax law.

Because most people will benefit from maximizing tax deferral on retirement savings, this chapter details valuable planning techniques and offers suggestions that can help to reduce overall tax bills and maximize income during retirement.

Employer Plans

Qualified Retirement Plans

When possible, you should think about participating in a qualified employer pension or profit-sharing plan, a 401(k) plan, a 403(b) plan, a Keogh plan, a SIMPLE, or a SEP plan. Qualified plans must meet complex participation, coverage, and nondiscrimination requirements, allowing sponsoring employers to immediately deduct their contributions. Employer contributions on your behalf are not taxed to you until you receive them. Your pretax contributions to these plans reduce your adjusted gross income (AGI) within specified limits as well as your current tax bill. This tax deferral is achieved in exchange for reduced liquidity because you give up immediate access to the funds. However, some plans permit you to borrow up to specified allowable limits from your account, giving you access to some of your savings if necessary.

> **Observation**
>
> It should be noted, however, that borrowing these funds is generally not as advantageous from a tax perspective as borrowing from a third party since this interest is not tax deductible and you are giving up the opportunity for pretax earnings on a larger base. This is particularly true when the investment return in the plan is greater than the borrowing rate.

> **Observation**
>
> The SIMPLE is available to employees of companies with 100 or fewer employees who do not have other types of retirement plans. Under this type of plan, employees may defer up to $10,500 for 2008 (or $13,000 if age 50 or older by year-end). Employers that offer a SIMPLE generally must make a nonelective or matching contribution on behalf of each plan participant.

There are two basic kinds of qualified employer retirement plans:
1. Defined contribution plans.
2. Defined benefit plans.

Defined Contribution Plans

A defined contribution plan allows your company or you—or your company *and* you—to contribute a set amount each year to the plan. Contributions are set aside in an account for you and are invested on your behalf. Sometimes you have the right to determine how the contributions are invested. With a defined contribution plan, you are not guaranteed a set amount of benefits when you retire. Instead, you receive the amount in the account, which depends on how much was contributed and how successfully the funds were invested over the years. You will receive a periodic statement advising you of your current account balance.

Defined contribution plan benefits are portable, so if you change jobs, you can transfer your vested benefits to an IRA or possibly to your new employer's plan. Most defined benefit pension plans, on the contrary, do not make your vested benefit available before you reach retirement age, unless your benefit is very small (in which case the plan may cash you out).

The most common defined contribution plans are profit-sharing plans, 401(k) plans, stock bonus plans, money purchase pension plans, and employee stock ownership plans.

Bigger Contributions Allowed The maximum contribution for 2008 increased $1,000 to $46,000 because of the annual inflation adjustment. The limit on the amount of compensation taken into account in figuring the contribution also increased in 2008 to $230,000, from $225,000 in 2007, because of the same inflation adjustment. These higher limits mean that larger contributions and benefits are possible for the more highly compensated.

In addition to the maximum dollar contribution, there are further limits based on a percentage of compensation. The maximum allocation to an individual account is 100 percent of salary. There is a 25 percent (of total payroll or of adjusted self-employment earnings) limitation on deductions for all contributions (except elective deferrals) to defined contribution plans for all covered participants, collectively. Thus, a sole proprietor or a one-employee corporation will be subject to the 25 percent limit.

> **Caution**
> Highly paid employees may still not be allowed to take full advantage of the increased contribution limits after nondiscrimination tests are applied.

Profit-Sharing Plans Profit-sharing plans are defined contribution plans that allow employees to share in the company's profits, usually through a discretionary employer contribution that is a percentage of compensation. Despite what the name implies, profit-sharing plans are not dependent on corporate profits for contributions to be made. Contribution levels may be changed from one year to the next. Plan participants generally do not control how the contributions are invested.

401(k) Plans Section 401(k) plans are defined contribution plans that are generically known as employee thrift or savings plans. You, as an eligible employee, elect in advance to defer part of your compensation to be held by the plan, and sometimes your employer will match some or all of it. Neither the amount deferred nor your employer matching contribution is included in your income until distributed from the plan.

A common level of employer matching contribution is $0.50 for every $1 the employee contributes up to a set percentage limit. For example, your employer may contribute 3 percent of your compensation if you contribute 6 percent. It is like a guaranteed 50 percent first-year return on the amount you contribute each year. Your own contributions are vested immediately, but your right to keep the matching contributions depends on the plan's vesting schedule. Matching contributions must vest either all at once after no more than three years or at a rate of 20 percent each year starting with the second year of service. Employer matching contributions made before 2002 are permitted to vest at a somewhat slower rate.

> ### Observation
> If you are eligible for matching contributions by your employer, make every effort to contribute at least the amount that will entitle you to the maximum available employer matching contribution.

As a 401(k) plan participant, you generally make your own investment decisions, usually by choosing among a variety of funds selected by your employer. The Pension Protection Act of 2006 permits qualified plan providers to offer individualized investment advice for the plan participants. This may be a new feature of your 401(k) plan and is worth looking into with your employer.

401(k) Contribution Limits For 2008, the maximum amount that you can elect to defer to a 401(k) plan is $15,500, subject to certain overall limits. Future contribution limits will increase as they are indexed for inflation. If you are over age 50 by the end of a year, you will be allowed to make even larger contributions, called catch-up contributions. For 2008, the catch-up contribution maximum is $5,000, and it will be indexed for inflation in future years. Also, contributions up to the dollar maximums are no longer limited by a set percentage of your compensation, unless provided for in your plan.

Observation

A change in the limitations means that you may contribute the maximum dollar amount to your 401(k) plan for a year, even if that amount is half, three-quarters, or all of your salary for the year. This important change will be especially useful in boosting retirement savings of a second family earner with modest earnings.

EXAMPLE

Sarah, who is 47 years old, reenters the workforce in 2008, on a part-time basis after a child-care hiatus of 15 years. Her employer maintains a 401(k) plan in which Sarah is eligible to participate after three months of service. Sarah's husband earns enough to support the family, and Sarah wants to put as much of her earnings as possible into a retirement

(Continued)

> **Continued**
>
> plan on a pretax basis. Sarah expects to earn $10,000 in compensation in 2008, during the time she is eligible to make elective 401(k) deferrals.
>
> *Result:* If Sarah wishes, she may contribute 100 percent of her compensation to the 401(k) plan. Only the annual dollar limit on 401(k) contributions (and her FICA tax liability) would reduce the amount she can contribute.

Note that even though these pretax contributions allow you to avoid immediate income tax, they are subject to Social Security tax.

Special nondiscrimination rules apply to 401(k) elective deferrals, but those rules will not limit the catch-up contributions you make if you are age 50 or over. If your employer chooses to match catch-up contributions, the matching contributions will be subject to the usual nondiscrimination rules that apply to other employer matching contributions.

> **Observation**
>
> The favorable tax rates for capital gains and qualified dividends should have little impact on the decision to participate in 401(k) plans. The combination of tax deductions, tax-deferred accumulation, and the potential for employer matching contributions should continue to make these plans the first-choice savings vehicle for retirement (despite the fact that distributions are subject to ordinary income tax rates). Psychological benefits are also associated with payroll deductions that make it painless and easy to invest. Further, access to the funds prior to retirement is restricted, thus reducing the temptation to spend.

The only taxpayers who should reconsider participation are older taxpayers who are close to retirement, receive no company match, and expect to be in a higher tax bracket in their retirement years.

Savings Incentive Match Plan for Employees Companies with 100 or fewer employees that do not offer other types of retirement plans can set up a SIMPLE. As its name implies, a SIMPLE is easier and less expensive to set up and administer than a standard qualified retirement plan. Under this type of plan, employees may defer up to $10,500 for 2008. Those employees age 50 and over may defer an additional $2,500 through catch-up contributions. Employers that offer a SIMPLE generally just make a nonelective or matching contribution in the 2 percent to 3 percent range on behalf of each plan participant.

The contribution limits on deferrals by employees to SIMPLE plans will be indexed for inflation increases on an annual basis.

Defined Benefit Pension Plans

Unlike a defined contribution plan, a defined benefit plan—commonly called a pension plan—generally pays a fixed monthly amount of income at retirement. The benefit is determined using a formula specified in the plan, usually based on your salary and the number of years you have worked for your employer. Some companies increase pension benefits during retirement to help overcome the impact of inflation.

You are entitled to your monthly pension benefit whether or not the plan contributions have been invested well. If the value of the investments falls below the amount needed to fund the promised benefit, the employer must contribute more to the plan, so you do not bear the risk of bad investments or a severe market downturn. If the plan ceases to exist, the Pension Benefit Guaranty Corporation (PBGC) pays promised benefits up to a certain level. Defined benefit plans generally do not require or allow employee contributions.

If you retire early, you will usually receive a reduced benefit, and if you work beyond normal retirement age, you receive an increased amount when you begin to collect benefits as indexed.

Increase in Benefit Limit The maximum annual benefit that a defined benefit pension plan can fund is $185,000 in 2008. This amount will be indexed for future inflation. The limit is somewhat lower for benefits beginning before age 62 and higher for payments beginning after age 65.

Nonqualified Deferred Compensation Plans

Nonqualified plans are used to reward individual executives, or other employees, without the need to treat all individuals similarly—if a company is willing to forgo current tax deductions for its contributions. (The company's deduction is delayed until the year the income is taxed to the executive.)

> ### Observation
> If you are a highly compensated employee, consider the benefits of coverage under a nonqualified plan. These plans offer the benefits of tax deferral on both the deferred amount and the income, as well as the ability to set aside larger amounts of retirement assets than do most qualified plans.

> ### Caution
> An employee is treated as a general creditor of an employer in the event that a company enters bankruptcy. This means that if your employer goes bankrupt, you have to get in line with all the other general creditors to get a portion of your employer's remaining assets, and you may lose some or all of your nonqualified plan benefits.

Under most deferred compensation plans, you elect to defer a portion of your salary or bonus until a future date (e.g., retirement). To obtain the tax savings, you generally must agree to defer the compensation before the year in which it is earned or awarded, and at the same time you must elect when and how your benefits under the plan will be paid.

Your Resources

Planning for retirement can include making contributions to Keogh plans or other self-employed retirement plans such as SEPs or IRAs, and making after-tax contributions to employer plans and 401(k) plans if they are available to you. Make sure you maximize the tax benefits by carefully considering the type of plan and whether contributions are deductible.

Observation

For most people, the decision to contribute to IRAs, SEPs, and Keoghs should not be impacted by the reduced tax rates on capital gains and qualified dividends discussed in Chapter 2. The immediate tax deduction combined with tax-deferred growth continues to provide an attractive after-tax potential (despite the ordinary income tax treatment on distributions). These accounts are particularly attractive for portfolios that produce significant short-term capital gains or ordinary income.

Observation

Beginning in 2007, participants in a qualified plan can roll over after-tax contributions to another qualified plan provided the rollover is made through a direct trustee-to-trustee transfer and the receiving plan accounts for the rollover separately.

Caution

The benefits of deductible retirement savings are not as certain for some taxpayers:

- Those who are over age 70½ (only Keogh and SEP contributions are allowed for these people, not IRA contributions) as a result of a shorter period in which tax is deferred.
- Those with an asset allocation heavy on dividend-paying stocks and low portfolio turnover, since in the current environment dividends are taxed at a historically low tax rate.
- Those who expect to be in a higher tax bracket during their retirement years.

Keogh Plans

If you are self-employed, you can increase your retirement savings by taking advantage of self-employed retirement fund (e.g., Keogh plan) contributions. You can make a deductible contribution to your own retirement plan for a given year up to the due date (including extensions) of your tax return for that year. The plan itself, however, must be set up by the end of the year for which the contribution is made to take advantage of this deferred-payment rule.

There are three general types of Keogh plans from which to choose:

1. *Profit-sharing plan:* Annual contributions may be discretionary, up to a certain percentage of self-employment income.
2. *Money purchase plan:* Yearly contributions based on a chosen percentage of self-employment income are mandatory.

3. *Defined benefit plan:* Contributions are based on complex calculations. Although this is the most expensive kind of plan to operate, older, highly compensated, and self-employed individuals usually find that it permits them to make the largest tax-deductible contributions.

Keogh contribution and deduction limits are the same as those for other qualified retirement plans, with adjustments for the way the self-employed individual's earned income is figured.

Observation

If you are self-employed and have employees, or you own another company with employees, you must remember that Keogh plans are subject to complex nondiscrimination and coverage rules. You generally cannot cover just yourself if you have part-time or full-time employees (or you own another company with employees) who are at least age 21 and who have worked for you for one year or more.

Simplified Employee Pension Plans

If you are self-employed or have a small company, you can also choose to use this IRA-type plan in which a percentage of net self-employment income is contributed to the plan (similar to a defined contribution Keogh plan). Unlike Keogh plans, SEPs can be established as late as the extended tax return due date for the prior tax year. A SEP must also provide comparable benefits for employees who satisfy certain liberal eligibility requirements. SEPs have a 25 percent contribution limit, which matches that of other defined contribution plans. While simpler to administer than regular Keogh plans, SEPs provide fewer options than Keogh plans do for accumulating large retirement benefits, especially for older plan participants. New SEPs also cannot offer 401(k) features such as income deferral by employees unless they were established before 1997.

Traditional and Roth Individual Retirement Accounts

Any person under age 70½ (or older for Roth IRAs) with earned income during 2008 can establish an IRA and contribute up to the lesser of earned income or $5,000. There are two very different types of IRAs:

1. *Traditional IRAs:* Contributions are deductible if the IRA owner is not covered by a qualified retirement plan or if income limits are not exceeded; distributions are fully or partly taxable. Those whose income level is too high to take deductions for these contributions may make nondeductible contributions. Distributions of pretax contributions and the appreciation on contributions from traditional IRAs are taxable when received and are subject to a 10 percent excise tax if taken before age 59½ (with certain limited exceptions).

2. *Roth IRAs:* While contributions are not deductible, earnings paid to you from these accounts are tax-free as long as certain requirements are met. Generally, the account must exist for at least five tax years, and you must receive the funds after you've reached age 59½ or as a result of death or disability. If you meet the income requirements to make Roth IRA contributions, you should seriously consider doing so. Roth IRAs are an excellent vehicle in which to save for retirement.

Observation

Consideration should be given to the types of assets in your IRA accounts to maximize the after-tax investment rate of return on your global portfolio.

The maximum amount that you can contribute to a Roth IRA for a year is phased out over an AGI range of $101,000 to $116,000 for unmarried taxpayers and $159,000 to $169,000 for married taxpayers who file a joint tax return. If you are not above these income levels, you may contribute even if you participate in an employer-sponsored retirement plan. If your income is above these full-phaseout levels, you are ineligible to contribute to a Roth IRA.

> **Observation**
>
> Contributing to a Roth IRA is still advantageous relative to taxable investments, even after the reductions in long-term capital gains and qualified dividend tax rates. Roth IRAs generate tax-free income and are not subject to the required lifetime distribution rules that govern other IRAs.

Roth 401(k)

Beginning in 2006, employers could offer Roth 401(k) accounts as an additional alternative to regular 401(k) contributions. The Roth 401(k) contributions are not deductible like regular 401(k) contributions, but can be rolled over to a Roth IRA or distributed tax-free after age 59½ and five years of plan participation. This feature may appeal to taxpayers who expect to be in a high tax bracket during retirement. The amount of the contribution is subject to the normal 401(k) contribution limits as discussed previously. To the extent that you use the Roth 401(k) option, your regular deductible 401(k) contribution is reduced. The Roth 401(k) was scheduled to sunset after 2010, but was made permanent by the Pension Protection Act of 2006.

Higher Contribution Limits

The maximum annual IRA contribution limit and catch-up contributions for those 50 or older as of the end of a year will increase, as shown in Table 4.1. The higher limits apply to both traditional and Roth IRAs.

Table 4.1 *Increased IRA Contribution*

Year	Regular ($)	Catch-Up ($)
2007	4,000	1,000
2008 and later	5,000	1,000

Observation

The increase in maximum IRA contributions gives you greater opportunities to save for retirement on a tax-favored basis and will help you to rely less on employer retirement plans and Social Security.

Observation

Nondeductible contributions to a traditional IRA are less attractive, because long-term capital gains and qualified dividend income are currently taxed at a maximum rate of only 15 percent outside of the plan, or 0 percent for those in the two lowest tax brackets. Because capital gains and dividends that are earned within an IRA are taxed at ordinary income tax rates when distributed, they lose the benefit of the preferential tax rates. Also, funds in the IRA are subject to required distribution beginning at age 70½, as described later in this chapter, whereas investments outside of the IRA do not have to be liquidated at any set time.

There has always been a school of thought that only long-term periods of deferral justify the use of nondeductible IRAs (because they can convert lower tax rate income into higher tax rate income).

The reduced tax rates on qualified dividends and long-term capital gains only add fuel to the debate. For portfolios that produce significant short-term capital gains or ordinary income, nondeductible IRAs may remain attractive, especially for those far from payout status. Also, younger taxpayers should continue to consider nondeductible IRAs, because long periods of tax deferral may overcome the other disadvantages associated with them.

One other point to consider is the implication of the sunset of the lower qualified dividend and long-term capital gains tax rates in 2011, leading to the potential for lost IRA opportunity. If these tax rates are not made permanent, taxpayers who passed on nondeductible IRAs for several years will not be able to make up those contributions.

Traditional Individual Retirement Accounts

Your ability to make tax-deductible contributions to a traditional IRA is limited by your income level if you are an active participant in your employer-sponsored retirement plan. The maximum deductible contribution you can make phases out over certain income levels (see Table 4.2).

If you are married, but you and your spouse file separately, your deduction phaseout range is from $0 to $10,000 of AGI, effectively preventing each of you from taking IRA deductions in almost all cases in which at least one spouse is an active participant in an employer-sponsored retirement plan.

Table 4.2 Phaseout of IRA Deductions for Employer Plan Participants

Year	Single and Head of Household Deduction ($) Full	Single and Head of Household Deduction ($) None	Married Filing Jointly Deduction ($) Full	Married Filing Jointly Deduction ($) None
2008	53,000	63,000	85,000	105,000

Tax Law Changes and Financial Planning

A nonworking spouse or a working spouse who is not a participant in a qualified retirement plan, but whose spouse is, has an opportunity to make tax-deductible contributions to a regular IRA on a joint return even though the working spouse is an active retirement plan participant. The availability of this deduction phases out for couples with an AGI between $159,000 and $169,000.

> ### Observation
> If you qualify, you should always make a contribution to a Roth IRA rather than making a nondeductible contribution to a traditional IRA. No deduction is allowed in either case, but the earnings on nondeductible traditional IRA contributions will be taxed to you at ordinary income tax rates when you take distributions, whereas there is the potential for completely tax-free distributions from the Roth IRA. Also, there is no requirement that amounts in Roth IRAs be distributed to you during your lifetime, as there is with traditional IRAs. This allows you to keep the Roth IRA's tax shelter going for your entire life, if you so choose, and pass the tax-free earnings on to your heirs.

> ### Observation
> Starting in 2007, if you are covered by a high-deductible health plan, you may be able to make a nontaxable health savings account (HSA) funding distribution from your IRA (not applicable to SEP or SIMPLE IRAs) that would otherwise be included in income. The distribution must be a trustee-to-trustee transfer to an HSA. This distribution will not be taxable to the extent that it is not more than the limit on your annual HSA contributions.

Conversions to Roth Individual Retirement Accounts

Traditional IRAs may be converted into Roth IRAs if your AGI is less than $100,000 (regardless of whether you are single or married). You will have to pay income tax on the amount converted, but not the 10 percent penalty that applies to early IRA withdrawals. Distributions from a Roth IRA within five years of the conversion that come from converted amounts will be subject to the 10 percent penalty tax. Beginning in 2010, the $100,000 ceiling on AGI will be removed and all taxpayers will be able to convert their traditional IRAs to Roth IRAs if they desire. The Tax Increase Prevention and Reconciliation Act of 2005 allows taxpayers to elect to spread ratably the recognition of income from Roth conversions completed in 2010 over tax years 2011 and 2012. However, income recognition is accelerated if a distribution occurs before 2012.

> **Observation**
>
> Consider converting (if your AGI makes you eligible) a traditional IRA invested in equities or stock mutual funds to a Roth IRA when stock values are depressed. The tax cost will be based on the low valuations at the time of the conversion, and no tax will be owed on future value increases. Beginning in 2010, you can convert regardless of the level of your AGI, and you can elect to spread the income from the conversion ratably over the 2011 and 2012 tax years.

> **Observation**
>
> After age 70½, required minimum distributions are no longer taken into account for the $100,000 income limit on Roth IRA conversion eligibility. This rule should allow more senior individuals to convert traditional IRAs to Roth IRAs than in past years.

> ### *Observation*
>
> Consider contributing currently to a nondeductible IRA if you do not currently qualify to make contributions to a deductible IRA or Roth IRA due to limitations previously discussed. In 2010, the nondeductible IRA funds can be converted to a Roth IRA since no income limits will apply. There should be little tax effect as only the appreciation in the account would be subject to tax. Due to the short time horizon, those gains could be relatively small. See Chapter 2 for more details and Caution regarding Roth IRA conversions.

You can change your mind and undo a conversion from a traditional IRA to a Roth IRA by transferring the funds back to a regular IRA in a direct trustee-to-trustee transfer. This eliminates the tax liability that otherwise results from the conversion. You might need to do this, for example, if your AGI for the conversion year exceeds the $100,000 AGI limit, making you ineligible to convert. Or you may want to switch back if the value of the assets in the Roth IRA has dropped after the conversion, and you do not want to pay tax based on the higher value of the assets on the conversion date. If you convert to a Roth IRA in 2008, you will have until October 15, 2009, to transfer it back to a traditional IRA, assuming you file a timely 2008 tax return. If you file your return before undoing the conversion, you'll need to file an amended return to report the reversal and eliminate your tax liability from the conversion.

If you have switched back to a regular IRA from a Roth IRA, you can reconvert to another Roth IRA and have your tax liability figured on the basis of the later conversion. However, you cannot reconvert until the start of the year after the original Roth IRA conversion was made, or, if later, more than 30 days after you switched the Roth IRA back to a traditional IRA.

Example

John converts a $200,000 IRA brokerage account (to which he has made only deductible contributions) to a Roth IRA in January 2008, giving him $200,000 of taxable income on the conversion.

Even though the value of that Roth IRA account falls to $170,000 in July 2008, John is nonetheless liable for tax on $200,000. However, if he transfers the $170,000 directly back to a traditional IRA, he will wipe out his tax liability from the conversion. Later he can reconvert to another Roth IRA after the waiting period has passed (explained earlier), perhaps before the value of the assets in the traditional IRA has fully recovered.

Observation

When it comes to IRAs, the earlier contributions are made, the better. Take the case of a 22-year-old who begins contributing $2,000 annually to an IRA for just 10 years, stopping after age 31. Assuming an annual growth rate of 10 percent, the assets in that IRA will increase to approximately $895,000 by the time the IRA owner is 65 years old, even though this person has contributed only $20,000 to the IRA account.

Contrast that with someone who waits until age 32 to start contributing to an IRA, but contributes $2,000 for 33 years— a total of $66,000. Assuming the funds also earn 10 percent, at age 65 this person's account balance is only about $540,000; it is $355,000 less than the IRA of the person who contributed for only 10 years starting at age 22, despite $46,000 more in contributions.

Once you establish the retirement savings vehicle or vehicles that are in line with your goals (and, obviously, for which you are eligible and from those that are available to you), you should contribute early and regularly to benefit more fully from the effects of tax-free compounding.

> ### *Observation*
> You do not have to wait until you are sure of your income for a year to contribute to an IRA. You can give to either a regular IRA or a Roth IRA at any time and switch the IRA account classification by October 15 of the following year, as long as you timely file your income tax return. For example, if you make a Roth IRA contribution or conversion during 2008, and it turns out that your income for that year is more than the allowable limit, you can transfer the funds and their earnings to a regular IRA (deductible or nondeductible, depending on your circumstances) by October 15, 2009.

> ### *Observation*
> Because many people in their teens and early twenties do not earn enough to save on a regular basis, this is an excellent opportunity for parents and grandparents to give their children and grandchildren a long-term gift that costs a fraction of its ultimate value. If your children or grandchildren work, consider helping them set up an IRA to capitalize on the big benefits of tax-deferred compounding (tax-free compounding with a Roth IRA) over long periods.
>
> It is amazing how much the investment can grow if a contribution is made to a tax-favored retirement plan early in life. For example, if you contributed $2,000 per year to an IRA for your child or grandchild while she was age 16 through 22 and never contributed another dime, assuming a 10 percent annual growth rate, she would have a retirement fund at age 65 of about $1.2 million, with only $14,000 in total IRA account contributions.

> **Observation**
>
> Giving funds to a Roth IRA for a child or grandchild will also allow the child or grandchild to withdraw $10,000 of earnings tax-free and penalty-free to put toward the purchase of his or her first home.

Tax Credit for Retirement Saving

Taxpayers with modest incomes now have another reason to save for their retirement. The Pension Protection Act of 2006 made the retirement savings contribution credit permanent. Taxpayers may be eligible for a nonrefundable tax credit if they contribute to qualified retirement plans and IRAs. The maximum annual contribution eligible for the credit is $2,000 per individual. The credit is in addition to any contribution deduction available.

For the lowest-income individuals (up to an AGI of $32,000 for joint return filers, $24,000 for heads of households, and $16,000 for all others), the credit is 50 percent of the eligible contribution. That would be a $1,000 tax credit for a $2,000 contribution. As AGI increases, the credit rate phases down from 50 percent to 10 percent of the contribution. It is totally phased out for those with an AGI above $53,000 for joint filers, $39,750 for heads of households, and $26,500 for singles. This credit is not available to students, taxpayers under age 18, or dependents.

> **Observation**
>
> This credit will be available to many young taxpayers who are out of school, but whose salaries are still modest. Be sure to tell your children about the new credit and encourage or help them to start their retirement saving.

Charitable Remainder Trusts

Another vehicle to consider for funding a portion of your retirement is a charitable remainder trust (CRT). A CRT is a trust that is generally a tax-exempt entity. The trust pays an annuity amount to an individual (usually the trust creator), and after a term of years or the annuitant's lifetime, the remaining trust assets are paid to one or more qualified charitable organizations. Although complex rules apply, funding such trusts with appreciated securities can provide an alternative to traditional qualified and nonqualified plans. The appreciated assets contributed to a CRT can be sold and diversified into a properly allocated investment portfolio without causing immediate capital gains tax on the entire sale. You can improve cash flow through a charitable income tax deduction in the CRT's first year of existence and by delaying the payment of taxes until distributions are received from the CRT. The CRT distributions can be made over your lifetime or a term of years to better help you plan retirement cash flow needs. Due to the complexity of the rules governing such a transaction, you should consult a tax professional to learn more.

Tax-Deferred Annuities

If you have contributed the maximum amount permitted to a 401(k) or 403(b) plan and have contributed to an IRA, and you have a portfolio of stocks designed to take advantage of favorable capital gains tax rates, then you may want to consider a tax-deferred annuity. The investment earnings (usually from name-brand mutual funds and other investment alternatives) can compound tax-deferred within the annuity vehicle until they are withdrawn. It is important to remember that annuities will ultimately be taxed at ordinary income tax rates (not capital gains tax rates) when distributed to you, similar to a traditional IRA. This is true even if the money is invested in mutual funds that would have been taxed at a 15 percent rate if held outside the annuity. Annuities are similar to IRAs in that there is a 10 percent excise tax generally applied to withdrawals prior to age 59½. Annuities offer a guaranteed payment option that will assure a fixed level of payments for your lifetime. Before investing in an annuity, however, you should examine the expenses and fees charged by the insurance company issuing the annuity to ensure competitiveness with other investment alternatives. You might also consider the universal variable life insurance policy alternative discussed next.

Observation

Deferred annuities are less advantageous now that long-term capital gains and qualified dividend income are taxed at a maximum tax rate of only 15 percent—except perhaps for the fact that these tax rates currently are not permanent. Because capital gains and dividends that are earned within an annuity are taxed at ordinary income tax rates when distributed, they lose the benefit of the preferential tax rates. However, younger taxpayers should continue to consider annuities, because long periods of tax deferral may overcome the annuities' other disadvantages.

Universal Variable Life Insurance

Instead of a tax-deferred annuity that is taxable on the withdrawal of funds from the annuity, you may want to consider universal variable life insurance. Like its cousin, the tax-deferred annuity, the universal variable life insurance policy has an investment component consisting of mutual funds or other investment choices. The investment earnings compound on a tax-deferred basis within the life insurance policy until they are withdrawn.

A universal variable life insurance policy is a common retirement savings vehicle. Many people purchase these policies due to their investment appeal and then take policy loans or withdrawals during their retirement years, as they generally are not subject to federal income tax. In essence, a pension-like vehicle can be created to supplement cash flow during retirement. See Chapter 5, which provides an in-depth discussion of universal variable policies as well as other insurance products.

Professional Retirement Services

You and your spouse may be able to take advantage of tax-free retirement planning services from your employer. Your employer can provide this service as a nontaxable fringe benefit.

> ### Observation
> Retirement planning has become a very complicated, difficult process, involving important income tax, investing, estate planning, and other family-related issues. This nontaxable fringe benefit should give you better access to professionals who can help you choose the right tools and make the right decisions when considering the complex options and opportunities now available when planning for your retirement.

Social Security

If you receive Social Security payments, you may be taxed on some of the payments you receive. Benefits must be included in income if your modified adjusted gross income (MAGI— generally including AGI, tax-exempt interest, and certain foreign-source income with other minor adjustments) plus one-half of your Social Security benefits exceeds a certain base amount. The base amount begins at $25,000 for single individuals and $32,000 for married couples filing jointly. The amount of benefits included in taxable income is the lesser of one-half of benefits received or one-half of the excess of MAGI plus 50 percent of benefits received over the base amount. A second threshold of $34,000 for singles and $44,000 for joint returns results in more of your benefits being taxable. If this threshold is exceeded, you must include the lesser of 85 percent of benefits or the sum of the lesser of the amount included under the old rules or $6,000 ($4,500 for singles) plus 85 percent of the amount by which MAGI, increased by 50 percent of Social Security benefits, exceeds $44,000 ($34,000 for single individuals).

> ### *Observation*
> The calculation of taxable Social Security benefits is not a simple one. It is often loosely stated that this provision will subject 50 percent or 85 percent of Social Security benefits to tax. In many cases, determining the amount of benefits actually subject to tax involves complicated calculations.

> ### *Observation*
> Because the second threshold for the tax on Social Security benefits for married filers is only $10,000 more than that for single filers, a substantial marriage penalty results. For example, an unmarried couple filing separately, each with total income of $37,000, $12,000 of which is from Social Security, would each be taxed on only $3,000 of Social Security benefits. If they were married and filed jointly, however, $20,400 of their Social Security benefits would be taxed.

> ### *Observation*
> The Social Security Administration now sends annual statements detailing an individual's earnings, contributions, and estimated future benefits. If you have not received these benefit statements, use Form SSA-7004, Request for Earnings and Benefit Estimate Statement, to obtain a listing of your lifetime earnings and an estimate of your Social Security benefit. There is a limited period in which to correct mistakes.

> **Observation**
> The earnings limit that reduced Social Security benefits for recipients age 65 through 69 with earnings over a certain limit was repealed several years ago. As a result, those who work beyond their full retirement age no longer have their benefits reduced. However, earnings limits and benefit reductions still apply before full retirement age (see Chapter 16).

To obtain information about the Social Security system, visit the Social Security Administration web site at www.ssa.gov.

Required Retirement Plan Distributions

You must begin to take at least a specified minimum amount of distributions from your qualified plans and traditional IRAs by April 1 of the year after the year in which you turn age 70½. However, if you are still working at that time and you are not at least a 5 percent owner of your company, you do not have to begin to take distributions from a company retirement plan until April 1 of the year after you retire. If you do not take the minimum distribution, you will have to pay a 50 percent excise tax. Obviously, this is something to avoid.

> **Observation**
> Minimum distributions are not required from Roth IRAs during the life of the owner. This allows the tax advantages of Roth IRAs to continue until the Roth IRA owner's death and allows the income-tax-free benefits to be passed to a spouse or other family member.

After years of criticism, the Internal Revenue Service (IRS) finalized and simplified these rules. The new rules generally spread payouts over a longer time, and give you more flexibility in naming and changing beneficiaries. You now figure your required distribution simply by dividing your account balance at the end of the previous year by a factor for your age that comes from an IRS table (see Table 4.3). You use this method even if you had been using the old rules in the past. You use the same factor whether or not you have named a beneficiary and, if so, regardless of the age of the beneficiary. (The only exception is if you have named your spouse as your beneficiary and he or she is more than 10 years younger than you. In that case, required distributions are based on your joint life expectancy and are even lower.)

Table 4.3 *Uniform Lifetime Table for Use by Retirement Account Owners*

Age	Distribution Factor	Age	Distribution Factor
70	27.4	87	13.4
71	26.5	88	12.7
72	25.6	89	12.0
73	24.7	90	11.4
74	23.8	91	10.8
75	22.9	92	10.2
76	22.0	93	9.6
77	21.2	94	9.1
78	20.3	95	8.6
79	19.5	96	8.1
80	18.7	97	7.6
81	17.9	98	7.1
82	17.1	99	6.7
83	16.3	100	6.3
84	15.5	101	5.9
85	14.8	102	5.5
86	14.1	103	5.2

(Continued)

Table 4.3 (Continued)

Age	Distribution Factor	Age	Distribution Factor
104	4.9	110	3.1
105	4.5	111	2.9
106	4.2	112	2.6
107	3.9	113	2.4
108	3.7	114	2.1
109	3.4	115 and over	1.9

Required distributions now are usually smaller than under the old rules. If you are taking distributions based on whom you named as beneficiary and whether you recalculate life expectancy, you are using the old, more complex, repealed minimum distribution rules.

Caution
Make sure that your required minimum IRA distribution is figured using the newest rules. For most people, the amount that must be distributed is much lower than the minimum distribution that was required under the old rules.

There also are now more workable rules for distributions after the account owner's death. If you have named a beneficiary, the remaining amounts in the account are usually distributed over the beneficiary's remaining life expectancy. If you have not designated a beneficiary, distributions can be made over a period no longer than your remaining life expectancy at the time of your death. If you have not started taking distributions and have not named a beneficiary, the balance remaining in your account at death must be paid out within five years after your death, which does not afford much of a tax advantage to your survivors.

As a result, it is very important that you name beneficiaries for your accounts and keep beneficiary designations updated as circumstances change.

> **Observation**
> Beneficiary designation planning can provide children or grandchildren with substantial funds for tax-deferred compounding during their lifetimes. It is generally not advisable to name as beneficiary either your estate or trusts that are not carefully structured to receive distributions.

Through postdeath planning, such as use of disclaimers, the postdeath distribution deferral can be maximized (i.e., stretched out). Note that postdeath estate or trust distributions cannot be used to stretch out distributions. If your surviving spouse is the sole beneficiary of your IRA, he or she is allowed to treat your IRA as his or her own IRA and name new beneficiaries, which can further extend the tax deferral.

> **Observation**
> Beginning in 2007, nonspouse designated beneficiaries may be able to make direct trustee-to-trustee transfers from eligible retirement plans of deceased employees to their own IRAs. The transfer will be treated as an eligible rollover distribution and the receiving IRA will be treated as an inherited IRA.

> **Observation**
> If you continue to work past age 70½, you can hold off taking distributions from employer retirement accounts, but not from regular IRAs, until your actual retirement date, as long as you are not a 5 percent owner of the business for which the plan was established.

Observation

Roth IRAs are exempt from the rules requiring distributions to begin at age 70½. Tax-free buildup can continue within a Roth IRA for your entire lifetime. If you do not need the money during your lifetime, this can increase the amount of income-tax-free accumulations in the account to pass to children and grandchildren.

Observation

Some participants in qualified retirement plans may have favorable tax treatment if they receive a lump-sum distribution that is not rolled over to another qualified plan or IRA. Employees who receive appreciated securities of the employer as part of the lump-sum distribution from a qualified plan pay ordinary income tax only on the original cost of the stock (to the plan trustee). Tax on the value above the plan's cost of the stock is at long-term capital gains tax rates only when the stock is later sold. This special exception is known as net unrealized appreciation on employer securities. Further, employees born before 1936 may be eligible for long-term capital gains treatment on any portion of the lump sum that represents accumulations before 1974. The lower long-term capital gains tax rate may encourage eligible employees to take advantage of these options.

Idea Checklist

- ☑ Maximize participation in employer plans, especially if your employer matches 401(k) plan contributions. Consider contributing the maximum amount permitted.
- ☑ Consider making extra catch-up contributions, if you are 50 or older.

Retirement Planning

- ☑ Make your IRA contributions at the beginning of each calendar year to maximize the tax-deferred buildup.

- ☑ Consider which self-employment retirement plan is best for you if you are self-employed. Remember that Keogh plans need to be established before year-end for a current-year tax deduction, although actual contributions can be made as late as the extended tax return due date.

- ☑ Consider reallocating investments between tax-deferred and taxable accounts to maximize tax breaks for capital gains and qualified dividends.

- ☑ Contribute to a Roth IRA if your income level permits. This may be done even if you are in a qualified retirement plan and are not permitted to make deductible contributions to a traditional IRA. A Roth IRA is especially desirable if you want to avoid making lifetime distributions required by traditional IRAs. Traditional IRAs have strict minimum distribution requirements.

- ☑ Consider whether converting an existing IRA to a Roth IRA makes sense for you and whether you can manage the tax liability generated from the conversion. This can be an especially good move when stock prices are depressed.

- ☑ Fund a Roth or other IRA for children and grandchildren who have earned income but insufficient cash flow to contribute to their own retirement plans. If you do this, the amount you contribute will be a gift, so make sure that it (along with any other gifts during the year) does not exceed the annual gift tax exclusion amount.

- ☑ Improve retirement cash flow by using a CRT funded with highly appreciated assets.

- ☑ Review your beneficiary designations on retirement accounts to maximize the family's income-tax-deferral opportunities. The tax law makes it easier than ever for Americans to be financially secure in their later years by saving in retirement plans and IRAs.

These retirement planning suggestions and techniques are not universally applicable; each person must pick and choose among them depending on his or her individual circumstances. The government is providing more tax help for retirement saving, and the tax breaks stretch across the income spectrum.

Whether all taxpayers are financially able, as well as willing, to make the change is another matter. This book attempts to smooth the learning curve for everybody.

The next chapter focuses on the personal financial planning aspects of life insurance. It discusses the various types of life insurance and their characteristics. It also highlights different types of life insurance needs as well as income tax consequences associated with various policies and transactions.

Chapter 5

Life Insurance

Life insurance is an important component of an individual's overall financial plan. Life insurance is especially important for estate tax planning purposes (amounts, ownership, and beneficiary). Many advisors have preconceived opinions about the uses of life insurance. Oftentimes, the advisors who understand most about life insurance (agents) have a financial interest in the outcome, however.

This chapter will first discuss the different types of life insurance and the important features associated with them. Then different type of life insurance needs will be addressed with specific tax and practical commentary. In particular, business owners should be very aware of how they own and pay for life insurance. Finally, some special income tax rules will be reviewed.

This is not an exhaustive discussion of any of these topics (any one of which could be a chapter by itself) but is meant to serve as a guide and reference as you are analyzing your financial situation.

Types of Life Insurance

There are a wide variety of life insurance products. Insurance carriers continue to add, delete, and change policy features to meet the demands of a competitive environment. There are no comprehensive sources for life insurance comparisons, investment performance, or fee structures (as there are for mutual funds).

Term Life Insurance (and Variations)

Term life insurance is pure insurance. You pay a premium in exchange for death benefit coverage. Term insurance has no cash or investment value, but the payment of relatively small premiums each year can provide large death benefits to beneficiaries. Many individuals have a form of term insurance through the group insurance coverage provided by their employer. Because the amount you pay is closely related to the actual risk of death each year, term insurance generally has premiums that increase with age, rising at an accelerating rate as you reach the age of 50 and beyond. Many carriers do not offer term insurance after age 70.

The most common types of term insurance are:

- *Annual renewable term:* Premiums typically increase each year, and the policy can be renewed to some maximum age.
- *Level premium term:* Premiums remain level for a specified period.
- *Mortgage insurance/decreasing term:* Premiums remain relatively constant, but coverage decreases each year. The death benefit usually is used to pay off an outstanding but decreasing debt, such as a mortgage.

> **Observation**
> Insurance linked to a consumer purchase is often very expensive.

The most popular form of term insurance today is *level premium term*. As the name implies, the premium stays the same for the number of years chosen. The policy can be continued after the stated term, but at an increased premium. Level premium term is available in 10-, 15-, 20-, and even 25-year increments. It is very competitively priced and can be shopped for using a variety of Internet sites that will provide quotes based on age. It is a very cost-effective way to insure the breadwinner or business owner.

Universal Life Insurance

Flexible premium insurance, adjustable life insurance, and other types of universal life insurance combine term life insurance protection with an investment or savings component. You deposit premiums into an accumulation account that earns a declared rate of interest. Universal life premiums can be paid in a single premium payment or annually over the life of the policy. Monthly charges are deducted for the cost of insurance and administrative costs.

The key to a successful universal life insurance program is to determine when the cost of coverage will consume the investment or savings components under a variety of earnings rates. Another key consideration is that the cost of the insurance element of universal life is not guaranteed (as it is with some other products), and can increase over time.

With universal life insurance, you can increase the death benefit (subject to evidence of insurability) or decrease it (subject to a required minimum). Similarly, you can select a different death benefit option, as well as increase or decrease the premium payment, which will directly impact the growth of the cash value. The policy will lapse, however, if the accumulation account balance cannot cover the cost of insurance and other charges.

In evaluating a universal life policy, be aware of the assumptions used in the illustrations. A low premium may be illustrated in anticipation of favorable interest and mortality experience.

If interest rates decline or the insurance charges increase, additional premiums may be required to maintain the policy. In fact, many policyholders who purchased coverage in prior years are discovering that higher premiums are required to continue coverage because interest rates (and the assumed earnings in the policy) have declined.

> ### Observation
> So much flexibility can be confusing for the consumer. Juggling multiple variables over long periods of time requires some assistance from knowledgeable advisors who have no stake in the transaction.

Whole-Life or Ordinary Life Insurance

Whole-life or ordinary life insurance provides a death benefit and the accumulation of a cash reserve. Annual premiums are fixed for the life of the policy and are based on assumptions about interest and mortality rates. These premiums may be payable annually for life (straight life) or for a limited number of years (for example, life to age 65, 10-pay life, 20-pay life). Because of the set premium payment, whole-life insurance is often used for permanent protection. As with universal life, dividend amounts on whole-life products vary with the current investment performance and are not guaranteed.

The flexible feature of a participating policy is the dividend (a refund of premium). The dividend can be used in one of the following ways:

- Received as cash.
- Applied to reduce premiums.

- Held by the company and allowed to accumulate interest like a money market account.
- Applied toward paid-up additional insurance (small, low-load, single-premium, dividend-paying mini whole-life coverage with guaranteed cash value and death benefits).
- Used to purchase one-year term insurance. Sometimes this option is used to maximize the death benefit.

> ### Observation
> Dividend options add flexibility to an otherwise inflexible product. For example, you can purchase paid-up additional insurance policies for several years and then surrender them to pay future premiums (eliminating the need to make additional premium payments). Dividend options also make it possible to combine whole-life with term insurance in several ways to reduce the initial premium without sacrificing long-term protection.

Flexibility and performance can be enhanced further with policy riders that allow you to purchase additional death benefits for an increased premium. The rider has a lower administration load and commission structure.

Mixed Whole-Life and Term Insurance

Many carriers offer a mix of whole-life and term insurance, which can be a cost-effective way to purchase whole-life insurance. The whole-life policy provides a base level of insurance, while the term rider provides additional temporary coverage. The dividends are used to buy paid-up additions. Eventually, the additions replace the term insurance, and the policy becomes entirely whole-life insurance.

Variable Life Insurance

Variable life insurance refers to any policy where the policy owner makes investment decisions. Unlike other life contracts, there is no minimum investment return. Variable life insurance can be universal life or whole-life insurance.

This type of life insurance is most appropriate for buyers seeking investment control over the investment account (for example, an increased investment in equities). You can pay premiums, choose the funds with the best prospects for long-term growth, and let the investment performance drive up the death benefit. The downside is that poor investment performance could rob the contract of needed cash value and require you to make additional premium payments to catch up for subpar investment performance.

As a practical matter, variable life is appropriate only if the investment allocation is heavily weighted to equities (increasing the chances of beating the carrier's portfolio-driven returns). Conservative variable life portfolio allocations will produce returns similar to the insurance carrier's own portfolio, but without the benefit of a minimum return.

The flexibility offered by variable life depends on the product, such as restrictions on the allocation of the account value among the investment options, withdrawals, and changes to the death benefit. Note that the insurance carrier earns high profits on the investment fees associated with the variable policy investment choices.

Second-to-Die or Survivorship Insurance

Second-to-die insurance (also known as survivorship insurance or joint life insurance) pays a benefit upon the death of the second of two insured lives. These policies are very useful in estate planning because their benefits can be used to pay estate taxes triggered by the death of a surviving spouse. This feature is further enhanced if the policy is owned by an irrevocable life insurance trust (ILIT), discussed later in this chapter.

A second-to-die policy is a permanent (cash value) life insurance policy covering two lives. Some policies mix both term and whole-life coverage to reduce premiums.

Premiums on second-to-die policies are generally lower than on single-life policies because the combined life expectancy of two individuals is always longer than the life expectancy of either individual alone. As with many permanent life insurance policies written today, second-to-die premium payments can be structured to suit present and future needs.

The most popular form of second-to-die insurance is universal life with guaranteed coverage. As long as you make premium payments on time, the insurance carrier guarantees the death benefit (regardless of investment performance). These policies are popular because the variability and risk of investment performance are eliminated.

Insuring the Breadwinner

The most common use of life insurance is to provide cash upon the death of the insured in order to care for surviving family members. The death proceeds can be set aside in income-producing investments (substituting for the breadwinner's wages) or to pay off mortgage obligations. Today's family often has more than one breadwinner and, therefore, may need a life insurance program providing coverage for several breadwinners based on the earnings levels and insurability of the family members.

Because the life insurance proceeds must be available at the death of the breadwinner, traditional single-life products are more appropriate (rather than second-to-die products).

Observation

While the loss of a breadwinner can be financially devastating for a family, it is important not to overlook the financial implications of the loss of a stay-at-home caregiver for children or other dependents. If the primary caregiver is deceased, it may be necessary for the family to hire a nanny, consider assisted living facilities for aging parents, and so on. Factors such as these should be considered in determining whether life insurance coverage for the nonbreadwinner partner is appropriate.

How Much is Enough?

No simple formulas can determine how much life insurance you need (such as a multiple of salary). Rather, you should consider many factors, including accumulated wealth, liquidity needs, earning power of surviving family members, projected expenses, family involvement and support, and other sources of income, such as pensions and Social Security.

Only you can evaluate needs of those who depend on you. When you evaluate these needs, keep in mind that you should aim to provide for your dependents from today until they reasonably can be expected to be self-supporting. The discounted present value of the amount you would need today to fill that future need should be available in case of your death. This amount can be provided through assets on hand with the difference provided through life insurance. Various financial engine web sites are available to help you make this calculation. We have included a very basic "Life Insurance Needs" worksheet on page 102.

For How Long?

Once you have calculated the amount of coverage you need, you should evaluate how long the coverage should be in effect. Choosing among the various types of insurance is often a function of how long coverage is needed and how much you can afford.

Term insurance is a type of low-cost, temporary coverage often appropriate for growing families with limited resources. Other types of life insurance such as universal life, whole-life, and variable life are more permanent and more expensive.

> **Observation**
>
> One of the most cost-effective term coverages in the marketplace is level premium term. The premium for the coverage is the same every year. You choose the number of years the coverage will remain in effect. Level premium term is available in 10-, 15-, 20-, and even 25-year increments. Multiple web sites are available that can provide instant premium cost data for different levels of coverage. The actual cost is then determined after the insurance company evaluates your application, including an examination of your medical history and the obtaining of a physical examination.

Group term insurance is an employee benefit available to many full-time employees through their jobs. This coverage should be considered as part of an overall life insurance needs analysis. Often additional coverage can be obtained through employer-sponsored arrangements. Because this coverage, when offered, is available to all employees without the need for a physical exam, it can sometimes be more expensive than coverage you purchase in the marketplace.

Life Insurance Needs		
Annual living expenses		_____
Annual income other sources	Spouse income Social Security benefits (widow, minor children) Pensions Investment earnings Proceeds of existing life insurance invested At assumed earnings rates $_____×_____ = Total	_____ _____ _____ _____ _____ _____
Additional income needed **Amount of insurance to make up shortage invested**		_____
	At assumed earnings rates $_____×_____ =	_____
Other cash needs		
	Estate settlement Education for children Liabilities	_____ _____ _____
Total		_____

The "Pension Max" Technique

Retirement pensions often come in many forms, including a pension for the employee only (life annuity), for the employee and spouse (survivor annuity), or for a set period of time (term certain). Most employer plans require a married employee to take a survivor pension unless the employee's spouse consents (in writing) to a different form. In a survivor pension, the monthly benefit during the employee's life is reduced to provide the survivor with a fraction of the pension payable to the employee.

The "pension max" technique involves the employee choosing a life annuity, rather than a survivor annuity, and using the additional monthly amount (compared to the survivor annuity) to purchase life insurance. The employee receives the greatest distribution option from the pension, and the survivor is protected via life insurance.

As a practical mater, the actuarial assumptions and calculations used to determine the pension reduction for survivor pension benefits are the same actuarial assumptions and calculations used to determine the cost of the life insurance replacement. Thus little, if any, economic gain results. Instead, the pension max technique protects the employee from the premature death of his or her spouse.

Liquidity for Estate Taxes

The estate tax can be a very large financial burden for a family, particularly if the estate contains closely held stock or other illiquid assets. Using life insurance proceeds to provide liquidity for estate taxes can be an effective planning strategy and can provide the family with cash to pay the estate tax without the necessity of selling assets at fire sale prices.

Moreover, with the judicious use of life insurance trusts (see pages 111–114) and annual gifts to the trusts, you can remove the proceeds of the life insurance from the taxable estate and pass them on to future generations free of estate taxes.

Whose Life?

Under current federal estate tax laws (as well as most state inheritance tax regimes), the major estate tax is not due until the death of the surviving spouse. Thus, estate taxes usually are postponed until the survivor's death. To provide cash to pay estate taxes, the policy should insure both the husband and the wife but not pay until the death of the survivor. This type of insurance is known as second-to-die insurance, or survivorship life insurance (see page 98).

> **Example**
>
> Bill and Jane are a married couple with $8 million in assets (each of them has $4 million). At Bill's death, he leaves all his assets to Jane and pays no estate tax. At Jane's death her estate contains $8 million and pays an estate tax of about $2,100,000 (in 2008). They have a second-to-die policy for $2 million that pays a death benefit that can be used to pay almost all of the estate taxes.

With survivorship policies, policy premiums are paid during both lives, even though death benefits are not paid until the survivor's death. This means that premium payments continue after the death of the first spouse (so both spouses should commit to the purchase and maintenance of the life coverage). The premium cost for second-to-die insurance is usually less than that required to cover each life separately.

Single taxpayers, widows, and widowers may need traditional life insurance to provide liquidity.

How Much Coverage Is Enough?

Although you can determine the amount of coverage needed in a quantitative way (by calculating the growth of your estate and the corresponding estate tax at various points in your career and retirement), many families also consider both a target inheritance for their children and grandchildren and a target premium in the analysis.

If you perform quantitative calculations, make sure they include a variety of sophisticated gift-giving strategies to control the growth of estate (and reduce the need for insurance). These strategies would include grantor retained annuity trusts (GRATs) and sales to grantor trusts (see Chapter 9).

For How Long?

To meet estate goals, the coverage must be in place at the death of the second-to-die of the couple. Thus, the policy must be supportable until well past the combined life expectancy of the couple.

What Kind of Insurance?

Survivorship insurance is a permanent type of life insurance. Survivorship *term* insurance currently is not available. The survivorship insurance available in today's market is universal insurance, whole-life insurance, or a mixture of whole-life insurance with term riders.

A very popular form of survivorship insurance is a universal product with guarantees. With this form of universal life insurance, the coverage is guaranteed regardless of changes to interest rates as long as you make premium payments on a timely basis. The cost for coverage can be easily compared from carrier to carrier. Unfortunately, some carriers are injecting additional variables into the pricing by changing the coverage guarantee.

> **Observation**
> The universal life with guarantees provides a very cost-effective way of purchasing second-to-die insurance with little potential for variation in most, but not all, cases. It is very popular in the marketplace.

Diversification

Life insurance is a promise to pay made by the insurance carrier. This promise is only as strong as the carrier. As with any investment, diversification among life insurance carriers is important. Large amounts of death benefit should be placed with a variety of carriers, since the best carrier today may not be the best and safest carrier 20 to 30 years from now. Several independent agencies (such as Fitch Ratings Ltd. and Moody's Investors Service) provide ratings for insurance companies, and these ratings can be helpful in selecting insurance carriers with financial strength and stability.

Owner and Beneficiary

The choice of policy owner and beneficiary are two of the most significant decisions in the purchase of life insurance. These decisions are important for nontax reasons in assuring that the objectives for providing coverage are met. However, from a tax perspective, careful choice of policy owner and beneficiary can also result in significant estate tax savings.

Policy Owner

The Insured as Owner

If the insured is the owner of the policy, the death benefit is included in the insured's estate. Ownership includes not only direct ownership of the policy but also indirect ownership through retained rights such as the ability to change the beneficiary, to cancel or assign the policy, or to borrow against the policy. Although the death benefits can pass free of estate tax to the surviving spouse (as beneficiary) using the unlimited marital deduction, designating the insured as the owner of a policy results in the imposition of an estate tax on whatever proceeds remain at the second spouse's death.

If estate taxes are not a concern (where combined assets are below about $2 million), the insured is most often chosen as the owner of the policy for simplicity. This also provides the insured with the maximum degree of control over the policy.

The Spouse as Owner

If the insured's spouse owns the policy, none of the proceeds are included in the insured's estate (see application of the three-year rule, page 110). Further, if the insured's spouse dies first, only the cash value is included in the spouse's estate. If the insured dies first and the spouse is named as beneficiary, any remaining proceeds are included in the surviving spouse's estate and, as in the case of an insured-owned policy, estate tax applies to these proceeds at the surviving spouse's death.

> ### Observation
> In most cases a spouse should not be the owner of an insurance policy on the other spouse's life.

The Children or Grandchildren as Owners

If the insured's adult children or grandchildren own the policy, the insurance proceeds are not included in either spouse's estate, and the children or grandchildren receive the death benefits free of both estate tax and income tax (see three-year rule, page 110). The children or grandchildren may elect to use the proceeds to purchase assets from the estate (providing liquidity to the estate) or choose another use for the funds (consumer spending). This is an excellent estate tax result. However, having children or grandchildren own policies on their parents/grandparents may not meet other objectives. For example, other ownership structures may be more appropriate if a primary objective is to provide the spouse with a continuing stream of income, or if the insured wishes to exert more control over the desired use of the policy proceeds.

A Qualified Plan as Owner

If a qualified plan—for example, a pension plan, profit-sharing plan, or employee stock option plan (ESOP)—owns the life insurance, the death benefit is included in the value of the plan for estate tax purposes (similar to an insured-owned policy). If the spouse is the beneficiary of the plan account, the assets typically pass free of estate tax. As with the insured-owned policy, any proceeds remaining at the surviving spouse's death are included in the spouse's estate and are subject to estate tax.

> ### Observation
> Having life insurance in a qualified plan is not estate tax effective. The life insurance can still retain its income-tax-free nature, but cannot be removed from the insured's estate unless it is removed from the qualified plan.

An Irrevocable Trust as Owner

The irrevocable life insurance trust (ILIT) (see pages 111–114) *is the primary estate-tax reduction technique available to the estate planner*. This is often the best choice for the owner of the policy.

If an irrevocable trust is the owner of the insurance (and the trust is properly structured), the death benefit is not included in the estate of the insured. Further, the proceeds can be made available for the insured's spouse, yet will not be included in the spouse's estate for estate tax purposes. Third, the insured can design the trust so the policy proceeds are restricted to the uses intended for the policy, protecting the assets from creditors and undisciplined spending habits. Finally, it is possible to accomplish generation-skipping objectives with an insurance trust and thereby avoid inclusion in a child's estate as well.

Thus, an irrevocable trust can be a device to pass significant sums to children and grandchildren free of estate tax.

> ### Example
> Bill and Jane have $6 million of assets. They also have $2 million of life insurance in an irrevocable trust. When Bill dies, the $2 million is available for Jane's needs (she can receive all earnings from the trust) but is not included in Jane's estate. At Jane's death, the $2 million is not subject to estate tax and may be distributed to the children.

The trust agreement gives the trustee specific guidance as to how, and for whose benefit, trust earnings and corpus should be used. The trust can give the trustee power to distribute principal to maintain a beneficiary's standard of living or for his or her comfort and happiness. Further, the surviving spouse can be given power to reshuffle the deck to meet a family's changing needs (e.g., to make distributions for the benefit of a grandchild suffering from a continuing illness). Thus, careful planning can build flexibility into the trust so it can meet the needs of the changing circumstances of the beneficiaries.

The original terms of the trust should be flexible enough to adapt to a variety of circumstances, since the insured loses all control over the policy once it is transferred to the trust. Such things as the desired use of death benefits, beneficiary designation, uses of policy cash values, and dividend options are all controlled by the trustee of the trust. Because the trust is irrevocable, you cannot change the terms even if family circumstances change.

Note that life insurance that is held for investment purposes typically should *not* be owned by a life insurance trust. Estate tax savings are generally a secondary consideration with these types of policies. Usually, if life insurance is being utilized primarily for its investment characteristics, the insured will wish to maintain access to the life insurance cash value during his or her life to make distribution as well as investment decisions.

The Three-Year Rule

Transfers of life insurance by the insured are not effective for removing a policy from the taxable estate of the insured for three years following the transfer. Transfers made within three years of death are included in the taxable estate of the insured just as if the transfer had not taken place. This rule applies only where the insured is the original owner of the policy. If an irrevocable trust is the original applicant and owner, then the three-year rule does not apply. For this reason, careful consideration should be given to the ownership of a policy before the policy is initially purchased.

A Partnership or Limited Liability Company as Owner

A partnership or limited liability company (LLC) may often own life insurance in order to facilitate business ownership transfers after the death of a partner. The value of any partnership or LLC interest owned by the insured will be included in his or her estate at death. Special allocation provisions in the partnership agreement can direct death benefits to the remaining partners. The use of partnerships and LLCs to own life insurance associated with business ownership transfers is a preferred method for business owners.

A Corporation as Owner

Sometimes corporations (either C corporations or S corporations) will own life insurance on shareholders in order to facilitate business ownership transfers after death. Such an arrangement is not as tax efficient as the partnership or LLC alternative. Some companies also own life insurance as a funding mechanism for deferred compensation or to protect against the loss of a key employee.

Policy Beneficiary

If the insured is the owner of the policy (where estate taxes are not a concern), then the choice of beneficiary should be dictated by testamentary desires (spouse, children, and trusts).

The beneficiary designation should be coordinated with will and trust dispositions to make sure estate planning objectives are met.

Where trusts are in place, naming the trustee (of an irrevocable life insurance trust, a revocable living trust, or a testamentary trust) as beneficiary is most appropriate. Payment of death benefits to the insured's estate is generally *not* the best alternative (due to application of state inheritance laws and creditor rights).

Failure of policy owners to designate the desired or appropriate beneficiary may result in proceeds not going to the desired heirs or may result in adverse tax consequences to remedy.

The Irrevocable Life Insurance Trust

The irrevocable life insurance trust (ILIT) is an excellent estate-tax reduction tool. These types of trusts are usually not suitable to receive other gifts, however, because of their unique terms and conditions.

> ### Observation
> An irrevocable life insurance trust should always be prepared by an experienced estate planning attorney and reviewed by an experienced estate planning professional. It depends on a series of complicated tax provisions to produce the intended estate tax savings.

The transfer of an insurance policy into a trust is treated as a gift to the trust's beneficiaries. As each premium payment is made, additional gifts take place. The beneficiary must have a present interest in the trust (see "Withdrawal Right," next) for the premium payments to qualify for the annual gift tax exclusion ($12,000 per person in 2008). The practical limit on the amount of life insurance that can be owned within an irrevocable trust is the amount of insurance that can be purchased using the annual gift tax exclusions available for gifts to the trust. The gift tax exclusions are usually limited by the number of children and grandchildren given withdrawal provisions and by the type of withdrawal right given. Gifts in excess of the annual exclusion will use up the insured's lifetime gift exemption (currently $1 million).

Any policy purchase within an irrevocable trust should take into consideration the long-term gift impact associated with the technique. This is especially important for policies with significant premiums. It is important to consider whether the payment of premiums will eventually exhaust your gift tax exemption over the life of the policy and result in costly gift tax liability to keep the policy in force.

Withdrawal Right

To create a present interest in the insurance trust, beneficiaries are often given the right to withdraw a stated amount after each contribution to the trust. These rights are known as Crummey powers (named after a court case involving the Crummey family and their trust). The withdrawal right is usually limited by the amount of the current contribution. Each person possessing a withdrawal right is permitted to withdraw his or her pro rata portion of the contribution. If a withdrawal right is not exercised in a specified period of time, it will generally lapse.

The withdrawal rights are effective in making the contribution a present interest only if the beneficiary has notice of the power. Each year, the beneficiary should receive written notice of the withdrawal right. The type of notice required, the amount of the withdrawal right, and the beneficiaries who have the withdrawal right should all be specified in the trust document.

The trust should allow the trustee to satisfy a withdrawal request with the policy itself, which also provides a method of removing the policy from the trust.

Contingent Marital Deduction

The transfer of an existing life insurance policy is not effective for estate tax purposes until three years after the transfer. Thus, an irrevocable life insurance trust should contain a contingent marital deduction or be drafted in such a manner that it can qualify for the marital deduction. This prevents unwanted estate tax consequences if the insured dies within the three-year period.

Choice of Trustee and Trustee Powers

The choice of trustee and the trustee's powers over income and principal must be carefully drafted to avoid inclusion in the estate of either the insured or the insured's spouse. The trustee should be authorized to purchase assets from or lend money to the estate. Further, removal and replacement of the trustee provisions must be drafted carefully. Trustee removal and replacement rights are very desirable features.

Finally, the trust should contain a provision allowing the trustee to terminate the trust and distribute life insurance policies to one or more of the beneficiaries. Therefore, the trustee must be someone on whom you can rely to follow your written instructions (i.e., the terms of the trust), and someone who will make the judgments you would make about needs that are not addressed by the trust's terms.

Generation-Skipping Consideration

An irrevocable life insurance trust with permanent life insurance is a good candidate for generation-skipping transfers. However, an irrevocable life insurance trust with term insurance is *not* a good candidate for generation-skipping. Generation-skipping is a planning technique where assets are held in trust for your children's lives and will eventually pass to your grandchildren or more remote descendants without inclusion in the taxable estate of you, your spouse, or your children (a triple estate-tax saving strategy). Gift tax returns may be important when generation-skipping results are anticipated even though gift tax returns might not otherwise be required.

Survivorship Life Insurance Complications

If an irrevocable life insurance trust owns a survivorship life policy (second-to-die policy), neither of the insured parties should be a beneficiary of the trust or a trustee. Careful drafting is required when dealing with survivorship life insurance.

Community Property Complications

For those who live currently or in the past have lived in community property states (Arizona, California, Idaho, Louisiana, Nevada, New Mexico, Texas, Washington, and Wisconsin), contributions to the trust should be made from separate property funds. In most community property states, it is possible to convert community property to separate property via a partition agreement. It is critical that separate property funds be used for life insurance premiums since using community property could cause unintended estate tax complications for the surviving spouse.

Life Insurance as an Investment

Sometimes life insurance is purchased not for the death benefit, but to obtain favorable tax consequences for the investment of the underlying cash values held within the policy. In these cases, the insurance policy is essentially used as an investment wrapper. Life insurance is attractive as an investment product since insurance policies have special income tax rules that apply to withdrawals and death benefits However, those same special tax rules can also drive up policy administration expenses, which can erode investment results. Finally, surrender charges and fees make any life insurance investment a very long-term commitment.

The most common types of investment-focused polices are known as variable life insurance. The term *variable* with an insurance product means that the policy owner has the ability to make investment decisions with respect to the cash value that will impact investment results; the variable nature of the investment results lends it name to the product.

Private Placement Variable Life Insurance

Private placement variable life insurance refers to a very customized life insurance policy designed for an elite class of investors. These custom-designed policies can accommodate special investments and carry reduced administrative pricing. The owner of the policy is free to choose the investment and is not restricted to the usual array of variable life insurance offerings provided by the insurance company.

Such policies are usually restricted to multimillion-dollar premium amounts and are designed to take advantage of the tax-deferred nature of life insurance policy earnings as well as the income-tax-free death benefit.

Private placement policies must be carefully constructed in order to fall within the IRS definition of life insurance. The investment choices within the policy must be available only to life insurance purchasers.

Hedge Fund Life Insurance

Many hedge fund investment and trading strategies produce significant amounts of taxable income each year. Further, much of the income is taxed at ordinary income tax rates (up to 35 percent in 2008). The current income tax reduces the after-tax return produced by the hedge fund.

By contrast, the investment activity within a life insurance policy is not subject to income tax until the policy is surrendered. Further, the death benefit of a life insurance contract is not subject to income tax at all.

Some advisors advocate holding hedge fund investments within a life insurance policy (the private placement variable life). However, there are some practical issues associated with this technique. For example, some hedge funds do not allow insurance policies as investors in their fund.

As noted, a significant number of technical issues must be addressed in order for these special types of policies to be respected as life insurance.

Education Funding

Using life insurance to fund education expenses involves purchasing a universal life, whole-life, or variable life policy. Policy premiums are calculated to accumulate a significant cash value at a target date (such as the year of beginning college). You access the cash value free of income tax via policy loans when needed to fund education. In the meantime, should you die before sufficient cash is accumulated within the policy to meet the educational objectives, the policy death benefit is available for this purpose.

The difficulty with this technique is that usually not enough time passes for the tax-free compounding within the policy to overcome the drag on earnings represented by mortality costs and administrative charges. As a practical matter, the borrowing to pay education costs, and the related interest expense on the borrowing, will be so great that the policy will lapse, creating an income tax event.

Retirement Accumulation, aka the Private Pension

The most widespread use of life insurance as an investment is as a pension supplement. Insurance agents often refer to this type of permanent life insurance policy as a "private pension." The private pension provides a method of forced savings for retirement as well as a death benefit during the employment years. The tax advantage of this technique is the tax-free compounding within the policy combined with the income-tax-free borrowing process.

The technique involves purchasing a universal life, whole-life, or variable policy. During your employment years, you pay premiums that are designed to accumulate a significant amount of cash value by a target retirement date. If you die prior to retirement, the death benefit is paid to your beneficiary.

At retirement, you access the accumulated cash value by borrowing from the policy. The annual borrowings create a stream of retirement income that is not subject to income tax. The policy borrowings attract an interest charge, and you borrow the annual interest from the policy as well. At death, the policy's death benefit is paid to your beneficiary after reduction for accumulated borrowings and interest charges.

Careful monitoring is critical to avoid an income tax disaster. During your employment years, premiums must be controlled to prevent classification of the policy as a modified endowment contract (i.e., putting too much into the policy too quickly). During your retirement years, the borrowing and interest accumulation must be managed to avoid the accidental termination of the policy (i.e., excess borrowing). The surrender or lapse of the policy triggers the imposition of income tax on all of the tax-deferred earnings in the policy. The optimum exit technique for the private pension strategy is death. At death, the policy proceeds first pay off the policy loans (with no income tax consequences), and any remaining policy funds pass to your beneficiary.

> **Observation**
>
> This planning technique has very interesting income tax benefits associated with it. However, it is labor intensive during the retirement years and becomes a significant maintenance issue during your twilight years (when you are least able to deal with it). The practical issues and dangers (accidental policy termination) often outweigh any tax advantages.

Charitable Contributions

Life insurance is often part of a charitable bequest either directly or indirectly.

Donations of Life Insurance

If you have a life insurance policy you no longer need and you do not want to surrender the policy, there are two ways to donate the policy to charity and obtain an income tax deduction.

The first alternative is to transfer ownership of the policy directly to charity (then the charity names itself as beneficiary). The difficulty with this technique is that an appraisal of the policy is required if it is worth over $5,000. A significant disadvantage to this technique is that the charitable contribution deduction is limited to the lesser of premiums paid or cash value. Therefore, a policy that has significant investment gains would *not* make a good candidate for a charitable donation.

The second alternative is to make a charity the irrevocable beneficiary of the policy. With this technique, you do not receive a current deduction for the value of the policy, but you do get an annual deduction as you continue to pay policy premiums.

Charitable Remainder Trust and Asset Replacement Trust

Charitable remainder trusts (CRTs) and asset replacement trusts offer tax-planning benefits for individuals who own low-basis assets they plan to sell (either because the assets produce too little income or as part of a diversification strategy).

Charitable remainder trusts can be used to dispose of low-basis assets without the imposition of a current income tax on the capital gain, to provide a current charitable income tax deduction, and to create an increased income stream for the donor's life. At the death of the income beneficiary, the remaining assets pass to charity (hence the name *charitable remainder*). Many donors are concerned that their heirs will receive less of an inheritance because of the gift to the charity. One solution is to purchase life insurance in an asset replacement trust to replenish the estate for the assets that went to charity.

The asset replacement trust is simply an irrevocable life insurance trust. The purchase of life insurance makes the heirs whole by replacing the assets passing to charity (using a portion of the increased income stream to pay premiums). By placing the life insurance in an irrevocable life insurance trust, you enable the proceeds to pass to the heirs estate tax free.

While the planning technique has merit, some advisors offer prepackaged arrangements that are loaded with fees and expenses. You should carefully evaluate the merits of the transaction, since the fees and expenses could make the technique uneconomical.

Insuring Businesses and Their Owners

Business owners use life insurance for many reasons, including:
- To continue operations after the loss of a key employee.
- To provide survivor income to the family.
- To provide liquid assets for payment of estate taxes.
- To provide an equalizing inheritance for other children.
- To fund buy/sell agreements.
- To fund cross-purchase agreements.

By carefully structuring ownership and beneficiary designations of the life insurance policy, you can reduce or eliminate income tax, gift tax, and estate tax consequences.

Key Person Life Insurance

Key person life insurance is designed to provide funds to continue a business after the death of a key employee (for example, financial manager, operations manager, ideas manager). Bank covenants sometimes require this type of insurance. The amount of insurance should be tied to the costs of searching for and hiring a suitable replacement (which could involve additional salary costs), as well as any temporary professional management costs.

Normally, the business owns and is the beneficiary of the key person life insurance policy. If the insured key employee is later replaced by another employee, many carriers will substitute the new employee for the prior employee in the existing policy rather than issue a new policy (although substitution often involves income tax consequences).

Income tax and estate tax issues are not the primary concerns with this type of insurance. Instead it is driven by business issues.

Survivor Income, Estate Taxes, and Inheritances

If the business owner is also the family's sole wage earner, the survivors may have additional problems. A business often finds it difficult to put funds into the hands of the surviving spouse and children due to technical tax rules. Therefore, many business owners purchase some life insurance to provide a temporary source of funds for the surviving family until the business's future is settled.

Most businesses, although quite valuable, can be illiquid in the hands of the estate administrator. By contrast, life insurance is very liquid at the death of the insured. Business owners often purchase life insurance to pay estate taxes, especially where it is desired that the business stay within the family.

Finally, insurance can provide a separate inheritance for children who will not share in business ownership. For example, one technique is to leave the ownership of the business to the children who will be involved in managing the business, and to use life insurance to create enough liquidity at death to provide for children who will not continue with the family business. This often avoids intrafamily conflict arising from ownership of the business passing to siblings as passive investors.

Insurance Funding for Buy-Sell Agreements

Life insurance for business transition must be arranged in a tax-efficient manner. Changes in the owner or beneficiary can produce radically different tax results. This is especially true with buy-sell agreements.

A common arrangement is for the company to purchase life insurance on shareholder lives. The company is the owner and beneficiary of the policy. The company makes all premium payments. The shareholder agreement calls for the company to purchase shares from any deceased shareholder's estate or family members. The technical tax term for this arrangement is a *redemption*.

A corporate redemption (buy-sell agreement) funded by corporate-owned life insurance is not a tax-efficient way to transfer ownership at death. The major issues are:

- Distortion of the business value (the insurance death benefit is added to the value of the business for estate tax purposes).
- Potential corporate-level income tax on insurance death benefit (alternative minimum tax).
- Complicated tax rules associated with purchasing stock from the estate, especially where payments take place over time.
- No basis increase in the stock held by the remaining shareholders.

Despite all these tax issues, the redemption buy-sell arrangement is the most common form of dealing with a deceased business owner. It is the easiest arrangement to put in place.

Insurance Funding for Cross-Purchase Agreements

A more tax-efficient (and flexible) arrangement than the traditional buy-sell agreement is a cross-purchase agreement. In this arrangement, the other business owners agree to buy the deceased owner's shares. The company itself is not part of the agreement.

The owners of the business purchase life insurance on each others' lives. Only one policy per owner is needed (multiple policies are not required). The owners create a special partnership to hold the life insurance. The partnership is the owner and beneficiary of the policies and makes all premium payments. At the death of a shareholder, the partnership distributes the cash to the remaining shareholders and they purchase the deceased owner's shares.

This arrangement has the following advantages:
- No distortion of the business value (the insurance death benefit is not added to the value of the business for estate tax purposes).
- No potential corporate-level income tax on insurance death benefit (alternative minimum tax).
- No complicated tax rules associated with purchasing stock from the estate.
- Full basis increase for the stock held by the remaining shareholders.

The types of policies used to fund cross-purchase arrangements typically are permanent types of life insurance (since the arrangement is likely to continue for a long period of time), such as whole-life, universal life, or variable life.

Nonqualified Deferred Compensation

Many corporations (both large and small) use life insurance as the investment mechanism to provide funds for employee perquisites such as deferred compensation plans and supplemental executive retirement plan (SERP) arrangements. These company-owned life insurance (COLI) policies involve special income tax, financial accounting, and investment features.

Congress more than once has changed the income tax treatment of life insurance policies owned by corporations (especially the interest expense on policy borrowings). Despite these changes, life insurance funding for deferred compensation remains a viable alternative.

In the typical arrangement, a corporation purchases life insurance policies on the lives of the participants in the executive benefit plan. Policy premiums are paid each year and reduce current earnings (but are not deductible for income tax purposes). New tax laws require that companies obtain the executives' permission before purchasing the policy and provide information on the policy to the IRS with annual tax filings. Policies on individuals who are not executives or employees at death have less favorable tax consequences.

The cash value in the policies builds during the employment years (and represents an asset of the corporation). When benefit payments are scheduled to begin, the employer borrows from the cash value to pay the benefits. The benefit payments produce compensation to the executive and a tax deduction to the corporation. Finally, the death benefit (which is paid to the company) is normally free of income tax (as long as the insured individual was an executive or a shareholder, or was an employee shortly before death).

As a practical matter, such arrangements require careful bookkeeping and can create cash flow issues for the corporation. In addition, it is often difficult to tell if you have an economically successful arrangement until all of the insured executives are dead. The arrangement is especially problematic if there is turnover in the executive ranks (which necessitates turnover in life policies—defeating the income tax advantages).

Split-Dollar Insurance Arrangements

A split-dollar plan is not a type of insurance but an ownership-sharing arrangement between two parties. The split-dollar arrangement is used for such purposes as providing insurance death benefits to business owners or key employees, as well as to significantly reduce the gift and estate tax consequences of life insurance coverage assigned to irrevocable trusts.

Life Insurance

One of the most attractive attributes of a split-dollar plan is its flexibility. An arrangement's design can split the death benefit and premium in a variety of ways. A split-dollar arrangement using second-to-die insurance is an excellent method of passing assets to children and grandchildren in a tax-efficient manner, because of the low gift tax amounts involved.

The income tax rules for split-dollar arrangements changed at the beginning of 2004. The rules now divide split-dollar arrangements into two different types. The more common type is where owner of the policy is not the primary premium payer (so-called collateral assignments). These arrangements look like loans, and that is how the IRS treats them (e.g., "loan regime").

> ### Example
> An employee is the owner of a policy, and the employer pays most of the premiums. The employer is entitled to a repayment of the premiums at the death of the employee (and holds a lien against the policy as collateral for this loan). Any death proceeds above and beyond the premiums paid would pass to the employee's family.

Arrangements where the primary premium payer is also the owner are known as endorsement arrangements. These arrangements are treated as part of the "economic benefit regime" for tax purposes.

> ### Example
> The employer owns the policy and pays the premiums. The employer is typically entitled to recover any premiums paid from the death benefits, but has agreed to endorse any remaining death proceeds to the employee's family. The employee chooses a beneficiary for the death benefit.

- **Loan regime** treatment means that the value of the arrangement for income tax or gift tax purposes is based on an interest rate and the amount of the premium lent to the owner to be repaid from the death benefits. There are a variety of special rules for determining what interest rate applies.

- **Economic benefit regime** treatment means that the value of the arrangement for income tax or gift tax purposes is based on the cost for the insurance protection each year plus any cash value or dividends that accrue to the benefit of the insured. The IRS and various insurance carriers provide tables to calculate the benefit of the insurance.

You do not choose which regime to apply. Instead, the terms of the arrangement are examined to determine which regime is more appropriate given the facts and circumstances.

> **Observation**
> Split-dollar arrangements in place before September 13, 2003, are not required to use the new split-dollar rules. Instead, they can continue to use the older less complicated rules.

Employee Split-Dollar

Employee split-dollar arrangements are between employers and employees. The employer pays the bulk of the premiums. The employee either pays a portion of the premium or has imputed income for the value of the benefit (using either the loan regime or the economic benefit regime). The imputed income is added to the employee's wages and reported on Form W-2. At the employee's death, the employer is repaid the insurance premiums, and any remaining death benefit goes to the employee's beneficiaries.

Shareholder Split-Dollar

Shareholder split-dollar arrangements are between the company and its shareholders. The company pays the bulk of the premiums. The shareholder either pays a portion of the premium or has imputed income for the value of the benefit. The imputed income is treated as a distribution from the business (a dividend in the case of a corporation). At the shareholder's death, the company is repaid the insurance premiums, and any remaining death benefit goes to the shareholder's beneficiaries.

A shareholder split-dollar plan can be an economical way to provide funding for a cross-purchase arrangement.

Private Split-Dollar

Private split-dollar arrangements are often between the insured and an irrevocable life insurance trust. These arrangements can keep the initial gift tax cost of the irrevocable trust low (although the cost can later skyrocket if the insured individuals live into their 70s and 80s). The value of the arrangement for gift tax purposes is determined based on either the loan regime or the economic benefit regime (depending on the terms of the agreement).

> **Observation**
> Carefully structured private split-dollar arrangements can significantly lower the initial gift tax costs associated with large life insurance policies owned by irrevocable trusts.

Arrangements before September 13, 2003

Arrangements in place before September 13, 2003, provide an opportunity and a trap for the unwary. These arrangements are allowed to use the old split-dollar rules (a simplified version of the economic benefit regime), which generally have more favorable tax results. However, the IRS has indicated that any termination of a split-dollar arrangement will be carefully scrutinized to determine if value has passed to the employee/shareholder. If value passes, it will be subject to income tax.

Also, arrangements prior to September 13, 2003, lose their grandfathered status if material changes are made to the policy or the split-dollar agreement.

Arrangements in place before September 13, 2003, that have continuing premium payments and policy cash value in excess of cumulative premiums are subject to additional rules affecting deferred compensation. These rules are punishing.

Income Tax Rules

The income tax treatment of life insurance policies generally is governed by three Internal Revenue Code sections (i.e., Sections 72, 7702A, and 7722), as well as a series of court cases and revenue rulings. The Code sections provide the definition of life insurance, special treatment for certain types of policies, and the general life insurance taxation rules.

Life Insurance Defined

Code Section 7722 contains the definition of life insurance for income tax purposes. The section sets forth a series of actuarial calculations that must be performed in order for a policy to qualify for life insurance income tax treatment. These calculations address the relationship between cash value and death benefits (the death benefit must be a multiple of cash value based on age). Most life insurance carriers have software to make these calculations and can advise whether the policy you buy will be treated as life insurance.

If a policy is not treated as life insurance, the income tax treatment of annual earnings, withdrawals, loans, partial surrenders, and even the payment of death benefits will be impacted. None of the special income tax rules associated with life insurance will apply.

Modified Endowment Contracts: When Life Insurance Is an Annuity

Life insurance policies categorized as modified endowment contracts (MECs) under Code Section 7702A receive unfavorable income tax treatment. A modified endowment contract is a life insurance policy with "excessive" premium payments or deposits in relation to the death benefit.

A series of complex actuarial tests must be met to avoid modified endowment contract status. Most carriers can test planned premium payment alternatives to avoid modified endowment status and can make representations to you about whether a particular policy avoids modified endowment status.

If a policy is classified as a modified endowment contract, distributions from the policy (whether by withdrawal, partial surrender, or policy loans) are treated as an annuity for income tax purposes. This means that the funds removed from the policy will first be treated as ordinary income rather than a recovery of original cost (not taxable). The death benefit remains income tax free.

> **Observation**
> Avoiding modified endowment contract status is an important goal. Life contracts that are treated as MECs lose all of their income tax flexibility. Flexibility is critical to any long-term financial plan.

Income Tax Advantages

Life insurance that meets the definition of life insurance and is not treated as a modified endowment contract has a number of income tax advantages.
- The death benefit normally is not subject to income tax.
- The cash value buildup is not currently subject to income tax.

- Removal of funds from the policy via policy loans is not treated as taxable income so long as the policy stays in force.
- Removal of funds from the policy via withdrawal is treated first as a return of premiums and second as taxable income.
- Policy dividends are treated first as a return of premiums and then as taxable income after all premiums have been returned.

The advantages associated with cash value accumulation and access to this cash value allow life insurance policies to compete favorably with other investment products.

Interest on Policy Loans

Unfortunately, a number of limits apply to the interest expense on policy loans. For individually owned policies, interest on policy loans typically is treated as personal interest expense and, therefore, is nondeductible. Only if the policy loan proceeds can be directly traced to traditional, taxable investments might the interest be deductible. For corporate-owned policies, the interest expense generally is not deductible unless the policy was purchased before June 21, 1986, or unless the insured is a key person and borrowings are limited to $50,000.

Lapse or Surrender of Policy

The lapse or surrender of a life insurance policy is treated as a taxable event. The amount received in cash (including previously borrowed amounts) in excess of premiums paid is treated as ordinary income. This is an especially severe result if the policy has being used as a private pension, because the borrowed funds may have been previously consumed to support a retirement lifestyle, and are not available to defray the income tax costs associated with the policy surrender.

> **Observation**
> An unplanned lapse of a life insurance policy can be an income tax disaster.

Foreign Life Insurance

Life insurance or assurance policies can be provided by non-U.S. life insurance companies. These policies cannot be sold in the United States unless the carrier and the agent are licensed under state law and become subject to state insurance regulations. However, these policies can be sold to U.S. citizens and residents if they venture offshore to make the purchase or are living outside of the United States.

Most life insurance policies sold by non-U.S. insurance companies will not qualify as life insurance under the U.S. income tax rules. This means that the annual policy earnings will be subject to U.S. income tax each year, and the death benefits will be taxable as well. Further, there is a U.S. premium tax imposed on funds deposited into the contract.

> **Observation**
> Another issue with non-U.S. insurance contracts is the lack of historic investment performance data and the oppressive fee structures associated with the product.

It is possible to find U.S.-tax-qualified life insurance sold by non-U.S. companies. However, it is up to the purchaser to verify the U.S. tax compliance and the economic viability of the contract.

Life Insurance Terminology and Illustrations
Quick Pay Premiums

A quick pay arrangement refers to paying larger premiums for a shorter period of time, sometimes referred to as vanishing premiums. The term *vanishing* is rarely used by agents today. To reduce the time over which premiums must be paid, the policy could also be structured to pay for itself by using dividends, by surrendering paid-up additional insurance, or by borrowing from the policy.

Quick pay arrangements are successful for life insurance purchases as long as funds are currently available and the policy is not in danger of losing its treatment as life insurance. Actual investment performance will impact the results. Therefore, if dividends are less than projected, premiums must be paid for a longer period than anticipated or may reappear at a later time.

Minimum Depositing

Minimum depositing, or "mini-dipping," is another method of funding a policy. This technique was popular in the 1970s and 1980s. It involves borrowing from the cash value of the policy to pay annual premiums, and sometimes the interest charges on policy loans, as well. The typical minimum deposit arrangement provides for the payment of four out of the first seven premiums and borrowing from the policy to pay all other premiums. The economic viability of the technique depends on the interest expense deduction. Since the deductibility of interest expense from policy loans is now limited, the technique is no longer viable. However, policies from this era still exist.

> **Observation**
> Life insurance policies with significant policy loans create economic and tax issues.

Life Insurance Illustrations

Life insurance illustrations are educated guesses as to how a policy will perform over a long period of time. Illustrations should be used to evaluate an overall proposed strategy, but may not assist with policy comparisons unless the same assumptions are illustrated for all policies compared.

There are several critical assumptions with any illustration. The most important are investment returns and mortality charges. Always insist on illustrations at various (lower) investment returns.

> **Observation**
> As with any multiyear illustration, minor changes to assumptions (policy earnings) can produce significant variations. It is possible for illustrations to show almost anything if the assumptions are manipulated enough.

Policy Selection and Servicing

Most life insurance is a long-term financial commitment. To ensure your family's security, review the financial health of an insurance carrier before purchasing a policy. You can do this my checking insurance company ratings from such sources as A.M. Best, Moody's, and Standard & Poor's. If possible and practical, try to diversify coverage among companies to reduce risk.

Further, today's complex life insurance products and planned payment alternatives require the continued attention of an insurance agent. Unfortunately, policy servicing is not a revenue-producing activity. Make sure your agent will continue to service the policy after the sale is concluded. This is critical to any investment-related life insurance purchase.

Idea Checklist

- ☑ Make sure you have the right type of insurance for your needs. Most popular forms of insurance are level premium term (breadwinners) and universal second-to-die with secondary guarantees (estate tax payment).
- ☑ Make sure you have the proper owner and beneficiary. Life insurance trusts make a good estate planning technique.
- ☑ Business owners should make sure they use the partnership-funded cross-purchase arrangement rather than a buy-sell agreement or redemption.
- ☑ Treat life insurance for investment purposes with caution, especially foreign life insurance.
- ☑ Consider split-dollar life insurance for low initial gift tax costs.
- ☑ Carefully review pre-September 13, 2003, split-dollar arrangements for tax traps (there are many).

Next, the effects of recent tax changes on home ownership are covered. Most people do not give much thought to the federal tax implications of owning a home. They know they can deduct mortgage interest and real estate property taxes, but many other aspects of owning a home have tax consequences as well.

Chapter 6

Tax Advantages of Home Ownership

Home ownership carries with it many special tax advantages. This chapter takes up the tax considerations of home ownership and explains how to use the tax code provisions to minimize federal tax bills. For instance, a home office has become easier to claim as a business deduction. There are tax advantages for vacation home rentals, but the rules on how to treat rental fees and expenses need careful study. Interest on limited amounts of home equity loan indebtedness is fully deductible for regular income tax purposes, regardless of how the proceeds are used. However, when calculating the alternative minimum tax (AMT), if the loan proceeds are not used for investment purposes, you can deduct home equity loan interest only to the extent that the loan was used to improve the house. Points paid to secure mortgages from a bank or other lender may be treated in several ways. Finally, there are special tax breaks on gains from the sale of a principal residence.

The 2001 Tax Act has had some interesting effects on homeowners' finances as the changes brought about in it continue to be phased in. Additionally, the 2003 Tax Act's tax-rate cuts and capital gains tax-rate reductions have impacted your decisions regarding how to maximize the tax benefits of owning a home. Now, the Housing Assistance Tax Act of 2008 provides instances of housing-related tax relief for weary taxpayers due to the downturn in the real estate market. However, the revenue offsets in this Act should not be overlooked, as they may have a significant impact on the decision to sell a home.

During recent years, wealthier individuals have found that long-term capital gains taxes for the portion of the profit on the sale of a principal residence that exceeds the amount that is tax-free has been only 15 percent. The good news here is that this favorable rate was extended, and it will not expire until December 31, 2010. A principal residence can be a house, houseboat, mobile home, cooperative apartment, or condominium.

Techniques and tools to help you maximize the tax benefits of owning a home are discussed in this chapter.

Tax Benefits of Owning a Home

Generally, you can deduct interest that is paid during the tax year on several types of debt related to your home, as long as it is secured by a qualified residence (your principal residence or one other home).

Mortgage Interest

You can deduct interest on debt incurred in acquiring, constructing, or substantially improving a qualified residence. Together, these debts are referred to as acquisition indebtedness. The combined amount of debt that can be considered acquisition indebtedness is capped at $1 million.

> **Observation**
>
> The $1 million cap is not indexed for inflation. As home prices have escalated over the years, more and more taxpayers are finding that a portion of their acquisition debt is not deductible because it exceeds this limitation.

> **Observation**
>
> Debt on a maximum of two residences is counted toward the $1 million limit. Thus, if you have a city home, a beach home, and a mountain home, only qualified debt related to your principal residence and one of the other residences can qualify as home acquisition indebtedness. If you have more than two residences, you are able to annually choose which residences you wish to use for purposes of the mortgage interest deduction. Thus, you will have the opportunity to choose those residences that produce the maximum interest expense deduction for you.

> **Observation**
>
> Margin interest cannot qualify as mortgage interest even where you borrow from your brokerage account to purchase a residence, because margin debt is secured by the assets in your account, not by the purchased home.

Home Equity Loans

Interest is deductible on up to $100,000 of home equity loans. For the interest to be deductible, the home equity loan cannot exceed the fair market value of the residence, reduced by any acquisition indebtedness.

Interest paid on a home equity loan is deductible in almost all situations, no matter how the loan proceeds are used (but there are exceptions—see *Caution*). For example, the fact that home equity loan proceeds are used to finance personal expenses, such as the purchase of a new car or paying college expenses, does not generally affect interest deductibility.

> **Observation**
>
> Consider refinancing nondeductible personal expenditures, such as an auto loan or credit card debt, with a home equity loan to make the interest expense deductible. You can then use your tax savings from the interest deduction to further pay down the principal portion of the loan, so the debt will be paid off sooner.

> **Caution**
>
> Keep in mind that home equity interest expense is not always deductible. If the debt proceeds are used to purchase municipal bonds, for example, the interest expense is not deductible. In addition, be aware that home equity interest that is not used to improve the home is not deductible for purposes of the AMT.

Mortgage Insurance Premiums

Qualified mortgage insurance premiums paid or accrued on your qualified personal residence are now allowed as an itemized deduction. This deduction is phased out by 10 percent for each $1,000 that your adjusted gross income (AGI) exceeds $100,000.

Vacation Homes

If your vacation home is a residence, the mortgage interest you pay is generally deductible. If your vacation home is partly your residence and partly a rental property (see the discussion that follows), your interest deduction must be prorated, along with your other expenses.

A vacation home is generally considered a residence if your use for personal purposes is more than the greater of 14 days per year or 10 percent of the number of days the home is rented out at a fair rental value. Personal use is use by you or a co-owner of the property, or a family member of either you or a co-owner, and use by other people who do not pay a fair market rental. Days when you are performing maintenance and repairs on a vacation property are not considered personal-use days. If you own a vacation home and rent it out to others, the amount of rental activity will affect the tax treatment of rental income, based on the following guidelines:

- *More than 14 days of personal use and rented fewer than 15 days:* If you rent out a home for 14 days per year or less, it qualifies as a second residence. Any rental income is tax-free, and any rental expenses are not deductible (except mortgage interest and real estate taxes).
- *More than 14 days of personal use and rented more than 14 days:* If you rent out your vacation home for more than 14 days per year, and your personal use exceeds the greater of 14 days or 10 percent of the rental period, the home is a personal residence subject to the vacation home rules. You can deduct a proportionate share of property taxes and interest attributable to your personal use. The balance of the interest and taxes can reduce the rental income. In addition, you can deduct depreciation and other operating expenses attributable to the rental to the extent of any remaining rental income. Note that you cannot deduct expenses in excess of the rental income.
- *Fewer than 15 days of personal use and rented more than 14 days:* If you rent your home for more than 14 days and your personal use does not exceed the greater of 14 days or 10 percent of the rental period, the vacation home is considered a rental property. Interest and taxes are allocated between personal and rental use of the property. In addition, other

expenses allocable to the rental activity can be considered in full, even if this results in a loss. The loss, however, will be subject to the passive activity loss rules discussed next (also see Chapter 12), and generally will be deductible only to the extent of passive activity income. Interest allocated to your personal use of the home is personal interest and may not be deductible because the home generally is not considered a residence.

Observation

It is important to remember the significance of fair rental value when renting your vacation home to friends and relatives. If the rent you charge is lower than fair rental value, the Internal Revenue Service (IRS) will consider the days rented as personal use, which can result in limits or elimination of rental deductions.

Observation

If the rental expenses on your vacation home are limited by gross rental income, consider taking an equity loan of up to $100,000 on your principal residence and use the proceeds to pay off the mortgage on your vacation home. Interest on this loan will generally be deductible on Schedule A, and you will still be allowed other rental expenses to offset the rental income.

Rental Properties

If your residential property is fully rented without any personal use, it is considered a rental property and is not subject to the special vacation home rules. As a rental property, taxes, interest, and other expenses are deductible, subject to the passive activity loss rules. Up to $25,000 of passive rental real estate losses can be deducted each year against other income, such as compensation and interest, if the owner meets certain "active participation" requirements.

However, the $25,000 exception is decreased for homeowners with an AGI over $100,000 and is fully phased out for homeowners with an AGI over $150,000. Passive activity losses that cannot be used currently are carried forward indefinitely, and can be deducted against future passive activity income, or are deducted in full when the activity that generated the losses is sold.

Home Office Deduction

Home is where the office is for a growing number of consultants, entrepreneurs, and telecommuters. Although the expenses associated with the use of a residence are generally not deductible, a home office deduction is permitted for certain expenses if a portion of the home is used exclusively and on a regular basis as the principal place of business or as a place to meet or deal with customers or clients in the ordinary course of the homeowner's trade or business.

In addition, home office deductions are available to homeowners who use a separate structure that is near but not attached to the home regularly and exclusively in connection with their trade or business.

Exclusive and Regular Use

To meet the exclusive-use requirement, you as the homeowner must use a portion of the residence solely for conducting business. There is no provision for *de minimis* personal use, such as typing a personal letter or making a personal phone call. If you are employed by a company, your use of the home office must be "for the convenience of the employer." Generally, if your employer supplies you with an office, your home office use would not pass this test.

Principal Place of Business

In the past, *principal place of business* was defined very restrictively for purposes of the home office deduction, preventing many who worked from their homes from claiming deductions.

However, a tax law change that went into effect in 1999 opened up the deduction to many more home office users. In addition to the place where the central functions of a business are performed, the term *principal place of business* now includes areas used for a business's administrative or management activities, if there is no other fixed location where the homeowner conducts these activities. This is the case even if most of the other work of the business is done outside of the home office. For example, it will be easier for salespeople, tradespeople, and manufacturers' representatives who work out of their homes, but perform much of their work at their customers' locations, to claim home office deductions. Here again, if you are an employee, use of your home must be for your employer's convenience to claim a home office deduction.

More people who work at home are able to take a home office deduction. Typical deductible expenses include a portion of rent, depreciation, repairs, utilities, mortgage interest, and real estate taxes.

> ### *Observation*
> Under this liberalized definition of principal place of business, more individuals also are able to deduct the cost of traveling between their home (as their principal place of business) and other business locations. In the past, these transportation costs were considered nondeductible commuting expenses.

> **Observation**
>
> The rules about home office deductions are still complex. A separate tax form is required with Form 1040 to claim the deduction. (Self-employed individuals claim home office expenses on Form 8829 and on Schedule C; employees use Form 2106 or Form 2106EZ and claim them as miscellaneous itemized deductions on Schedule A of Form 1040, subject to the 2 percent of the AGI floor.)

Another consideration in evaluating whether it makes sense to take the home office deduction is that the portion of the home for which home office deductions are claimed may not qualify for the principal residence exclusion of gain described later in this chapter.

Personal Residence Trust

A first or second home is an ideal asset to transfer to a personal residence trust—a popular gift tax planning technique (see Chapter 9). In this case, the property is transferred to the trust for a period of years, during which you retain the exclusive right to live in or use the property. At the end of the term, the property passes to whomever you choose, either in further trust or outright. The value of the transfer is discounted for gift tax purposes because of your retained right to live in the residence. In addition, all future appreciation in the value of the home is transferred free of gift tax.

Although your beneficiaries will own the residence (either in trust or outright) at the end of the trust term, you can lease the property from them at a fair rental value. If you die before the end of the trust term, the property remains in your taxable estate. Consequently, the retained right to live in the property or to use it should be for a reasonable period given your age and general health.

> **Observation**
>
> The personal residence trust's governing instrument (the document that creates the rules of the trust) must prohibit the trust from selling or transferring the residence, directly or indirectly, to you, your spouse, or an entity controlled by you or your spouse, during the time in which the trust is a grantor trust (a trust in which the grantor keeps some rights and control and therefore is taxed on any income from the trust). This means that the grantors will not be able to get the income tax basis step-up at death if they live beyond the trust term. This makes a personal residence trust less attractive for homes that are already highly appreciated.

Home Sales

Principal Residence Gains Exclusion

As a home seller, you may exclude up to $250,000 of gain from the sale of your home as long as it is owned and used by you as your principal residence for at least two of the five years before the sale. Qualifying married taxpayers filing jointly may exclude up to $500,000 of gain. The full exclusion is not available if, within the two-year period before the sale, you sold another home for which you claimed the exclusion.

Note that the sale of surrounding land on which your principal residence is located is not excludable unless the house itself is sold. Personal property, such as furniture or drapes included as part of the sale, is also not excludable (although these personal assets generally are not sold at a gain). Additionally, if you own two residences and live in both of them, your principal residence is the one you live in most of the time.

Qualifying for the $500,000 Exclusion

A married couple filing jointly may exclude up to $500,000 of gain from the sale of their home if:

- Either spouse owned the home for at least two of the five years preceding the sale.
- Both spouses used the home for at least two of the five years preceding the sale.
- Neither spouse sold another home at a gain within the previous two years and excluded all or part of that gain using the exclusion.

Those in the military on official extended duty (stationed at least 50 miles from home or required to live in government quarters) may elect to suspend the five-year period for up to 10 years.

Partial Exclusion

A partial exclusion may be available if you do not meet the two-year ownership and use requirement, or sell your home within two years of a previous home sale for which you used the exclusion. If you fail to meet either requirement because of a change in employment, health, or certain other unforeseen circumstances as determined by the IRS (e.g., separation, divorce, or multiple births arising from the same pregnancy), the exclusion is based on the ratio of qualifying months to 24 months (or, if less, on the ratio of the number of months between the sale date of a previous home for which the exclusion was claimed and the sale date of the current home to 24 months).

For example, suppose a single person owned and used a home as a principal residence for 12 months (and did not use the exclusion on another home sale within the previous two years) and must move for job-related reasons. The partial exclusion rule allows this person to exclude up to $125,000 of his or her gain from the sale of the residence ($250,000 exclusion times 12 months divided by 24).

Partial Exclusion Rule for Joint Filers

If a married couple filing jointly does not meet all the conditions for claiming an exclusion of up to $500,000, the gain that is excluded on the home sale is the sum of the exclusion each spouse would be entitled to if both were single. For this purpose, each spouse is treated as owning the home for the period that either spouse owned the home.

For example, assume a couple sells a home that one spouse owned and used as a principal residence for 10 years and the other spouse used as a principal residence for only one year. They sell the home because of illness. They may exclude up to $375,000 of profit from the sale ($250,000 for one spouse, plus $125,000 for the other spouse).

Property Previously Used for Nonresidential Purpose

Under the Housing Assistance Tax Act of 2008, gain from the sale of a principal residence will no longer be excluded from gross income for periods the home was not used as a principal residence (nonqualifying use). This new rule applies to sales after December 31, 2008. A period of absence generally counts as qualifying use if it occurs after the home was used as a principal residence. Also, the new rule will only apply to periods of nonqualifying use that begin after January 1, 2009.

The amount of gain allocated to periods of nonqualifying use is calculated on a pro rata basis. The amount of gain is multiplied by a fraction, the numerator of which is the aggregate period of nonqualifying use while owned by the taxpayer, and the denominator of which is the period the taxpayer owned the property.

Additionally, the amount of gain that may be excluded is reduced by the amount of depreciation attributable to periods after May 6, 1997. A special capital gain rate of 25 percent will apply to any gain that is included in income due to this depreciation recapture rule.

Example

John buys property on January 1, 2009, for $500,000 and rents it for two years claiming $25,000 of depreciation. On January 1, 2011, he begins using the property as his principal residence. He moves out of the property on January 1, 2013, and sells it for $800,000 on January 1, 2014. The years 2009–2010 are a period of nonqualifying use, as the property was not used as his principal residence during that time. The year 2013, after John moved out, is treated as qualifying use. Of the $300,000 gain, 40 percent (two years out of the five years owned), or $120,000 is not eligible for the exclusion from income. The balance of the gain, $180,000, may be excluded. The $25,000 gain attributable to depreciation is taxable at 25 percent.

Observation

Special care and planning are needed to preserve the full home sale exclusion in divorce situations.

Observation

Home sellers in many real estate markets will have to pay capital gains tax on any profit above the $250,000/$500,000 limits. The rollover break that used to defer unlimited amounts of home sale gain, provided an equally expensive residence was purchased as a replacement, is no longer available. However, the lower long-term capital gains tax rates generally mean that gain that is not excludable is currently taxed at only a 15 percent federal rate plus any applicable state taxes. Because the exclusion is available once every two years regardless of whether it has been used before, some homeowners may decide to sell before their gains exceed the limits. Then additional gain on their replacement residence could also qualify for the exclusion in another two years.

> **Observation**
>
> Because a vacation home is not your principal residence, it does not qualify for the exclusion when it is sold. A residence that you use as a vacation home also cannot be swapped tax-free for another property in a like-kind exchange. Only investment and rental real estate qualify for a like-kind exchange.

> **Observation**
>
> A vacation home can become your principal residence and therefore qualify for the home sale exclusion. For example, if you own a principal residence where you have lived for two or more years and a vacation home, you can sell your principal residence and get the benefit of the home sale exclusion. Then if you move into your vacation home and establish it as your principal residence for at least two years, you can get the home sale exclusion on its sale. This result is subject to the new rules discussed previously on gain related to periods of nonqualifying use that begin after January 1, 2009.

Home Purchases

Real Estate Taxes

In general, real estate taxes can be deducted in the year paid on all residences you own. You are not limited regarding the number of residences as you are with interest expense (see previous example). In the year of a home sale, however, the tax code requires the deduction for real estate taxes to be apportioned between the buyer and seller according to the number of days each held the property during the year. It does not matter that your sales contract contains a different division of responsibility for the taxes.

Currently, only individuals who itemize may deduct real estate taxes. The Housing Assistance Tax Act of 2008 gives nonitemizers a limited deduction for real estate taxes by increasing the amount of their standard deduction by the lesser of (1) actual real estate taxes paid during the year or (2) $500 ($1,000 for a married couple filing jointly). This temporary deduction is available only for 2008.

> **Observation**
> Even though the buyer or seller of a property might pay the entire real estate tax, the deduction is limited by the statutory formula.

> **Observation**
> You will need your closing statement from a home sale or purchase to calculate the amount of deductible real estate taxes. You will also need to know whether the state in which you purchased or sold a home requires prepayment of real estate taxes or whether such taxes are paid in arrears.

Mortgage Points

Mortgage points incurred with a home loan can be significant. A point is a charge paid by a borrower for taking out a loan. Each point is 1 percent of the loan amount. You must amortize most points over the life of the loan; however, you can immediately deduct the points you pay for acquiring or making improvements to your main residence in the year the points are paid. The deductibility of points depends on whether the lender assesses them as additional interest or as a service charge. This is sometimes a difficult determination. Points are generally considered additional interest if the lender is charging for the use of money. If points are assessed for application preparation or processing, they are treated as a service charge and added to the purchaser's basis in the residence and thus are nondeductible.

> ### Observation
> Do not assume you should pay points when purchasing a new home. Think about how long you are likely to own the property. If you expect to sell the property within five years or less, it may be more advantageous to pay a slightly higher interest rate to get a no-points or low-points mortgage loan.

Points may be deducted in full for the year during which they were paid, if the following requirements are met:

- The points are paid directly to the lender by the borrower.
- They are treated as paid directly to the lender if the borrower provides unborrowed funds at least equal to the points charged at the closing or as a down payment or escrow deposit.
- The points are clearly designated as such on the settlement form.
- They are expressed as a percentage of the loan amount.
- Payment of points is established as a business practice for the area in which the loan originates (i.e., banks and other lending institutions in that geographical area typically impose points when granting mortgage loans).
- The dollar amount of the points is typical for the area in which the loan originates.
- The loan is incurred for the purchase or improvement of a principal residence.

Thus, points paid on most mortgage loans financing the purchase of principal residences are deductible. However, borrowers who do not satisfy these requirements must amortize the points over the life of the loan.

> **Observation**
>
> The most common situations in which points must be amortized include the purchase of a second residence and refinancing the mortgage on the principal residence.

> **Observation**
>
> The unamortized points remaining when an underlying mortgage is paid off after a sale or refinancing are deductible in full. But points on a satisfied mortgage cannot be deducted immediately on refinancing if the same mortgage lender holds both mortgages.

First-Time Homebuyer Tax Credit

The Housing Assistance Tax Act of 2008 gives first-time homebuyers a temporary refundable credit equal to the lesser of 10 percent of the purchase price of a home or $7,500 ($3,750 for a married individual filing separately). The credit is effective for homes purchased on or after April 9, 2008, and before July 1, 2009.

The availability of the credit is subject to income limitations and begins to phase out for taxpayers with adjusted gross income in excess of $75,000 ($150,000 in the case of a joint return). The credit completely phases out for married couples filing jointly with adjusted gross income over $170,000 and for single filers with adjusted gross income over $95,000.

Unlike other individual credits, the first-time homebuyer credit must be repaid in equal installments over 15 years. Repayments start two years after the year of purchase. This essentially makes the credit an interest-free loan.

The credit will be disallowed if the residence is disposed of or ceases to be used as a principal residence before the close of the tax year for which the credit would be allowed (2008 or 2009). Further, if a taxpayer sells or no longer uses the home as his or her principal residence before repaying the credit, the unpaid balance becomes due in the year in which the residence is sold or is no longer used as a principal residence. The recaptured amount will not exceed the gain from the sale to an unrelated person.

Reverse Mortgages

A reverse mortgage is a loan available to seniors age 62 and older that allows them to access the equity in their home in one lump sum or multiple payments. The lender bases the mount of the loan on the value of the home, the amount of equity in the home, and the homeowner's age at the time of the loan. The loan is deferred until either the owner dies, the home is sold, or the owner permanently moves. The proceeds of a reverse mortgage may be used for any purpose, but the borrower must first use the proceeds to pay off any existing mortgage on the property.

In a reverse mortgage, the owner makes no payments, so the amount of money owed to the lender increases over time. If the home is sold, the owner may keep any proceeds in excess of the loan amount. Although the proceeds received from the lender are generally tax-free, the interest paid on the loan is not tax-deductible until the loan is paid off in part or whole.

Idea Checklist

- ☑ Convert nondeductible interest expense into tax-deductible home equity interest expense.
- ☑ Know the vacation home rules before renting out your second home.

- ☑ Consider placing a principal residence or second home in a personal residence trust.
- ☑ Review closing documents from real estate sales or purchases to find deductible real estate tax amounts.
- ☑ If you refinance your home, any remaining unamortized points on the paid-off loan are generally deductible on your tax return for that year.
- ☑ Rather than paying tax on a large gain on a vacation home, consider converting it to your principal residence for two years before the sale to make up to $250,000/$500,000 of your gain tax-free. Keep in mind the new rules on nonqualifying use that begin after January 1, 2009.
- ☑ Higher-income taxpayers should consider paying off educational loans with a home equity loan because the phaseout limitations for the deductibility of interest payments on educational loans generally mean that higher-income taxpayers will not benefit from education loan interest.
- ☑ Keep detailed records of all home and vacation property improvements in order to verify basis upon sale.

Owning a home is a cornerstone of the American Dream, and a home is usually a taxpayer's most valuable asset, both financially and emotionally. The tax law gives home ownership numerous tax-saving opportunities, which this chapter has described.

The next chapter discusses saving for education—a high priority for many taxpayers, given the rapidly rising cost of higher education. In the past, many of the tax code's incentives for education savings were not available to taxpayers in the higher tax-rate brackets. Now, however, families with relatively high incomes may be able to put away more after-tax money and withdraw the gains tax-free, which increases their flexibility for funding education for children and grandchildren. Chapter 7 looks at maximizing education savings in detail.

Chapter 7

How to Maximize Savings for Education

To pay for a child's quality education, many parents will do just about anything, even spend their life savings, assume second mortgages, and work multiple jobs if that is what is necessary. It gets harder and harder to keep up with college tuition rates that are growing far faster than the inflation rate.

Fortunately, the tax code offers some real incentives to help parents fund their children's educations. This chapter describes a number of helpful tuition-financing techniques. Despite the fact that there are more available tax breaks, the best advice is to put aside as much as you can, as early as you can.

Until recently, many of the education tax incentives were not available to those with higher incomes. Now, families with higher incomes can take advantage of some tax breaks, including what is by far the best educational tax break, the much-improved Section 529 plan. Also, many of the restrictions that previously prevented taxpayers from bundling various education tax breaks together in the same year have been eliminated.

> **Observation**
>
> Parents should consider the impact that Section 529 programs and Coverdell Education Savings Accounts (formerly called Education IRAs) will have on their chances of obtaining financial aid for college. Some advisors suggest that families who wish to maximize their financial aid use the types of investments that are favored in the federal financial aid formulas. These investments include retirement savings, life insurance, and home equity. However, there are many reasons not to engage in this type of planning:
>
> - The financial aid rules may change before your child is in college.
> - The favored assets under the federal formula may not be favored for your child's university-provided financial aid.
> - Most financial aid is in the form of loans, not grants—why burden yourself or your child with debt?
> - Only a small percentage of parental assets is applied to reduce each year's financial aid.

Qualified Section 529 Tuition Programs

For a number of years, the Internal Revenue Code has allowed states to set up qualified state tuition programs, often referred to as Section 529 plans after the part of the tax code that authorizes them. States are permitted to offer two types of plans:

1. *Prepaid tuition plans that allow a parent, grandparent, or other person to prepay tuition costs and certain other education expenses:* Participants are generally allowed to put aside future tuition by contributing money to these plans, thus assuring tuition at today's tuition rate. The dollar amount required to participate in the plan is generally fixed based on the age of the child and the number of college credit hours you wish to purchase. The state essentially

takes the investment risk to assure that your contributions will grow sufficiently to purchase the desired number of college credit hours by the time the student matriculates. These types of plans are generally available only to state residents and are meant to be used for tuition at in-state public schools. Not all states offer these plans for their residents. Programs differ from state to state, so carefully review the details of your own state's plan.

2. *College savings plans that offer more flexibility on contribution limits and investment choices and can be used at almost any higher education institution:* They can be used to pay tuition, room and board charges, and other expenses required for enrollment. All 50 states currently sponsor at least one college savings plan—and most of these plans are available to out-of-state residents. This means that you have a large number of college savings plans available to you, and you can pick and choose the one best suited for your needs.

Parent-owned Section 529 college savings plans are treated like any other parental asset under federal financial aid guidelines. This means that only 5.64 percent of the plan assets are counted toward a family's expected contribution. This is much lower than the expected contribution from a student-held asset such as a Coverdell Education Savings Account or a custodial account. And because higher education distributions from these plans are excluded from income, the distributions will not be included as student income in the financial aid formula used in determining the family's expected financial contribution to tuition and other expenses.

Distributions from state tuition programs that are used to pay qualifying higher education expenses are completely tax-free. This applies to both prepaid tuition plans and college savings plans. The Pension Protection Act of 2006 made permanent the tax-free treatment of plan distributions used to pay higher education expenses. The 2006 Act also extended the ability to roll over from one plan to another once per year and the ability to invest in both a 529 plan and a Coverdell Education Savings Account in the same year. Coverdell accounts are discussed in detail later in this chapter.

Private educational institutions are now permitted to establish prepaid tuition programs (but not college savings plans) that have the same tax benefits as state tuition plans. These private plans could be attractive to many parents and future students, especially families with a history of attendance at a particular private college. Currently, at least one organization has created a nationwide prepaid tuition program. The 529 plan permits the purchase of prepaid tuition that can be used at more than 200 private schools.

Section 529 tuition programs offer a number of advantages over other college savings alternatives. First, unlike most other tax-advantaged education savings vehicles, there are no limits to prevent high-income individuals from using them. Second, the amount that can be contributed to the college savings plan alternative is very flexible and can be tailored to fit any budget. Substantial sums can be accumulated for a beneficiary in these plans—more than $300,000 in some plans. Finally, a rollover option allows transfers between the tuition plans of different states, between a state's prepaid tuition plan and its savings plan, or between a state tuition plan and a private plan. Rollovers are also allowed from one beneficiary to another beneficiary in the same family. While the federal tax law permits rollovers, plans are not required to do so. If flexibility is important to you, make sure that the plan you choose permits rollovers.

What Expenses Qualify?

Tax-free qualified tuition plan benefits (both state and private) are available to fund tuition, fees, books, and supplies. Most room and board expenses for students who attend school at least half-time will also qualify. Expenses that would otherwise qualify must be reduced by tax-free scholarship grants, veterans' benefits, tax-free employer-paid educational expenses, and amounts that qualify for higher education tax credits to determine the amount that can be received tax-free.

Distributions of earnings from a Section 529 plan that exceed qualified expenditures are taxed to the beneficiary and are generally subject to a 10 percent excise tax. Amounts not used by the beneficiary can be rolled over to another beneficiary's account as long as the new beneficiary is a family member (including a spouse or first cousin), thus keeping the tax benefits working for other family members. Earnings not used for qualified higher education expenses that are returned to the contributor are taxed at the contributor's tax rate plus the 10 percent excise tax. Earnings that are distributed because of the beneficiary's death or disability, or because of the beneficiary's receipt of a scholarship, are not subject to a penalty. Also not subject to the 10 percent excise tax are distributions of earnings that are taxable because the taxpayer elects to take the credits or deductions described in the prior paragraph.

Observation

The Internal Revenue Code imposes a 10 percent tax penalty for taxable distributions from Section 529 plans that are not used for education expenses. Some states have incorporated a penalty for nonqualified use of funds. However, this should not be a factor in choosing a state-qualified tuition plan as long as the plan permits rollovers. If there are funds in the account that will not be used for education expenses, the account could be rolled over and later distributed from a plan that does not impose a penalty of its own.

Contributions to qualified tuition plans may be made only in cash. Unlike Coverdell Education Savings Accounts, discussed later, contributors and beneficiaries are not permitted to self-direct the investments in qualified tuition plans. However, most savings plans permit an initial investment selection among different investment types, and the account owner is generally allowed to switch investments once every 12 months and whenever any change in account beneficiaries occurs.

Many states also offer tax incentives to their residents, including state income tax deductions for some contributions to their state's qualified tuition plans. A small number of states permit a deduction for contributions to a Section 529 plan sponsored by another state. Some states have changed or are considering changing the tax treatment of these programs to conform more closely to the federal tax exemption. Also, some states require a recapture of the state income tax deduction if funds are withdrawn and/or rolled over to another state's plan. The recapture is necessary to prevent the abuse of making contributions solely for the purpose of receiving state income tax deductions.

Caution

A number of special rules coordinate the benefits of various tax-favored education savings vehicles. For example, if you take distributions in the same year from a Coverdell Education Savings Account and a qualified tuition program, and the cumulative distributions exceed the amount of higher education expenses that qualify for the tax breaks, the expenses must be allocated between the distributions to determine how much of each can be excluded. Also, you may claim a higher education tax credit (i.e., Helping Outstanding Pupils Educationally [HOPE] scholarships or lifetime learning credits), if you otherwise qualify, and receive a tax-free distribution from a qualified tuition plan in the same year for the same student (but only to the extent that the distribution does not cover the same expenses for which the tax credit was claimed).

In addition to the tax advantages, Section 529 plans generally offer professional investment management. The plans of some states offer little flexibility in this regard, and their investment choices are somewhat limited. In these plans, your funds usually are invested on an age-based scale, with investments being somewhat more aggressive and stock market based when your child is younger and converting to less aggressive, fixed-income investments as the time horizon to begin paying for college nears. Other plans allow you to choose among various types of mutual funds. However, do not expect to be able to time the market too closely. Federal tax law allows investment changes within a plan to be made no more than once a year. Because you are not limited to using your own state's plan, you can shop around and find one that gives you the kinds of investment management and choices that suit you. However, keep in mind that state tax deductions for contributions are usually available only to state residents who invest in their own state's Section 529 plan (not all states allow this deduction). To learn the details of programs offered by various states, go to www.collegesavings.org/index.aspx or www.savingforcollege.com and click on your state.

Another thing to keep in mind is that anyone can set up a Section 529 plan. You do not have to be the parent of the beneficiary. You can establish a plan for the benefit of a grandchild, nephew, or niece, or even an unrelated individual. As the owner of the account, you control the amounts and timing of distributions to the beneficiary, changes in beneficiary, or cancellation of the account. Some plans permit you to be both the owner and the beneficiary. If you later want to change the beneficiary without incurring income tax, you can name another family member of the original beneficiary as the new beneficiary. You will need to supply the beneficiary's Social Security number, but there is generally no reason that the beneficiary would have to be informed of the plan's existence. With the exception of a few prepaid tuition plans, the beneficiary has no rights of any kind regarding a Section 529 plan. Therefore, the account owner must carefully consider who will become the successor owner when the original account owner dies. The successor owner could choose to direct the money away from the intended beneficiary.

Gift and Estate Tax Breaks

Payments made to qualified tuition programs are considered completed gifts at the time payment is made into the program, even though the student-beneficiary may not receive the benefit of the gift for many years, and even though you retain control over the account. The payments are eligible for the annual gift tax exclusion ($12,000 in 2008). In fact, five years' worth of annual-exclusion gifts can be made in one year to a qualified tuition plan. As a result, a married couple could give $120,000 or $60,000 each to a plan for the same beneficiary in a single year. However, if you or your spouse contribute more than $12,000 to a qualified tuition plan in a single year, it is necessary to file a gift tax return to elect to take advantage of the five years of annual exclusions at once. In addition, if five years of annual exclusions are used for a qualified tuition plan contribution, no additional gifts from the couple can then be made to that beneficiary for the next four years without being subject to further gift tax filings (see Chapter 9 for details). Furthermore, contributions and earnings in Section 529 plans generally will not be included in your taxable estate. Therefore, contributions to qualified tuition programs can assist you in transferring your assets and help optimize your estate plan.

Coverdell Education Savings Accounts

Coverdell Education Savings Accounts allow individuals to contribute up to $2,000 per year for a child to save for education. To make a full contribution, contributors cannot have an adjusted gross income (AGI) above $190,000 on a joint return or $95,000 if single. The allowable contribution phases out for AGIs between $190,000 and $220,000 on a joint return (between $95,000 and $110,000 for singles). Contributions are nondeductible, must be made in cash, and cannot be made after the beneficiary's 18th birthday.

Tax-free Coverdell Education Savings Account distributions can be used for kindergarten, primary school, and secondary school tuition and expenses as well as for higher education expenses. The ability to use the Coverdell Education Savings Account for educational expenses before college sets this alternative apart from the Section 529 plan. Distributions may be made for qualified expenses, including not only tuition and fees but also tutoring costs, room and board, uniforms, transportation, and extended-day programs. Even some computer equipment and Internet access qualifies if used by the beneficiary and the beneficiary's family during a year that the beneficiary is enrolled in school.

Any unused amounts in a Coverdell Education Savings Account must be either distributed before the beneficiary turns 30 or rolled over into a Coverdell Education Savings Account for another family member under age 30. Undistributed amounts are taxed to the beneficiary at that time if not rolled over. Eligible family members include the beneficiary's spouse, children, brothers and sisters, nieces and nephews, and first cousins. If a distribution is not used for educational expenses, the beneficiary is taxed on the earnings and must pay a 10 percent penalty.

The HOPE scholarship and lifetime learning credit are available in the same year in which an income exclusion is claimed for distributions from a Coverdell Education Savings Account as long as expenses for which a credit is claimed are not the same ones for which the exclusion is claimed.

> ### Observation
> Your children and grandchildren may be able to benefit from a Coverdell Education Savings Account even if your income exceeds the AGI threshold. Anyone can contribute to a Coverdell Education Savings Account for your child or
>
> *(Continued)*

Continued

grandchild. Grandparents, aunts, uncles, or even siblings can make the contributions, provided their income is below the modified AGI (MAGI) limitation. A child may even contribute to his or her own Coverdell Education Savings Account. Also, companies may make contributions to Coverdell accounts. If a parent's income is too high to make a contribution, his or her company may make the contribution to the child's Coverdell account. (Such a payment would be taxable compensation to the parent, the same as if the company paid the parent, who, in turn, made the contribution to the account.)

Observation

Parents who intend to send their children to private elementary and secondary schools may want to use Coverdell Education Savings Accounts to help pay those costs and use qualified tuition programs to build a higher education fund. Contributions to a Coverdell Education Savings Account can be made until April 15 following the end of a year to which the contribution relates.

Observation

The low 15 percent tax rate on qualified dividends and long-term capital gains should have little impact on the decision to participate in state-sponsored college savings programs (Section 529 plans) or Coverdell Education Savings Accounts. These plans offer the potential for tax-free appreciation on stocks (dividend paying or otherwise) as long as funds are used for education.

Roth IRAs

Roth individual retirement accounts (IRAs) have a special distribution payout rule that makes them a good source of tax-advantaged cash for education funding. If you withdraw funds from a regular IRA to pay for college while you are under age 59½, the withdrawal is mostly, if not completely, taxable. With a Roth IRA, however, you can withdraw up to the amount of your contributions tax-free for any purpose, even if you are under age 59½ (if the plan was established at least five years prior to the withdrawal). Earnings on the contributions are deemed withdrawn only after you have withdrawn all contributions. If you need to withdraw earnings on the contributions to pay for qualified education expenses, they will be included in your gross income but will not be subject to the usual 10 percent early withdrawal penalty.

> ### Example
> John Smith contributes $5,000 a year to a Roth IRA for 10 years. At the end of that period, he can withdraw his $50,000 cumulative contribution free of income tax and with no penalty. Amounts earned on the contributions remain in the account to further compound for his retirement.

Individuals with adjusted gross income above certain limits are not allowed to contribute to a Roth IRA. See Chapter 4 for a discussion of these limits.

Traditional IRAs

Traditional IRAs are generally not as good a source for funding education expenses as the other vehicles described in this chapter, because all distributions are included in income for tax purposes if all contributions were deductible. If nondeductible contributions were made, part of each distribution is taxable and part is considered to be a return of capital. However, if an IRA withdrawal is used to pay for qualified educational expenses for you, your spouse, child, or grandchild, no 10 percent early withdrawal penalty is imposed. Qualified educational expenses include tuition, fees, books, supplies, and required equipment at a postsecondary school.

> ### Observation
> This penalty exception for higher education expenses does not apply to premature distributions from qualified retirement plans, but it does apply to simplified employee pension (SEP) distributions, which are treated as IRAs for this purpose.

HOPE (Helping Outstanding Pupils Educationally) Scholarships and Lifetime Learning Credits

Taxpayers may be eligible to claim a nonrefundable HOPE scholarship tax credit or a lifetime learning tax credit against their federal income taxes for qualified tuition and related expenses.

A HOPE scholarship tax credit provides up to $1,800 in tax credits per student, but only for each of the first two years of at least half-time college enrollment. A lifetime learning tax credit is also available, which provides an annual 20 percent tax credit on the first $10,000 of tuition and related expenses, for a maximum of $2,000 per year. The lifetime learning credit maximum applies per household, not per student, and can be claimed for yourself, your spouse, or your child. Note that only one of these credits can be claimed in any year for the expenses of a given student.

Students claimed as dependents may not claim either credit on their own tax returns. Qualifying educational expenses that a dependent student pays are treated as paid by the person who claims the student as a dependent for purposes of figuring that person's HOPE credit. Amounts paid to educational institutions by third parties, such as grandparents, are treated as paid by the student (and, in turn, by the student's parents if they claim the student as a dependent).

Even if you are above the income threshold in 2008 for these credits (availability of the credits phases out between a MAGI of $48,000 and $58,000 for singles; $96,000 and $116,000 for married couples filing jointly), there may still be some opportunities to benefit from the credits. If you forgo claiming your student/child as a dependent, and the child has sufficient taxable income to be able to use the credit, the tax value of the credit may be more than you lose by giving up the dependency exemption. There is no restriction on the type of income that may be offset by the tax credit, so a child's investment income would qualify.

Observation

For higher-income taxpayers in particular, it may be beneficial to forgo claiming a student as a dependent since the ability to claim dependency deductions on a 2008 joint return starts to phase out at $239,950 of AGI and reaches total phaseout when AGI is above $362,450. However, you should consider that with the reduction of the phaseouts as part of the 2006 Tax Act, all taxpayers will receive the benefit of at least two-thirds of the dependency exemption in 2008—regardless of their income level.

U.S. Savings Bonds

On your tax return, you may exclude income from interest received on the redemption of U.S. savings bonds purchased after 1989 when you (the bond purchaser) were age 24 or older if your qualifying educational expenses (including the educational expenses of your dependents) for the tax year exceed the aggregate proceeds received from the redemption of the bonds. However, if your AGI is too high, you do not qualify for the interest exclusion.

> ### Observation
>
> The ability to use the provision for exclusion of interest from savings bonds in 2008 begins to phase out for single individuals with an AGI of $67,100 and married couples with an AGI of $100,650. The phaseout range for the interest exclusion is $15,000 for singles and $30,000 for joint-return filers. Because the income level is measured in the year the bonds are redeemed (which might be years into the future), you may not be able to take advantage of the provision if income levels are too high at that time. The interest income would then be subject to tax at ordinary rates.

If you are concerned that your income may be too high in the year of redemption, it might make more sense to invest in growth stocks. This can allow you to manage the recognition of capital gains income, and you could transfer the stock to your child on a just-in-time basis, to be sold at reduced long-term capital gains tax rates (see "Income Shifting and Capital Gains," page 170).

> ### Example
>
> Ms. Jones redeems series EE bonds in the amount of $20,000. She paid $12,000 for the bonds in 1991 and would have to recognize $8,000 of interest income upon the redemption. If she has qualifying education expenses of at least $20,000 during the tax year in which she redeems the bonds and her income is low enough, she avoids income tax on the interest income from the bond redemption. Qualifying educational expenses include tuition and fees spent for the taxpayer, the taxpayer's spouse, and dependents of the taxpayer.

Home Equity Loans

If you need to borrow to pay college expenses, consider a home equity loan. You can claim the loan interest as an itemized deduction, up to a maximum loan amount of $100,000. However, be aware that home equity debt interest in this case would not be deductible for alternative minimum tax (AMT) purposes.

Student Loans

You may deduct up to $2,500 of interest paid (even if you do not itemize deductions) on qualified education loans (i.e., loans taken out and used solely to meet higher education expenses) that you are liable to repay. Interest on loans from relatives or other individuals cannot be deducted.

The student-loan interest deduction phases out in 2008 at a MAGI level between $55,000 and $70,000 for single taxpayers, and between $115,000 and $145,000 for married joint-return filers.

Observation

Due to the phaseout thresholds, many parents are shut out of student-loan interest deductions because their family income is too high. If borrowing is necessary in these situations, it usually makes sense for the student rather than the parent to take out as much of the loan as possible to generate maximum tax benefits. The deduction is not available to a child for any year when the child is claimed as a dependent on the parents' tax return. However, the child is not likely to be a dependent when the loan is being repaid following graduation. At that time, parents can make gifts to help the child with loan repayment.

In 2007 there was a deduction for up to $4,000 for certain higher education expenses. This deduction was taken above the line, which means that it reduces your gross income before taking itemized deductions into account. As of this writing this deduction is not available in 2008. However, we mention it because it is possible that Congress may extend this tax break.

Relatives

Relatives, especially grandparents, with taxable estates (those that exceed the $2 million estate tax exemption that applies in 2008) may be looking for methods to reduce their estates despite additional future increases in the exemption amount that may escape estate tax (see Chapter 9). Payments of tuition made directly to an educational institution should be considered because they do not count as taxable gifts, and do not count against the gift tax annual exclusion amount, as explained on page 196.

Income Shifting and Capital Gains

As discussed in Chapter 3, the lower long-term capital gains tax rates make it worthwhile to consider shifting income to children who may pay a 0 percent tax on capital gains. However, consider the kiddie tax rules that now apply to children who are under age 19 and full-time students under age 24 (see Chapter 3). As a result of the expanded kiddie tax rules, the law severely limits the ability to shift income to children who are in school, since most children will complete their undergraduate education before the age of 24. Of course, from age 24 and on, the kiddie tax will not apply and the income shifting strategy could be effective.

> ***Observation***
>
> If you expect to have capital gains from selling stock to pay a major expense for a child who is not subject to kiddie tax (age 19 and not a full-time student or age 24 or older), consider giving the asset to the child, who can then sell it. Assuming that the child is in a 10 percent or 15 percent tax-rate bracket, the child will pay tax at a 0 percent long-term capital gains tax rate (even if the asset is sold the next day) as long as the combined holding period exceeds 12 months. Keep in mind that both your purchase price and your date of purchase will transfer to gift recipients.

> ***Observation***
>
> Remember, in 2008 the gift tax may apply to gifts over $12,000 from single individuals and $24,000 from married couples. See the discussion of these rules in Chapter 9.

> ***Observation***
>
> If qualifying for financial aid is a possibility, it may be wise to keep assets in the parents' names and transfer them to the student on a just-in-time basis. This is because the federal financial aid family contribution formula requires parents to contribute a smaller percentage of their assets than students must contribute.

Employer Education Assistance

Many employers, especially larger ones, have benefit plans that provide up to $5,250 a year of education assistance to employees. This benefit is tax-free to employees if it applies to tuition and related expenses, such as fees, books, and certain associated supplies and equipment. Other related expenses, such as meals, lodging, and transportation, are not covered by the income exclusion. The courses do not have to be job-related for the benefit to be tax-free. For example, a person who works as a clerk or secretary at a company could take courses toward a degree in literature, history, or economics and receive tax-free benefits. Tax-free assistance is not available, however, for courses involving sports, games, or hobbies.

An employee whose employer's plan permits can receive tax-free benefits to attend graduate school part-time while working. Tax-free benefits are not available to companies whose education assistance plan discriminates in favor of highly compensated employees and their dependents. However, union employees do not have to be covered if education assistance was the subject of good-faith bargaining.

If your employer does not have an education assistance plan as such but does reimburse you for education expenses, the reimbursement is tax-free if the education is job-related (i.e., it maintains or improves a skill currently used in your trade or business or is required to continue your employment). However, the courses cannot qualify you for a new profession (e.g., law school courses taken by a certified public accountant) or be needed for you to meet the minimum educational requirements for your current position.

If you pay for job-related courses on your own without being reimbursed by your employer, you can deduct the expenses on your own tax return as miscellaneous itemized deductions.

However, you can only claim otherwise deductible miscellaneous expenses that exceed 2 percent of your AGI, and these deductions are not allowed in calculating the AMT.

■ ■ ■

For a summary of education tax breaks, see Table 7.1.

Table 7.1 Tax Breaks for Education		
Type of Arrangement	**Main Features**	**Income Limits**
Qualified tuition plan	Distributions for higher education expenses are tax-free.	None
	Large gift-tax-free contributions can be made.	
	Amounts can be transferred to other family members.	
Coverdell Education Savings Account	Per-child contribution limit: $2,000	Contribution limit phases out between a MAGI of $95,000 and $110,000 for singles; $190,000 and $220,000 for joint filers
	Tax-free distributions for education	
	Can be used for kindergarten through postgraduate school, including school-related computer equipment and room and board	
	Broad investment choices	
U.S. savings bond interest education exclusion	Interest is tax-free on redemption for higher education expenses (but not room and board).	Exclusion phases out for 2008 between a MAGI of $67,100 and $82,100 for singles; $100,650 and $130,650 for joint filers.
	Proceeds can be transferred to Coverdell Education Savings Account or qualified tuition plan.	
	Child cannot own bonds.	

(Continued)

Table 7.1 (Continued)

Type of Arrangement	Main Features	Income Limits
Student loan interest deduction	Up to $2,500 of student loan interest is deductible, even by nonitemizers. Deduction cannot be claimed by tax dependent.	Maximum deduction phases out for 2008 between a MAGI of $55,000 and $70,000 for singles; $115,000 and $145,000 for joint filers.
Higher education tax credit	HOPE credit: up to $1,800 per student per year for the first and second year of postsecondary education Lifetime Learning credit: $2,000 maximum per household	Credit phases out between a MAGI of $48,000 and $58,000 for singles; $96,000 and $116,000 for joint filers.
Roth IRA distributions for higher education expenses	Tax-free after 59½ if plan has been established at least five years Distributions tax-free and penalty-free up to amount of contributions Exempt from premature distribution penalty	None for favorable tax treatment of distributions
Traditional IRA distributions for higher education expenses	Taxable to same extent as other IRA distributions, but exempt from 10 percent premature distribution penalty	None
Education assistance plan	Up to $5,250 of employer-provided education assistance is tax-free. Does not have to be job-related education Includes graduate study	None

Idea Checklist

- ☑ Fund a qualified Section 529 tuition plan, especially if your income exceeds the threshold for Coverdell Education Savings Accounts.
- ☑ Fund a Coverdell Education Savings Account and a qualified tuition plan (if you qualify) if you plan to send your children to a private elementary or high school.
- ☑ Have lower-income family members establish Coverdell Education Savings Accounts for children and grandchildren; alternatively, have children contribute to their own Coverdell Education Savings Accounts.
- ☑ Shift capital gains income to a special 0 percent tax bracket by giving stock to your children or grandchildren who are older than 18 if not full-time students or age 24 or older if they are full-time students and whom you expect to be in the 10 or 15 percent tax bracket with respect to their ordinary income in the year in which the stock will be sold.
- ☑ Consider a home equity loan first if loans are needed to help pay for educational expenses, since the interest may be tax deductible.
- ☑ Be sure relatives know that tuition can be paid directly to an educational institution and not be considered a gift subject to the annual exclusion. Also make sure that relatives know that up to five years' worth of annual exclusion gifts can be made at one time to a qualified Section 529 tuition program.
- ☑ Consider funding a Roth IRA (if you qualify) so you can withdraw your contributions tax-free and penalty-free to pay for college.
- ☑ Be aware of the higher income thresholds for some education tax incentives to know if you qualify for any that you could not use in past years.

- ☑ Consider not claiming your child as a tax dependent if your child has enough income to benefit from a higher education tax credit.
- ☑ Determine whether lower long-term capital gains and qualified dividend tax rates make saving for higher education outside of special tax-qualified vehicles a viable option, after taking into account financial aid implications.

The tax law makes paying for college much more affordable for many (see Table 7.1). Parents need creative ways for turning tax burdens into tuition tamers—a need that Congress has begun responding to in the ways this chapter has described.

Higher education can be a large expense for a family. But medical expenses can also be very costly. Fortunately, the tax law provides some ways in which to pay for medical expenses favorably, as discussed in Chapter 8.

Chapter 8
Account-Based Health-Care Arrangements

The Medicare Prescription Drug, Improvement, and Modernization Act, which was designed in 2003 primarily to create prescription drug programs for Medicare beneficiaries, also established health savings accounts (HSAs), which provide individuals with a tax-advantaged vehicle for paying medical expenses. Moreover, over the past few years, the Internal Revenue Service (IRS) has supported company plans to provide medical benefits to employees on a tax-advantaged basis by issuing a number of favorable rulings, including the recognition of health reimbursement arrangements (HRAs). The HSA and HRA plans are in addition to health flexible spending accounts (FSAs) that employers have traditionally made available to employees. This chapter discusses HSA, HRA, and FSA plans.

Health Savings Accounts

You can use HSAs to pay for qualified medical expenses. To be eligible to contribute to an HSA, you must be covered under a qualifying high-deductible health plan (HDHP). You and/or your employer may contribute to the HSA up to a specific limit. You can make contributions and claim a tax deduction, or, if your employer allows, you can make pretax contributions through your employer's cafeteria plan. If your employer contributes to your HSA on your behalf, those contributions are not taxable to you (and are not subject to Social Security and Medicare taxes). Once money is in your HSA, it belongs to you. You own the account and can take it with you when you leave the company.

Funds in your HSA build up on a tax-free basis and are carried forward year to year. You can withdraw money and use it tax-free to pay for qualified medical expenses that you, your spouse, or your dependents incur (including long-term care expenses and insurance premiums). Withdrawals for any other purpose are taxable and, if you are under age 65, subject to a 10 percent penalty. However, if you are 65 or older, withdrawals for nonmedical purposes are considered retirement income and are only subject to income tax. Therefore, this account can also be used to save for retirement purposes with similar tax benefits to an individual retirement account (IRA).

When the account owner dies, his or her spouse can become the owner of the HSA and use it as if it were his or her own account. If the owner is not married, the account will no longer be treated as a HSA and will pass to a beneficiary or the estate and be subject to income tax.

Observation

Nobody currently monitors withdrawals from HSAs to see that they are used for medical purposes. It is your responsibility to keep receipts and other proof to show the IRS (in the event it ever asks) that you used the withdrawals for a tax-free purpose.

Eligibility

Whether you are covered by an HDHP from your employer or by your own policy, make sure it meets the tax law requirements so you can contribute to an HSA. Premiums for an HDHP are lower than for traditional, more extensive medical insurance.

An HSA is open to anyone who, on the first day of the month, meets the following requirements:

- Covered by a plan that meets the definition of an HDHP.
- Not covered by another type of health coverage (other than certain specific types of coverage, such as workers' compensation, long-term care, disability, vision, or insurance for specific illness or disease).
- Not enrolled in Medicare.
- Not able to be claimed as a dependent on someone else's tax return.

For 2008, an HDHP is defined as a plan with an annual deductible of at least $1,100 for self-only coverage or $2,200 for family coverage, and the sum of the annual deductible and other annual out-of-pocket expenses is no more than $5,600 for self-only or $11,200 for family coverage (these dollar limits are adjusted annually for inflation).

Contribution Limits

For 2008, contributions to your HSA by you and/or your employer are limited to $2,900 if you have self-only coverage or $5,800 if you have family coverage (i.e., any plan other than self-only), regardless of your plan deductible. These limits are adjusted annually for inflation.

If you are age 55 or older by year-end, the contribution limit is increased by $900 in 2008 (increasing to $1,000 by 2009).

Contributions are fully deductible as an adjustment to gross income. You do not have to itemize medical expenses to claim this deduction.

Like IRAs, you have until April 15, 2009, to make HSA contributions for 2008. If you are an eligible individual for an HSA for at least the last month of your tax year, you are deemed to be an eligible individual for the entire tax year for contribution purposes. This means you may be able to make a full year's contribution even though you were eligible to participate in only the last month of the tax year.

There are now other ways to make contributions to your HSA. You can elect to make a one-time trustee-to-trustee transfer from your IRA into your HSA. The amount of the transfer is limited to the HSA contribution limits discussed earlier. Your employer can also make a one-time transfer of the entire balance of your HRA or your FSA. The maximum allowable transfer is the smaller of your HRA or FSA balance on September 21, 2006, or on the date of transfer. The amount transferred from your IRA, HRA, or FSA is not included in your income and is not deductible. The amount transferred from your IRA reduces your HSA contribution limit for the year (transfers from your HRA or FSA do not limit your HSA contribution for the year).

Health Reimbursement Arrangements

Generally, health reimbursement arrangements (HRAs) are notional accounts to which your employer credits an amount on your behalf. Only your employer can contribute to an HRA—you cannot. You can draw from the account to pay qualified medical costs that you, your spouse, or your dependents incur that are not covered by insurance. You are not taxed on the contributions or the withdrawals.

Your employer may provide you with a credit or debit card to use in accessing funds in your account or require you to submit bills and receipts to obtain reimbursements. Your employer may allow you to carry over some or all of the funds in your HRA from year to year to increase your available funds in the following year. Most employers do not allow their employees to take their HRA balances with them when they terminate employment.

Flexible Spending Accounts

Your company may allow you to contribute a portion of your compensation to a medical FSA. Your contributions are made on a pretax basis; therefore, you do not pay income tax on the salary reduction amounts you commit to the FSA. Your employer may also contribute to your FSA.

You can access funds already contributed as well as funds you agree to contribute. For example, if you agree to a $200 monthly salary reduction amount for 2008, you can submit for reimbursement a $2,400 medical expense incurred in January 2008 (even though you may have actually contributed only $200 to your FSA at that time).

Funds in your FSA that are not used by the end of the year are forfeited; you cannot carry them over to the next year or take a withdrawal for any other purpose. However, back in 2005, the IRS extended the period immediately following the end of the plan year during which unused FSA funds can be reimbursed to plan participants for qualified expenses. Employers can now amend their plans to add up to a two-and-one-half-month grace period in which employees can use any remaining FSA funds for a given year. The fact that excess funds in an FSA are forfeited means that you must fund your account with an amount that you are relatively sure you will incur in medical expenses for the year. In deciding on your amount to contribute, it is better to underfund the FSA account than to overfund it.

Funds in FSA accounts can be used for a wide range of qualified medical expenses, including over-the-counter nonprescription medications (e.g., antacids, allergy medications, cold remedies, and pain remedies) taken to alleviate or treat an illness or personal injury.

> ### *Observation*
> Withdrawals from FSAs are not permitted for medications taken to maintain general good health, such as dietary supplements.

Chapter 9
Estate Planning Ideas

The federal estate tax is in a state of transition. The phaseout and eventual repeal of the tax as embodied in the Economic Growth and Tax Relief Reconciliation Act of 2001 provides less relief from estate planning chores than most people expected; this Act repealed the estate tax for only the calendar year 2010. Given the scheduled increase in the estate tax exemption amount in 2009, decrease in the transfer tax rates, and repeal in 2010, planning for wealth transfer has become increasingly important.

As the law is now written, the federal maximum estate tax rate began to phase down starting in 2002 (from 55 percent in 2001 to 45 percent in 2008), and the estate tax will be completely eliminated for 2010. During the transition period, the estate tax exemption amount has increased as the maximum rate of tax on estates and gifts has decreased. The tax rate on lifetime gifts will benefit from the tax-rate reductions, but it is important to note that the gift tax exemption does not increase from the current level of $1 million. Further, the gift tax is not scheduled to be repealed.

> ### Observation
>
> If you previously used your full lifetime gift tax exemption at a time when the maximum exemption amount was $675,000, you may think that you can make an additional $325,000 of tax-free gifts, in addition to your annual exclusion gifts, to reach the current maximum gift tax exemption amount of $1 million. However, due to the way prior gifts are figured when calculating the gift tax owed on current gifts, that is not the case. People who are already subject to the maximum 45 percent (for 2007 to 2009) gift tax rate bracket (because of prior taxable gifts) can make only $278,333 of additional gifts before paying gift tax. This is because the increased exemption amount of $325,000 is implemented through an increase of $125,250 in the applicable credit amount, and $125,250 divided by 0.45 equals $278,333.

Some of the advantages of the full estate tax repeal in 2010 will be offset by some generally unfavorable changes to the income tax rules for inherited property, especially for those people with large estates. For example, the repeal brings with it a limitation on the current step-up in tax basis for assets acquired from a decedent. The loss of the income tax basis step-up that currently exists, in conjunction with the estate tax, will increase the income tax burden of many people who inherit property. And tracking the basis in assets that your parents or grandparents acquired many years ago could prove to be a nightmare.

Another reason you may wish to review your current estate planning documents is to make sure that your current plan continues to distribute your estate to the intended beneficiaries in light of the changing estate tax exemptions. During the phasedown period, when the estate tax exemption reaches $3.5 million (in 2009), complications with preexisting estate plans may arise that could cause a surviving spouse to receive no property outright. But proper planning during this period may result in large tax savings for some.

Because the tax law changed in 2001, many states have also added to or increased their own estate taxes (because they are losing revenue as a result of the repeal of the state death tax credit that previously offset federal estate taxes). Residents of these states, or nonresidents owning property in those states, must factor differing state rates and exemptions into their estate planning considerations.

After 2010, the repeal of the estate tax is scheduled to sunset. This will return the estate and gift tax rules to the 2001 level: a 55 percent maximum tax rate in 2011, coupled with a $1 million unified estate and gift tax exemption amount.

As was previously the case, estate and gift tax planning strategies can still protect significant amounts of property from being subject to transfer taxes. However, there is less certainty as to what the best solutions will be. This chapter focuses on important planning ideas to consider.

How Estate and Gift Taxes Work

Estate and gift taxes currently work in tandem as a unified transfer tax system, with the same tax rates (but differing exemption amounts) applying to both taxes. Gift tax exemption used during a lifetime is subtracted from the available estate tax exemption amount on death. Transferring wealth amounts to "pay me now or pay me later." However, although the amount exempt from estate tax has increased to over $1 million (it is $2 million for persons dying in 2008 and $3.5 million for persons dying in 2009), the gift tax exemption amount is frozen at the $1 million level. In addition, the gift tax will continue, although at a reduced maximum tax rate of 35 percent, in 2010 when the estate tax is scheduled to be repealed. See Table 9.1.

Table 9.1 Estate and Gift Tax Exemption Allowances

Year	Estate Tax Exemption (in $ Millions)	Gift Tax Exemption (in $ Millions)
2008	2	1
2009	3.5	1
2010	N/A (tax repealed)	1
2011 and later	1	1

Amounts Exempt from Tax

In 2008, you may transfer $12,000 ($24,000 for most married couples) to each of an unlimited number of individuals free of gift tax. These amounts are expected to increase in 2009 to $13,000 and $26,000 respectively. To qualify for the annual gift tax exclusion, the recipient generally must have immediate access to the gift, although some gifts in trust can qualify, as can contributions to a qualified tuition program (e.g., Section 529 plans).

In addition to the 2008 $12,000 annual exclusion, unlimited amounts can be transferred directly to an educational institution or health-care provider free of gift tax to pay someone else's tuition or medical expenses.

Aside from the annual exclusion amount, there are even larger tax breaks. You can transfer unlimited amounts to your spouse (if your spouse is a U.S. citizen) free of gift or estate tax by way of the unlimited marital deduction. In addition, you may transfer $1 million in total to children and others without paying any gift tax through the lifetime gift tax exemption. If you and your spouse agree to split your gifts, you can give a total of $2 million by using the lifetime exemptions of both spouses. Annual exclusion gifts, tuition, medical, and spousal transfers are in addition to and do not count against the lifetime exemption. (Special rules apply, however, if your spouse is not a U.S. citizen.)

Gift and Estate Tax Rates

After you have exceeded the exemption amount, the gift tax rates outlined in Table 9.2 apply for 2008. For 2008, the maximum gift tax rate (which also applies to estates greater than $2 million) is 45 percent. In future years, the maximum tax rates are as shown in Table 9.3.

Currently, the recipient of most property transferred at death receives an income tax basis equal to the fair market value (FMV) of the property at the date of death. This means that income tax is avoided on the property value increase that occurred during the decedent's life, and the estate or heir can sell the asset immediately after the decedent's death, generally without paying any income tax.

The rule is different for gifts made during life. For property where the fair market value is equal to or exceeds the donor's

Table 9.2 *Gift Tax Rates*

For Taxable Gifts ($)	Marginal Tax Rate (%)
1,000,000–1,249,999	41
1,250,000–1,499,999	43
1,500,000 and above	45

Table 9.3 *Maximum Estate and Gift Tax Rates*

Year	Highest Estate and Gift Tax Rates (%)
2008 and 2009	45
2010	35 (gift tax) 0 (estate tax)
2011 and later	55

income tax basis at the time of the gift, the recipient receives the donor's basis in the property. Thus, if he or she sells the property immediately after receipt, there is an income tax on any appreciation that has occurred since the donor acquired it. On the plus side, gift recipients get to include the donor's holding period in determining whether their sale qualifies for favorable long-term capital gains treatment.

For property where the fair market value is less than the donor's basis at the time of the gift, the recipient receives the donor's basis in the property for purposes of calculating gain and the recipient would use the lower FMV at the time of the gift for purposes of calculating loss. In other words, one cannot generally *gift* a capital loss to the recipient of the property.

With long-term capital gains tax rates as low as 15 percent—and 0 percent for those (e.g., children and grandchildren) who are in the 10 percent or 15 percent income tax brackets—it still may be worth considering whether lifetime giving makes sense in spite of the lack of income tax basis step-up for lifetime gifts. Be sure to consider both the income tax and the transfer tax consequences of your gifts.

In 2010, when the estate tax is scheduled to be repealed, the income tax basis step-up (basis increase to the property's FMV at the time of death) for assets received from a decedent will be limited. The heirs of decedents dying in 2010 will receive an income tax basis step-up that will generally eliminate income tax on a total of no more than $1.3 million of gain that occurred during the decedent's life. Property inherited by a surviving spouse will generally get an additional $3 million of tax basis increase, allowing a total tax basis increase of no more than $4.3 million.

Observation
The dollar limits on tax basis step-up will not affect smaller estates. However, they will add income tax complications to estate planning considerations for those with larger estates.

Observation
Only property transferred outright to the surviving spouse or held in a special form of trust known as a qualified terminable interest property (QTIP) trust qualifies for the additional $3 million of income tax basis increase for property passing to a surviving spouse. Many persons have estate plans in which bequests to surviving spouses are held in other forms of trusts that qualify for the marital deduction for estate tax purposes, but not for purposes of the $3 million tax basis increase (e.g., general power of appointment trusts or estate trusts—often put in place for state tax purposes). Although these types of transfers may be adequate if death occurs before 2010, these trusts may not be optimal for federal estate tax purposes if death occurs in 2010, because the opportunity to step up the tax basis by an additional $3 million would be lost.

Observation
In the past, estate plans often provided that retirement assets or other assets that may not be stepped up be left to the surviving spouse rather than to children or other heirs. Under the post-2009 rules, the reverse may be desirable because it may be necessary to use the maximum amount of tax basis step-up for post-2009 transfers to a surviving spouse. However, when deciding on the beneficiary of retirement plan assets, for example, it is important to consider all of the income tax consequences of that decision.

An estate's executor will choose which of a decedent's assets will receive the tax basis increase. Donors and executors will also be required to report information about certain transfers, including tax basis and holding period information, to the IRS and to donees and estate beneficiaries.

> ### Observation
> If some beneficiaries receive property with a higher tax basis, other beneficiaries may be burdened with higher capital gains on the sale of the property they inherit. Planning will be needed to make the most of available tax basis step-up and to keep the potential for family strife over this issue to a minimum.

> ### Observation
> For those interested in leaving assets to charity, retirement assets remain an excellent choice because retirement assets do not qualify for a step-up in tax basis either before or after the scheduled repeal of the estate tax. Because a charity is a tax-exempt entity that will not have an income tax liability from the retirement plan distributions, it makes sense to fund charitable bequests with retirement plan assets and to allocate other assets that receive a step-up in tax basis at death to heirs.

Planning for Phasedown and Repeal of the Estate Tax

What will all of these changes mean for you? They will mean more—not less—estate planning. First, you will have to make sure that during the transition period from now through the end of 2009, when exemption amounts are increasing and the maximum tax rates are dropping, your existing will and your overall estate plan still do what you intended. If not, you will have to make adjustments.

Second, you will need to stay on top of future changes to the estate and gift tax rules. Most estate planning experts doubt that the current rules, which include full repeal of the estate tax for 2010, will be fully implemented. There are ongoing discussions in Congress regarding significant changes, including increasing the overall estate tax rates in lieu of making the estate tax repeal permanent. The political and economic environment, including budget deficits, will be a factor in determining whether and when change is made. As for complete repeal of the estate tax—even for one year—many professionals advise not to count on it. The political or economic climate over the next couple of years is not predictable; only time will tell.

Planning will be easiest for those whose estates fall below the increases in the exemption amounts through 2009, which would eliminate all federal estate tax liability. Many people will be able to implement simple wills, without even the usual credit shelter trusts, to avoid estate taxes during this time. However, if estates increase in size, or if the estate tax rules return to their 2001 status after 2010, or if you live in a state with an inheritance tax that is not tied to the federal exemptions, this will not be true. New plans that are more complicated will again be necessary.

During the phaseout period, flexibility will be needed. Some estate planners have suggested increasing the use of disclaimers (i.e., an election by the planned recipient of inherited property to decline the receipt of the property) to give surviving spouses the ability to balance estate tax savings with other financial needs. Wills may benefit from contingency language that would cause alternative provisions to kick in if the expected estate tax changes, repeal, and/or reinstatement do not occur as scheduled.

There are many tax-saving ideas you can use to reduce your estate. They are particularly helpful to high-net-worth individuals. One quick way to figure out whether you need estate tax planning is to look at your net worth (the value of the assets you own minus the liabilities you owe). Be sure to include the face value of the life insurance on your life that you own. If the total exceeds the exemption amount, you may want to consider some planning ideas.

The sooner you take action to update and implement your plan, the better. A gift made now also removes future appreciation from your estate.

Example
An individual used her exemption to make a $600,000 gift of property in 1987, when that was the maximum exemption amount. She dies in 2008 when the property's value has grown to $2.5 million. Thus, she effectively removed the growth on $600,000 ($2.5 million less $600,000, or $1.9 million) from her estate by acting early. In addition, the first $1.4 million of her remaining estate is sheltered by the balance of her exemption allowance ($2.0 million allowance for 2008 less $600,000 used in 1987). Had she not made the gift but instead held the property until her death, her gross estate for tax purposes would have increased by $1.9 million.

Observation
Those with large estates should consider maximizing the early giving strategy using the $1 million gift tax exemption.

Draft a Will

Many people do not have a will. As a result, their state of residence generally determines who receives their property at death and how and when the property is received. If you are married with children, in many states not having a will means your surviving spouse will not receive all of your assets. In addition, you will miss the opportunity to generate some significant estate tax savings for your family.

Even if your estate is less than the estate tax exemption, you may need to use a will to name a guardian for your minor children, and to specify whom you wish to inherit your assets and when they should receive them.

Review How Your Property Is Owned

Unless you live in a community property state (i.e., Arizona, California, Idaho, Louisiana, Nevada, New Mexico, Texas, Washington, Wisconsin, and, under certain circumstances, Alaska) in which generally all property acquired during marriage is treated as half-owned by each spouse, it is important for a married couple to consider how their property is owned.

For married couples, joint ownership with right of survivorship can defeat an otherwise excellent estate plan, because the surviving spouse will automatically receive the property at the death of the first spouse. You may want it to go to your children or someone else. Although no estate tax will result on the first spouse's death because of the unlimited marital deduction, there might not be enough property to fund other estate planning options, such as the credit shelter trust.

A review of the ownership of assets can also help determine whether lifetime gifts or transfers of property should occur between spouses to ensure that each spouse has sufficient assets in his or her name alone to help fund a credit shelter or family trust without regard to the order in which the spouses die. For example, assume husband and wife have $500,000 and $3,500,000 of assets in their own names, respectively. If the husband predeceases his wife, there will not be sufficient assets in his name alone to fully fund a credit shelter trust. It may be wise for husband and wife to consider lifetime gifts to each other to better equalize the respective sizes of their estates so the credit shelter trust can be funded regardless of which of them dies first.

> **Observation**
> A review of your assets will be more crucial than ever given the increased exemption amounts.

Consider State Death Taxes

The state death tax credit allowable against the federal estate tax was repealed for those dying after 2004 and was replaced by a deduction against the decedent's gross estate for taxes actually paid to any state. Many states have enacted a stand-alone state inheritance tax, and the implications of these state taxes must be considered as part of your overall estate planning.

> **Observation**
> Almost all states formerly had a state death tax equal to the amount allowed as a federal credit. This generated tax revenues for the states without actually increasing the total amount of estate tax due by decedents' estates. Before its repeal (and conversion to a deduction), the state death tax credit was an important source of revenue for many states, and these states have experienced a loss in revenue with the repeal of that credit. As a result, many states have enacted or revised their state death tax so it is no longer tied to the federal credit. This issue is continuing to evolve, and ultimately could influence the state in which you choose to reside.

> ***Observation***
> Some states (but not the federal government) allow for a deduction for transfers to domestic partners. Special will drafting may be advisable in such states to take full advantage of such deductions.

Give Gifts

Over time, an annual giving program can remove hundreds of thousands of dollars from your estate on a tax-free basis. In 2008, you can give up to $12,000 ($24,000 if your U.S. spouse joins in the gift) to each of any number of people each year, and you will not have to pay gift tax. The annual gift tax exclusion will be increased for future inflation, which would allow you to give $13,000 in 2009 or $26,000 if you and your U.S. spouse give jointly. Making annual exclusion gifts removes property from your estate at no gift or estate tax cost and often shifts income-earning property to family members in lower income tax brackets. The future appreciation in the value of the gifted property is also removed from your estate.

> ***Observation***
> It is generally better not to wait until late in the year to make gifts. Instead, it is a good idea to get in the habit of making gifts in January each year. In a good year, an asset that is worth $13,000 in January could be worth significantly more by the end of December. By giving early, you enable the postgift appreciation also to escape gift tax. Even though this strategy might not have worked well during down years for stocks, its prudence in the long run has been proven by the stock market's history. Over the years, there have been vastly more up than down years in the stock market.

In addition to the $12,000 annual exclusion, there is an unlimited exclusion for any tuition you pay directly to a school or for medical care payments you make directly to a health-care provider on someone else's behalf. These tuition and medical payments are fee of gift tax, and they do not count toward the annual gift tax exclusion. Even multiyear advance tuition payments may be structured to be free of gift tax. Thus, grandparents can pay tuition directly to a school on behalf of a grandchild, as well as pay the insurance company for the grandchild's health insurance premiums and the orthodontist for the grandchild's braces, and still each give the grandchild $12,000 in 2008 without using any of their $1 million lifetime exemption amount.

> ### Observation
> Tuition payments made directly to a private elementary school, secondary school, or college all qualify for the unlimited gift tax exclusion. However, room and board, books, and similar expenses do not qualify for the tuition exclusion.

It should be noted that payments by parents or other friends and family members to a qualified tuition program (e.g., 529 plans) do not qualify for the unlimited tuition gift tax break. Instead, payments to these tax-favored college savings programs count toward the annual gift tax exclusion limit. You can, however, elect to treat a contribution for a beneficiary in 2008 that is more than $12,000 as made equally over five years (the current year plus four more years). Thus, a $60,000 gift to a qualified tuition program for a single beneficiary in a single year can be free of gift tax. A gift tax return must be filed to make this election, and for the next four years you could not give the same beneficiary any additional annual exclusion gifts. From an income tax standpoint, the assets in the program can appreciate free of income tax provided the funds are ultimately withdrawn for qualified higher education expenses.

> ***Observation***
> The 0 percent tax rate on qualified dividends and long-term capital gains for taxpayers in the 10 percent or 15 percent tax-rate bracket increases the benefit to a parent (who is in a high income tax bracket) of making a gift of appreciated or dividend-producing property to a child over 18 years of age (who is in one of the two lowest income tax brackets). In 2008, the benefit does not apply to a gift to a child under age 24 if the child is a dependent and a full-time student. In addition to the gift and estate tax benefits associated with such a gift, the family may realize an additional income tax benefit of reducing the income tax imposed on future dividends and capital gains generated by the gifted property from 15 percent in the parent's hands to 0 percent in the child's hands.

Consider Valuation Discounts

Transfers of certain types of assets, typically a minority interest in a business enterprise, may permit the use of a valuation discount for gift and estate tax purposes (so that the value for transfer tax purposes is below the value that might result from a sale of the entire enterprise). How the property is owned may result in valuation discounts, even if the value of the underlying property does not change.

Example

The fair market value of an asset is $100. For valid business reasons, the asset is placed into a vehicle that may yield a valuation discount, such as a limited partnership. When all the limited partnership interests are given to multiple children, the sum of the values of each gift to a child as reported on the gift tax return might be only $75, reflecting a discount from the underlying FMV of the asset because of the minority interest and lack of marketability of the limited partnership interests. An appraisal is likely to be necessary, but in this example, the discount is 25 percent. Limited partnerships and limited liability companies also offer many nontax advantages, including significant control for the general partner and some protection from creditors of the limited partner(s).

Observation

The IRS has challenged valuation discounts taken when family limited partnership interests are given away. Full consideration of the potential tax risks involved with such planning is recommended before undertaking such a plan. Also, you must disclose claimed valuation discounts on your gift tax return or lose the benefit of a statute of limitations that ends the IRS's ability to adjust the value of the gift.

If you own a majority interest in a business, you can make gifts of nonvoting shares (or less than controlling amounts of voting shares) and could be entitled to a minority discount that would be unavailable if the shares were transferred at your death. The shares given away would not receive an income tax basis step-up at your death, but future appreciation would be outside of your estate. If your lifetime gifts of voting shares brought your voting rights to 50 percent or less, then all of your shares held at death may also be entitled to a discount for lack of control for estate tax purposes.

> **Caution**
> If at your death you own a limited partnership, limited liability company, or nonvoting shares while still controlling the entity, you may not get a minority discount on any of the interests you own, and may risk inclusion in your estate of assets previously given away.

Consider Trusts

Credit Shelter or Family Trust

Married couples should have a credit shelter or family trust in their estate plan if their combined assets exceed the per-person estate tax exemption allowance of $2 million for 2008. Failure to have this type of trust in your estate plan can cost your family hundreds of thousands of dollars in estate taxes that could have been easily avoided.

The use of credit shelter trusts for each spouse ensures that both spouses' estates get the full estate tax exemption. Their purpose is to fund trusts for children or other heirs with the maximum amount that can pass without estate tax and to give the surviving spouse only a limited interest (generally limited to use of the trust assets only if the spouse needs them) in that portion of the estate. Use of these trusts was often designed around the old exemption amounts ranging from $600,000 to $1 million. Now that the exemption has increased after the 2001 Tax Act, however, these trust arrangements will be funded with larger and larger amounts—and in 2010 possibly all—of a decedent's assets, in some cases leaving no assets to pass outright to the surviving spouse. If the surviving spouse has sufficient assets in his or her own name and maximizing estate tax savings is the prime consideration, this may be a desirable outcome.
In other situations, use of the credit shelter trust could cause serious financial problems for the surviving spouse. This issue

will become even more important in 2009 when the estate tax exemption amount is scheduled to increase to $3.5 million, and in 2010 when the estate tax is repealed in its entirety. At the same time, the increases in the estate tax exemption amount will require those with relatively modest estates to reexamine the impact of credit shelter trusts. Spouses with very large estates still need fully funded credit shelter trusts.

> **Observation**
> Many wills now automatically increase the credit shelter trust's funding with the rise in the exemption amount. You can avoid this by specifying in your will the maximum amount of your estate that you would like to fund a credit shelter trust or the minimum amount that should be available to the surviving spouse.

Irrevocable Life Insurance Trust

Life insurance policies that are owned by you are an asset of your estate; therefore, if the policy is on your own life, the death benefit proceeds will be subject to estate tax. To shelter the proceeds from estate tax, you can transfer existing policies into an irrevocable life insurance trust (ILIT) that has been created for the purpose of holding the policy and managing or distributing the death benefit proceeds. While the transfer of the policy to the trust and the payment of all future premiums are gifts, the death benefit may be removed from your estate and not be subject to estate tax. Transferring an existing life insurance policy, however, does not provide immediate estate tax relief. An existing life insurance policy that is transferred to an irrevocable trust will not be effectively removed from your estate for a period of three years from the date of transfer. To avoid the three-year transfer rule and achieve immediate estate tax relief, consider transferring cash to the life insurance trust and having the trust acquire all new life insurance policies directly from the life insurance company. If the trust acquires the policy (rather than receiving it from you or someone else), then the death benefit proceeds escape estate taxation right from the outset (i.e., no three-year rule). See Chapter 5 for more detail on irrevocable life insurance trusts.

> **Observation**
> Life insurance needs for estate liquidity may decrease as the estate tax is phased out and repealed, but the need will not be eliminated because of the loss of full tax basis step-up and the possibility of reinstatement of the estate tax in 2011. You will have to take a variety of contingencies into account in drafting and funding an irrevocable life insurance trust, particularly the anticipated need by your survivors for quick access to cash.

Grantor Retained Annuity Trust

The grantor retained annuity trust (GRAT) arrangement is popular because it permits you to give away future appreciation on the property that you place in the trust while retaining for yourself the property's initial value plus a fixed return. The fixed return is legislatively provided and prescribed over the entire life of the arrangement based on the prevailing interest rate in the month the arrangement begins. If the trust assets provide an actual economic rate of return that exceeds the fixed return, the trust's beneficiaries will receive the excess (either in further trust or outright) at little or no gift tax cost.

Typical assets placed in this type of trust include S corporation stock, publicly traded stock, and other assets that are expected to grow quickly. The higher the rate of return on trust assets, the greater the amount that will go to the trust's beneficiaries free of gift tax.

> **Observation**
> Gifts to grantor retained annuity trusts are particularly attractive in periods of low interest rates (e.g., current rates) because it should be easier to exceed the benchmark rate of return. (The benchmark rate of return varies from month to month based on the prevailing interest rates on U.S. Treasury securities.)

Qualified Personal Residence Trust

You can transfer a personal residence (either a principal residence or a vacation home) to the beneficiaries of a qualified personal residence trust at a discount from the home's current fair market value. You can live in the home for a term of years and continue to take a mortgage interest deduction as well as a real estate tax deduction. When your term interest in the trust ends, you can then make arrangements to rent the home from the trust or its beneficiaries at FMV rental rates (while this is an excellent means of further reducing your estate, the nonfinancial emotional impact also needs to be considered).

A qualified personal residence trust is especially desirable if significant appreciation is expected in the value of the home over time, because the appreciation that occurs after the trust is established can also escape estate and gift taxation.

> **Observation**
> Unlike grantor retained annuity trusts, gifts to qualified personal residence trusts are less attractive in periods of low interest rates because the gift tax cost is higher than it would be in periods of higher interest rates. Please note that, irrespective of interest rates, the gift tax cost of implementing a qualified personal residence trust can be substantial relative to a grantor retained annuity trust, where the gift tax cost can be nominal.

Dynasty Trust

A dynasty trust can be established during your life or in your will. The dynasty trust allows you to set aside assets for your descendants (usually your grandchildren and more remote descendants) without incurring gift, estate, or generation-skipping transfer (GST) taxes at each generation.

Such trusts are typically designed to last for the longest possible period allowed by law. Typically, the trustee (an individual or entity other than the grantor) who manages the trust assets and income will have the discretion to pay trust income and principal to your descendants. The trusts are intended to take advantage of some portion or the entire amount of the GST tax exemption, which allows you to transfer assets to your grandchildren or more remote descendants without incurring the GST tax. The amount of the GST exemption for 2008 through 2009 is equal to the estate tax exemption amount as shown in Table 9.1 on page 186.

Charitable Remainder Trust

If you are charitably inclined, have highly appreciated assets, and wish to sell them while creating a regular stream of cash flow, a charitable remainder trust (CRT) may help. A CRT allows you to sell assets in the trust today and defer the income tax cost until the income is distributed from the trust as part of an annual annuity. The annual annuity can be a fixed dollar amount, a percentage based on the assets contributed to the trust, or a variable annuity that is defined as a percentage of the assets as measured on an annual basis. While the trust allows you to defer a portion of the income tax liability and to retain an annual annuity, it also provides for a remainder interest that will pass to charity when the trust ends. The value of this remainder interest is based on the term of the trust, which may be for a term of years (not to exceed 20 years) or for your lifetime. Although the charity does not receive its interest until the end of the trust term, you will receive an income tax charitable contribution deduction in the year the trust is funded that is equal to the present value of the remainder interest that is calculated to go to charity. This trust may be a great vehicle to replace current cash flow, such as in the year after retirement, while also providing a current charitable deduction for an interest that will pass to charity at some time in the future.

> ### Observation
> You can use some of the extra cash flow that you receive from a CRT asset transfer and establish a life insurance trust for your family to replace the assets placed in the CRT, which go to charity at your death. However, life insurance is not a required adjunct to a CRT.

> ### Observation
> The current income tax rate reductions and the decrease in the income tax rates imposed on qualified dividends and long-term capital gains diminish the tax benefits of CRTs, making them relatively less attractive than they have been in the past. In addition, CRTs are less attractive in periods of low interest rates.

Charitable Lead Trust

A charitable lead trust (CLT) provides that the charity receives an income stream for a period of years and the remainder goes to a family member or other noncharitable beneficiary. A CLT is the opposite of a CRT (discussed earlier). There are two types of CLTs: the charitable lead annuity trust (CLAT) and the charitable lead unitrust (CLUT).

Upon creation of a CLT, the donor is entitled to an income tax charitable deduction if the charitable interest is in the form of a fixed percentage of trust assets or a guaranteed annuity, and if the donor is taxed on the trust's annual income as it is earned (i.e., a grantor trust). The tax liability can be mitigated if the trustee invests in tax-exempt securities. If the donor establishes a nongrantor CLT, he or she will not receive a charitable income tax deduction, but will not be taxed on the trust's income each year, either. In that case, the trust pays its own tax and can claim a charitable contribution deduction for the annual amounts distributed to charity.

Individuals who are charitably inclined can achieve important gift tax and estate planning objectives through the use of a CLT. In return for promising to make a certain level of annual charitable contributions, it can be possible for an individual to transfer the property remaining in the trust at some future date, with minimal gift or estate tax consequences. The CLT is particularly beneficial in the low interest rate environment of the past several years.

Observation

Charitable lead trusts generally benefit from income tax reductions, as if the grantor held the CLT assets directly. However, there are factors that may make nongrantor CLTs less beneficial. Generally, a nongrantor CLT is entitled to an income tax deduction each year for the annuity amount that it pays to charity. This deduction is available only to offset CLT income, as opposed to other income the grantor may have. There also may be factors that make nongrantor CLTs more beneficial. A CLT's charitable deduction is not subject to adjusted gross income (AGI) limitations or the 2 percent of AGI threshold (in 2008) on itemized deductions.

Intentionally Defective Trust

Transfers into an intentionally defective trust are gifts, but the person making the gift is still liable for the federal income tax on income earned by the trust. Why is this a great idea? This income tax payment provides an economic benefit to the trust beneficiaries, because what they receive from the trust will not be diminished by income taxes owed by the trust, yet the grantor's payment of the income tax is not considered a gift to the trust. The defective aspect refers to the fact that the person setting up the trust is liable for the income taxes of the trust. At one time, when income tax rates were 90 percent, paying the trust's income tax was considered bad. But for high-net-worth individuals, a defective trust can save a family a significant amount of estate taxes. Further tax savings may be obtained by selling property to the trust for a promissory note. If this is properly structured, the growth in the trust assets above the interest rate on the note may pass to your heirs free of gift or estate taxes.

Qualified Domestic Trust

A qualified domestic trust (QDOT) is a special trust that qualifies for the estate tax marital deduction even if the surviving spouse is not a U.S. citizen. Generally, the estate tax is deferred until the death of the surviving spouse, at which time an estate tax must be paid based on the value of the trust principal remaining. If distributions of trust principal are paid out to the surviving spouse before death, estate tax is also generally payable based on the value of that distribution. Because of the scheduled repeal of the estate tax, QDOT principal will escape estate taxation at death if the surviving spouse dies in 2010. Also, for persons dying before 2010 whose assets pass into a QDOT, any distributions of principal from the QDOT to the surviving spouse remain subject to the estate tax through 2020 but will be free of estate tax in 2021 and thereafter. (Because 2021 occurs after the December 31, 2010, sunset date, this latter provision is, in effect, nullified.)

> **Observation**
> It is possible to completely avoid estate tax for a QDOT established before 2010 where the surviving spouse dies in 2010. A QDOT, therefore, should be considered for use in the estate plan of any person married to a non-U.S. citizen.

Stock Option Trust

Consider putting some or all of your nonqualified stock options in trust for your children. Although you must pay income tax on the value of the options when they are exercised, you could save a substantial amount of estate and gift tax. Option plans may need to be amended to allow this type of transfer.

Effect of Reduced Tax Rates on Dividends

The reduced income tax rates (15 percent or 0 percent) on long-term capital gains and qualified dividends (see Chapter 3) also apply to trusts. The lower income tax rates on qualified dividends are particularly beneficial for dividends that are retained by and taxed to a trust, because the trust income tax brackets are extremely compressed. For 2008, trust income above $10,700 is taxed at the highest rate of 35 percent (compared to married individuals filing jointly, who do not reach the 35 percent tax bracket until their income exceeds $357,700).

Many trusts give the trustee the discretion to distribute income to beneficiaries (in which case, the income is generally taxable to the beneficiaries) or to retain the income in the trust (in which case, the income generally is taxable to the trust).

The relative tax brackets of the trust and the beneficiaries frequently are a factor used by a trustee in deciding whether to make distributions to the beneficiaries. In the past, retained dividends may have been taxed at the highest tax rate due to the compressed income tax brackets for trusts. Conversely, if the trustee distributed the dividends to the beneficiaries, this income may have been taxed at a lower tax rate because the beneficiaries may not have been in the highest income tax bracket.

The reduction in the income tax rate on qualified dividends for both trusts and individuals generally means that the dividends are taxed at the same rate, whether or not they are distributed from the trust. This should allow the trustee to decide whether to make distributions based on other factors, such as the needs of the beneficiaries or the grantor's original purpose in establishing the trust.

Trustee's Investment Decisions

The reduction in the income tax rate on qualified dividends gave trustees an additional factor to consider when making investment decisions for the trust. For example, in the past, interest and dividends generally were taxed at the same tax rate. Therefore, a trustee may have decided to invest the trust assets in a way that generated significant interest income. Trustees may need to consider whether the preferential treatment of qualified dividends warrants a change to an investment strategy designed to produce less interest income and more dividend income. However, any shift in investment strategy should consider that the preferential tax rate on qualifying dividend income is now set to expire on December 31, 2010, so that a strategy that was previously switched might need to be switched back.

Allocation of Expenses

Generally, the trustee can choose how to allocate trust expenses among the different categories of trust income (e.g., interest and dividends). Because dividends and interest are taxed at different tax rates, a trustee should allocate expenses to income (e.g., interest) that is taxed at a higher tax rate.

Give a Roth IRA

It is wise to provide funds for a Roth IRA contribution each year to family members who have earned income and who do not exceed the income limitation for Roth IRA contributions (see Chapter 4). Providing the funds will be considered a gift to the family member. Unless other gifts have been made, this gift should qualify for the annual gift tax exclusion. This permits the Roth IRA owner to accumulate wealth in a vehicle that is not subject to income tax and to avoid income tax when the Roth IRA assets are later distributed.

> ***Observation***
> Gifts of IRA contributions are an excellent way for parents and grandparents to help their children and grandchildren accumulate significant retirement assets. The early start allows the tax-free compounding to build significant asset value.

Pay Gift Taxes Now

While the tax rates imposed under the estate and gift tax systems are the same, the method of calculating the taxes is very different. Therefore, greater economic benefits may result from transferring assets during your lifetime and reporting the transfers under the gift tax system. You must survive at least three years after the payment of the gift tax to realize the benefits; any gift taxes paid within three years of death are included in your taxable estate. A second benefit of a gift is that it allows the donor to remove all postgift appreciation from the donor's taxable estate. However, transferring an asset during a donor's lifetime does have its downside. An asset transferred during a lifetime will carry over the donor's tax basis to the recipient and will not receive the step-up in tax basis that currently results from assets that are taxed in an estate.

With the prospect of an estate tax repeal in 2010 or increased estate tax exemptions, the idea of paying any substantial amount of gift tax now is not appealing. However, the strategy of paying gift tax now may still make sense for more elderly or unhealthy taxpayers or in the case of property with substantial appreciation potential.

Idea Checklist

- ☑ Review your will and estate plan to determine what adjustments are needed to benefit from changes to the estate and gift tax and to avoid potentially costly pitfalls. Especially consider whether you need to change or eliminate an existing credit shelter trust arrangement.
- ☑ Use asset ownership forms that may maximize estate tax savings (e.g., limited liability companies or limited partnerships).
- ☑ Review the use of joint ownership. Make sure each spouse has enough assets in his or her own name to fund credit shelter trusts or other testamentary objectives.
- ☑ Make annual exclusion gifts each year ($12,000 per donee in 2008, and $13,000 in 2009).
- ☑ Give appreciated capital assets to children and grandchildren in the lower tax brackets, so that they will be liable for only a 5 percent income tax on the recognition of long-term capital gain (however, beware of the kiddie tax rules).
- ☑ Pay tuition expenses directly to an educational institution or make a payment to a health-care provider on behalf of a donee. Consider a multiyear tuition gift (529 plan), where appropriate.

- ☑ Transfer existing life insurance policies into an irrevocable life insurance trust. Acquire any new life insurance policies within a life insurance trust.
- ☑ Put rapidly appreciating assets into a grantor retained annuity trust or sell them to an intentionally defective trust.
- ☑ Reconsider the investment mix of trust assets to take advantage of lower dividend and capital gains tax rates.
- ☑ Structure asset ownership to take advantage of valuation discounts.

The bottom line is that Congress has opened a window of opportunity for taxpayers to optimize their estate and gift planning. It is important to take advantage of these opportunities as soon as possible.

Chapter 10

Charitable Giving

This chapter examines the tax rules governing charitable contribution deductions, including gifts that qualify for the deduction, as well as timing issues, valuation issues, and qualified charitable organizations. Also discussed are some of the different charitable giving vehicles that can provide meaningful tax benefits while helping you achieve your charitable objectives.

Defining Charitable Deductions

To receive a tax benefit from a charitable contribution, donors must itemize deductions on their tax returns. Specific rules relating to donations determine whether a deduction can be claimed for a charitable contribution. A charitable deduction will be allowed only after the rights of actual possession in the donated property shift from the donor (and those parties related to the donor) to a qualified charitable organization. In addition, specific tax rules apply to donations of tangible personal property as well as to different types of charitable organizations receiving the donation.

A contribution is considered made when mailing or delivery occurs. For example, mailing a check to a charitable organization constitutes an effective contribution on the date of delivery or mailing (identified by the postmark date). As a result, a check mailed December 31 will qualify the gift for a charitable deduction for that tax year. Similarly, a gift of a properly endorsed stock certificate will be considered completed on the date of delivery or mailing to the charity. Alternatively, if the stock certificate is delivered to a broker or the issuing corporation, the gift will be completed on the date the stock is transferred on the books of the broker or issuing corporation.

Payment of a charitable contribution by credit card is deductible by the donor on the date the payment is charged to the credit card, rather than the date the authorization to charge is mailed to the charity. A pledge to make payment to a qualified charitable organization, however, generally is not deductible until payment has been delivered.

Making Charitable Contributions

The Internal Revenue Code provides little guidance in defining the term *charitable contribution*. It states that a charitable contribution is a contribution or gift to certain enumerated organizations (generally known as Section 501(c)(3) organizations) that are organized and operated exclusively for religious, charitable, scientific, literary, or educational purposes or to governmental units or entities for a public purpose. Each year, the Internal Revenue Service (IRS) issues a list of qualified charitable organizations in Publication 78, *Cumulative List of Organizations Described in Section 170(c) of the Internal Revenue Code*.

The IRS lists qualified charitable organizations on its web site (www.irs.gov). On the IRS web site, type "Publication 78" in the search box and you will be directed to the online version of the list. The organizations listed by the IRS have generally obtained an exemption letter from the IRS that verifies their tax-exempt or Section 501(c)(3) status. Certain charitable organizations, such as churches or smaller charities, however, need not obtain an exemption letter from the IRS and may not be listed in Publication 78. If you are contemplating a gift to an organization that is not listed in Publication 78, you may wish to exercise other due diligence to make sure your gift will qualify for a tax deduction.

For a contribution to qualify for a charitable deduction, there must be a gift. A gift is generally defined as a transfer of something of value with no consideration given or expected in return. Thus, if there are strings attached to a donation, it may not qualify as a gift. In addition, donative intent is an important element of a charitable contribution. The courts and the IRS will look for such factors as a lack of consideration expected or received (i.e., no quid pro quo) and for "detached and disinterested generosity."

Deductible Contributions—Quick Guide

Contributions of money or property are generally deductible if given to:
- Churches, synagogues, temples, mosques, and other religious organizations.
- Federal, state, and local governments if made solely for public purposes (e.g., a gift to reduce the public debt).
- Nonprofit schools and hospitals.
- Public parks and recreation facilities.
- Salvation Army, Red Cross, CARE, Goodwill Industries, United Way, Boy Scouts, Girl Scouts, Boys and Girls Clubs of America, and other similar charities.
- War veterans' groups.

Charitable deductions may also be taken for expenses paid for a student living with the donor, if the student is sponsored by a qualifying organization; and deductions may be taken for out-of-pocket expenses paid by a donor who serves a qualified organization as a volunteer, if certain conditions are met. In addition, actual travel expenses or a mileage deduction of 14 cents per mile is allowed for each mile of travel specifically related to charitable activities.

Nondeductible Contributions— Quick Guide

Contributions are not deductible if made to:
- Political action committees.
- Social and sports clubs.
- Chambers of commerce.
- Trade associations.
- Labor unions.
- Certain social welfare organizations.
- Most foreign charities.
- Political parties.
- Organizations that primarily engage in lobbying activities.
- Other nonqualified organizations.

In addition, payments made for tuition; payments for raffle, bingo, or lottery tickets; dues, fees, or bills paid to country clubs, lodges, fraternal orders, or similar groups; as well as the value of a donor's time or services or the value of blood given to a blood bank are all nondeductible as charitable contributions.

A charitable organization that provides goods or services to the donor in exchange for a contribution in excess of $75 is required to furnish a written statement to the donor of the deductible amount and a good-faith estimate of the value of the goods or services provided.

Valuation Issues

A donation that qualifies as a charitable contribution must be valued to determine the deductible amount. Valuation is the responsibility of the donor who is claiming the charitable contribution deduction. Proper valuation is doubly important because undervaluing a contribution reduces the available charitable deduction, but overvaluing could subject the donor to additional taxes, interest, and penalties.

For contributions of cash, value simply equals the dollar amount donated. For contributions of property, valuation becomes more difficult (see Table 10.1). The IRS regulations state that charitable contributions of property, other than money, will be valued at "fair market value" at the time of the contribution, subject to certain reductions discussed later. Fair market value is defined as "the price at which the property would change hands between a willing buyer and a willing seller, neither being under any compulsion to buy or sell." Encumbrances or debts on such property will also affect the value of the contribution and the tax consequences to the donor.

In determining the fair market value of donated property, one or more of four different factors are most often used:
1. Opinions of experts.
2. Cost or selling price.
3. Sales of comparable properties.
4. Replacement cost.

See Table 10.2 for questions the IRS indicates you should consider when using these factors for valuing property contributed to a charitable organization.

The following discussion describes the valuation rules for several types of property that are commonly contributed to charity.

Table 10.1 *Guidelines for Determining Fair Market Value*

Assets	Valuation Guidelines
Cash	Amount donated
Retail property	Retail price
Stocks and bonds	Exchange price
Closely held businesses	Appraised value (could be subject to discounting)
Notes	Unpaid balance plus accrued interest
Life insurance	Cost/replacement cost
Real estate	Appraised value (comparable sale, capitalization of income, or replacement cost)
Artwork	Appraised value (or cost if donated by artist)
Jewelry and gems	Appraised value
Used cars, boats, and aircraft	Gross sale proceeds
Used clothing and household goods	Consignment price
Hobby collections	Appraised value

Retail Property

For purposes of charitable contributions, the value of property generally sold to the public equals the price at which the property would be sold at retail. For example, a passenger van donated by an individual to a charitable organization to be used by that organization to fulfill its charitable purpose would be valued at the price the van would sell for to the general public rather than to an automobile dealer.

Table 10.2 *Questions for Determining Fair Market Value*

When Using This Factor	Questions to Consider
Opinions of experts	Is the expert knowledgeable and competent?
	Is the written opinion thorough and supported by facts and experience?
Cost or selling price	Was the purchase or sale of the property reasonably close to the date of contribution?
	Was any increase or decrease in value, as compared to actual cost, at a reasonable rate?
	Do the terms of purchase or sale limit what can be done with the property?
	Was there an arm's-length offer to buy the property close to the valuation date?
Sales of comparable properties	How similar is the sold property to the property donated?
	How close is the date of sale to the valuation date?
	Was the sale at arm's length?
	What was the condition of the market at the time of sale?
Replacement cost	What would it cost to replace the donated property?
	Is there a reasonable relationship between replacement cost and fair market value?
	Is the supply of the donated property more or less than the demand for it?

Stocks and Bonds

Contributions of stocks and bonds are valued at the fair market value of the stock or bond as of the date of the gift. For stocks and bonds traded on a stock exchange or other public market where values can be easily ascertained, the fair market value is the average between the highest and lowest selling prices on the date of the contribution. If the stock or bond was not traded on the date of contribution, but was traded within a reasonable period of time before or after that date, the donor would use a weighted average of the highest and lowest selling prices before and after the date of contribution. You can also use the weighted average where the stock or bond was not traded within a reasonable amount of time, or you can use bona fide bid-and-ask prices on the date of the contribution even if no trade was made.

Closely Held Businesses

Contributions of interests in a closely held business pose particularly difficult valuation problems. The IRS often employs a willing buyer/willing seller analysis to determine value, but provides that the following additional factors should be used in valuing the business interest:

- A fair appraisal as of the date of the contribution of all tangible and intangible (including goodwill) assets of the business.
- The demonstrated earning capacity of the business.
- The company's dividend-paying capacity, the economic outlook of the industry, the company's position in the industry, the degree of control of the business represented by the block of stock to be valued, and the value of any other comparable business whose stock is traded on a stock exchange.

Observation

The practice of *discounting* (reducing the value to reflect the lack of control connected with minority interests or lack of marketability of nonpublicly traded stock) has become a popular technique to reduce gift or estate tax liability. It is possible that the IRS may apply the concept of discounting the value of a charitable gift to discount the value of charitable donations of such stock. Charitable gifts of closely held stock will likely receive more IRS scrutiny due to the inherent valuation concerns. Care should be taken to ensure that proper valuation procedures are followed. Generally, an outside appraisal by a qualified appraiser is obtained in this context.

Notes

The fair market value of any note is calculated by adding the unpaid balance and the accrued interest at the date of the contribution. The donor may be required to report a different value if there are factors to warrant an alternative valuation. Such factors include interest rate fluctuations, the ability to collect on the note, and whether the property pledged as security is sufficient to satisfy the obligation.

Life Insurance

The valuation of contributions of life insurance can depend on whether the insurance policy has been paid in full at the time of the contribution. The fair market value of a single-premium policy transferred immediately after payment is the cost of the policy. The fair market value of a paid-up insurance policy is the amount that the issuer of the policy would charge for a similar policy of the same specified amount on the life of a person who is the same age and health as the insured at the time of the contribution.

For contributions of insurance policies with premiums still due, determination of the fair market value is more complex. Typically, the insurance company can assist donors of unpaid insurance policies in determining the fair market value for charitable contribution purposes. Each premium payment made after the contribution of the insurance policy will result in an additional charitable contribution that is deductible in the year that each premium is paid.

Real Estate

Contributions of real estate often present unique valuation problems. Competent appraisers are needed to determine the fair market value for charitable contribution purposes. Generally, real estate is appraised by using one of three valuation methods, or a combination of these methods:

1. *Comparable sale:* Compares the donated property to other similar properties that have been sold. Such factors as the time of prior sales, location of properties, and interest rates need to be considered in valuing donated real estate.
2. *Capitalization of income:* Incorporates an analysis of the present value of income to be produced in the future.
3. *Replacement cost:* Determines the cost required to replace the donated property. Contributions of real property subject to a mortgage are deductible only up to the amount of value in excess of the mortgage.

Artwork: Paintings, Antiques, and Other Art Objects

For deductions related to paintings, antiques, and other objects of art over $5,000, the deduction must be supported by a written appraisal from a qualified and reputable source. A claim for a deduction of $20,000 or more must be accompanied by a complete copy of the signed appraisal attached to the donor's tax return. For individual items valued at $20,000 or more, a photograph of a size and quality that fully shows the object must be provided if requested.

For artwork that has been appraised at $50,000 or more, the donor may request a Statement of Value for the item from the IRS in advance of claiming the charitable deduction.

> **Caution**
>
> The donor must pay a user fee of $2,500 to obtain a Statement of Value for one to three items of art. This fee is not refundable unless the IRS refuses to issue the Statement of Value "in the interest of efficient tax administration."

Jewelry and Gems

An appraisal by a specialized jewelry appraiser is almost always required to support the claimed value of a donation of jewelry or a gem. The appraisal should describe (among other things) the style of the jewelry, the cut and setting of the gem, and whether it is still in fashion. The stone's color, weight, cut, brilliance, and flaws should be reported and analyzed.

> **Observation**
>
> Sentimental personal value has no effect on the value of donated jewelry. However, if the jewelry is or was owned by a famous person, its value might increase.

Used Cars, Boats, and Aircraft

If a used vehicle is sold by a charity, the charitable contribution will generally be limited to the gross sales proceeds that the charity receives on the sale of the car, boat, or airplane. If the charity sells the property, it is obligated to report to the taxpayer within 30 days of the sale the amount of proceeds realized on the sale. If the donor plans to claim a deduction greater than $500 for a donated vehicle, boat, or plane, the donor should receive a Form 1098-C from the charity reporting the sale transaction and should attach it to the return on which the deduction is taken. This valuation rule does not apply if the vehicle is substantially used by the charity for charitable activities.

If the vehicle is not sold by the charity prior to significant charitable use, the fair market value can be deducted. Commercial firms and trade organizations publish periodic guides to dealer sale prices for recent model years of cars and other vehicles. These prices are not official for valuing specific donated property, but they do provide clues for making an accurate appraisal of fair market value. The IRS has indicated it will continue to closely examine values, and donors should carefully consider this in making a final determination of value.

Used Clothing and Household Goods

The value of both used clothing and household goods is usually much lower than the price paid when new. The price that buyers of used items actually pay in stores selling these goods, such as consignment or thrift shops, is an indication of fair market value.

> **Observation**
>
> The law now requires that used clothing and household goods must generally be in good condition in order for a deduction to be claimed.

Hobby Collections

Collectibles are often the subject of charitable donations. Most common are rare books, stamps, coins, natural history items, manuscripts, and autographs. Many of the rules applicable to paintings and other objects of art (discussed previously) also apply to miscellaneous collections. Publications are often used to help determine the value of many types of collections.

> **Observation**
>
> Be certain to use the price guide's current edition at the date of contribution. These sources are not always reliable indicators of fair market value and, where the collection has significant value, should be accompanied by an appraisal from an expert.

Appraisals and Substantiation Requirements

Any charitable deduction claimed in connection with a contribution of property valued in excess of $5,000 ($10,000 for gifts of closely held stock) from an individual, a closely held corporation, a partnership, a C corporation, or an S corporation must be supported by a qualified appraisal. The required appraisal for donations above $5,000 is not just to support the claimed value but also to meet a statutory requirement to claim any charitable contribution deduction. If a taxpayer fails to get the appraisal, the allowable deduction is $0. This rule does not apply to publicly traded securities.

For gifts of closely held stock not requiring an appraisal, a partial summary of the property is required. If a deduction of $20,000 or more is claimed for a contribution of art, and for any other noncash contribution in excess of $500,000, a complete copy of the signed appraisal must be attached to the tax return. All similar items of property donated to one or more organizations are treated as one property for purposes of determining the applicable thresholds.

Form 8283 has been designed to provide this information. This form is required to be signed by the appraiser and a representative of the charity when an appraisal is required. The IRS can disallow a charitable deduction if a required appraisal is not secured. A qualified appraiser is generally someone who holds himself or herself out to the public as an appraiser, or performs appraisals on a regular basis, and has qualifications to value the particular type of donated property.

The weight given to an appraisal depends on the completeness of the report, the qualifications of the appraiser, and the appraiser's demonstrated knowledge of the donated property. An appraisal must give all the facts on which to base an intelligent judgment of the value of the property.

While additional guidance in the form of final regulations on qualified appraisals is pending, the IRS issued a notice that taxpayers can rely on for additional guidance in the appraisal area. Specifically, the notice directs that a qualified appraiser of real property must be a licensed or certified appraiser for the type of property being appraised in the state in which the appraised property is located. For property other than real property, the appraiser must have successfully completed college- or professional-level coursework that is relevant to the property being valued; must have obtained at least two years of experience in the trade or business of buying, selling, or valuing the type of property being valued; and must fully describe in the appraisal the appraiser's education and experience that qualify the individual to value the type of property being valued.

In addition, qualified appraisals must include a statement that the appraiser understands that a substantial or gross valuation misstatement resulting from an appraisal of the value of property that the appraiser knows, or reasonably should have known, would be used in connection with a return or claim for refund may subject the appraiser to a civil penalty.

> ### *Observation*
> The IRS may accept the claimed value of the donated property, based on information or appraisals sent with the return, or may make its own determination of fair market value.

> ### *Observation*
> A charitable deduction may not be taken for fees paid for appraisals of donated property. However, these fees may qualify as a miscellaneous deduction (subject to the 2 percent threshold) on Schedule A (Form 1040) if paid to determine the allowable amount of a charitable deduction.

Charitable Giving

The substantiation rules and IRS enforcement have become considerably more strict. No deduction is allowed for any contribution in excess of $250 that is not substantiated by the charitable organization. The substantiation statement must indicate the amount of the contribution and the value of any goods or services provided to the donor. The substantiation statement must be obtained from the charity before the taxpayer files his or her tax return. Waiting to secure the substantiation statement to respond to an IRS audit request will not preserve the contribution deduction. For single contributions in excess of $250, a canceled check is not considered a valid form of substantiation. When value is received by the donor in connection with any contribution that exceeds $75, such as a dinner dance sponsored by a charity, the charitable organization is required to inform the donor of the value of any goods or services received, so that the donor can adjust the amount of the contribution by the value of the benefit to the donor.

Finally, you can no longer deduct a cash contribution, regardless of the amount, unless you keep as a record of the contribution a bank record (such as a canceled check or a bank statement containing the name of the charity, the date, and the amount) or a written communication from the charity. The written communication must include the name of the charity, date of the contribution, and amount of the contribution.

> ***Observation***
>
> Donors may wish to use a check or credit card to make a charitable contribution, as gifts of cash may be hard to substantiate upon audit.

Penalties for Overvaluation

Penalties can be assessed for overstating the value of a charitable contribution, and they can be quite severe. The tax underpayment attributable to the valuation misstatement must exceed $5,000 for a penalty to be assessed. If the value reported on a donor's tax return is 200 percent higher than the allowed value, the IRS will subject the taxpayer to a penalty equal to 20 percent of the tax underpayment. If the valuation misstatement is deemed "gross" (reported value is 400 percent greater than the allowed value), the penalty is equal to 40 percent of the underpaid tax.

There is a reasonable cause exception to be excused from this penalty. For valuation misstatements related to charitable contribution property, the donor must prove that the value claimed was based on an appraisal performed by a qualified appraiser and that the donor made a good-faith investigation of the value of the donated property.

Reduction of Contribution Amount

Sales of certain property held for longer than one year will produce long-term capital gains. A contribution of this type of property to certain charities (rather than a sale of the property) usually generates a deduction equal to the fair market value of the donated property. In addition, a contribution, rather than a sale, avoids recognition (and tax) of any gain. This provides a double benefit to taxpayers and an obvious incentive for a donor to contribute appreciated long-term capital gain property to a charity rather than to sell the property and donate the proceeds.

Observation

Current legislation imposes a recapture requirement for donated items of appreciated tangible personal property (such as artwork) to charity when the item is sold within three years. This provision requires a recalculation of that deduction. If the charity sells the property in the same year as the donation, then the donation is limited to the donor's tax basis (rather than the asset's fair market value). If the recipient sells the asset in the next two years, the donor must include as ordinary income an amount equal to the unrealized gain at the time of the donation. The recapture rules do not apply if the charity provides a written statement concerning the original planned use and the reasons why that use was impossible or not feasible. The written statement must be provided to the IRS and the donor at the time of the sale.

Observation

If property has declined in value, it generally would be more beneficial to first sell the property and recognize any potential loss, and then donate the cash proceeds to charity.

The income tax law and related regulations require certain charitable contributions to be reduced in value when determining the amount of the allowable charitable deduction. In effect, these rules prevent a donor from claiming the full fair market value deduction as explained previously.

Contributions of ordinary income property (defined as property that would not produce long-term capital gains if sold at the time of the contribution) must be reduced in value for charitable deduction purposes. Examples of this type of property include inventory, a work of art created by the donor, and letters and memoranda written by the donor. In addition, contributions of short-term capital gain property (property held for not more than one year) must be reduced.

The reduction rules require that the deduction for donated property be computed by reducing the fair market value by the amount of gain that would not have been long-term. In effect, the rules require donors to use their tax basis in the property, rather than the fair market value, to determine the allowable charitable deduction for ordinary income property. These reduction rules also apply to contributions of tangible personal property, if the property is unrelated to the exempt function of the charitable organization, and to gifts of long-term capital gain property, other than qualified appreciated stock, if the gift is to or for the use of a private foundation. The exception for "qualified appreciated stock" applies to gifts of publicly traded stock as long as the aggregate amount of gifts of that stock by the donor and donor's family does not exceed 10 percent of the value of all the outstanding stock of the corporation. Thus, gifts of closely held stock to a private foundation are subject to the reduction rule.

Limitations on Your Deduction

After determining that a transfer of property is a contribution eligible for a charitable deduction, a donor is often surprised to find that there are limits on the amount that can actually be deducted in a given tax year. These limitations are based on an individual's annual contribution base, generally equal to the individual's adjusted gross income (AGI). The limitations in Table 10.3 are calculated based on the characterization of the charitable organization receiving the contribution (e.g., public charity versus private foundation) and the type of contributed property (e.g., long-term versus short-term capital gain property and other ordinary income property). Again, the rules are complex and this discussion has been simplified. Donors should consult with their tax professionals prior to making substantial charitable contributions.

Table 10.3 Percentage Limitations

Type of Gift	Deductible Amount	AGI Limitation Public Charity[a]	AGI Limitation Private Foundation
Cash	Fair market value	50%	30%
Ordinary income property	Lesser of fair market value or adjusted basis: • Inventory • Short-term capital gain property • Depreciable property	50%	30%
Appreciated long-term capital gain property	Fair market value except: • Certain contributions to a private foundation—limited to adjusted basis • Personal property not related to tax-exempt purpose—limited to adjusted basis	30%[b]	20%
Publicly traded stock	Fair market value	30%	20%
Carryover		5 years	5 years

[a]Private operating and pass-through private foundations are subject to the same AGI limitations as public charities.

[b]The donor may elect to apply the 50 percent of AGI limitation by decreasing the deductible amount for any potential long-term capital gain. The election applies to all gifts given that year.

Notes: These percentage limitations apply to contributions made directly to charities. Lower percentage limitations may apply to contributions made for the use of charities (such as contributions to some trusts).

For estate purposes, there are no limitations on the deduction available to a decedent's estate. All contributions made by bequest are deductible based on the property's full fair market value.

The 50 Percent Limitation

Charitable contributions made to publicly supported charities (e.g., churches, hospitals, and educational organizations) and certain private operating foundations may be deductible up to 50 percent of a donor's contribution base. For charitable contributions that are greater than this base, the excess may be carried forward and deducted in the five tax years succeeding the year of the original contribution. The amount carried forward is added to current-year contributions in the succeeding years, and the total is subject to the 50 percent limitation of the donor's contribution base for each subsequent year in the carryforward period.

For example, assume a couple has an AGI (contribution base) of $200,000. In a single tax year, they make a $125,000 cash donation to a university as part of its capital campaign. If the couple made no other charitable contributions in that tax year, they could deduct $100,000 (50 percent of the contribution base) and carry forward the remaining $25,000 to be deducted over the next five years, subject to the 50 percent limitation on each succeeding year's contribution base.

The 30 Percent Limitation

Contributions of cash and property (i.e., not appreciated) to charitable organizations (generally, private foundations) that are not designated as 50 percent organizations are deductible up to 30 percent of a donor's contribution base. In addition, charitable contributions of appreciated long-term capital gain property to public charities are subject to the 30 percent limitation. If a donor uses up more than 20 percent of AGI with cash contributions to public charities, the 30 percent limitation must be reduced so that the aggregate amount of contributions does not exceed the 50 percent limitation.

There is an alternative to the treatment of gifts of long-term capital gain property. This alternative allows donors to use the 50 percent limitation if they deduct an amount equal only to their tax basis rather than using the 30 percent limitation. This election should be used cautiously because it will apply to all such property that has been carried forward from prior tax years.

The 20 Percent Limitation

The 20 percent limitation applies to contributions of appreciated long-term capital gain property to private foundations.

Private Foundations

A private foundation is a tax-exempt organization that is organized and operated exclusively for religious, charitable, scientific, literary, or educational purposes and does not meet the requirements that would classify it as a public charity. Both private foundations and public charities are called Section 501(c)(3) organizations.

Every tax-exempt charitable organization is classified as a private foundation unless it receives broad public support (in the form of financial contributions) or is a church, school, hospital, or organization operated to support another public charity.

A private foundation often is established by an individual or a family. In addition, many corporations establish foundations in their names.

It should be noted that like the increased scrutiny affecting charitable gifts, the IRS has stepped up its review of private foundations to ensure that no inappropriate acts of self-dealing between donors and their private foundations exist. It is critical to understand the special tax rules governing the operation of private foundations before a private foundation is implemented.

Nonoperating Foundations

Most private foundations do not actively conduct their own charitable activities (e.g., operating a museum or nursing home) and therefore are classified as nonoperating. These foundations are required to make distributions equal to at least 5 percent of the average fair market value of their assets each year. The charitable contribution deduction for an individual to a nonoperating foundation generally is limited to 30 percent of the individual's AGI for gifts of cash and unappreciated property, and 20 percent for gifts of appreciated property such as publicly traded stock.

Operating Foundations

An operating foundation is one that actively conducts a program of charitable activities, rather than merely providing passive financial support to other charities. Individuals can claim a charitable deduction of up to 50 percent of AGI—the same as public charities for contributions to these entities. The charitable contribution deduction for an individual to an operating foundation is generally limited to 50 percent of the individual's AGI for gifts of cash and property that is not appreciated and to 30 percent for gifts of appreciated property.

Usually, operating foundations are museums, libraries, or care facilities for the elderly.

Pass-Through Private Foundations

If a private foundation distributes (to qualified charitable organizations) all of its annual gifts plus its investment income in any given year, the higher 50 percent AGI limit applies. The decision to make distributions and achieve pass-through status can be changed from year to year.

Tax Compliance and Operating Rules for Private Foundations

Private foundations file tax returns annually to report their activities. Most foundations will pay a 2 percent excise tax on their net investment income, including realized capital gains. In some instances, it is possible to reduce the excise tax to a 1 percent tax rate.

Failure to follow the tax rules associated with the operations of a private foundation can subject the founder and the foundation itself to severe penalties.

Alternatives to Private Foundations

Because of the rather strict rules that apply to private foundations, some donors desire alternatives to a private foundation:

- *Community foundations:* A community foundation is a fund that is designed to attract assets for the benefit of a particular geographic area. Community foundations are treated as public charities (not as private foundations), so the donor has a large degree of flexibility both in structuring the gift and in advising the foundation on how to benefit the surrounding community. Because the community foundation is a public charity, there are no excise taxes to worry about.
- *Supporting organizations:* A supporting organization is similar to a private foundation in that typically it is privately organized and the donor retains some influence over the organization (however, outright legal control by the donor or the donor's family is not permitted). To qualify for public charity status, it must support a named, publicly supported charity.
- *Donor-advised funds:* This is another way of retaining a degree of influence (but not legal control) over contributions (see the following subsection).

Donor-Advised Funds

Generally, a public charity establishes a donor-advised fund and allows the donor to serve on an advisory board or to make suggestions as to the use of funds. Some mutual fund families have established donor-advised funds that facilitate charitable giving.

> **Observation**
>
> Donor-advised funds have become a popular way to contribute to charitable organizations and maintain a continuing active role in how the contributions are used. A donor-advised fund or group of funds is established by a public charity and allows the donor or the donor's family to give advice or make recommendations regarding distributions made by the fund.

These funds are alternatives to establishing a private foundation, and they avoid the record-keeping, filing, and other administrative chores associated with maintaining private foundations. The funds can generally be established with smaller contributions than would be needed to justify the expense of maintaining a private foundation. Excise taxes that can apply to private foundations also do not apply to donor-advised funds. In addition, contributions to donor-advised funds are deductible as contributions to public charities, and, therefore, are not subject to the lower AGI limits that apply to private foundation contributions.

Although donors and their families may recommend how distributions from these funds should be made, the public charity that maintains the fund must have final decision-making authority. In practice, however, donors' wishes are taken very seriously by these funds. Commercial investment firms have also established charitable organizations to maintain donor-advised funds that have attracted billions of dollars of contributions. The commercial funds benefit from their sponsors' investment experience, and the sponsors derive significant fees for their services.

Currently, guidance is lacking on the extent to which donors may be involved in decision making, and the IRS has not been vigorous in enforcing limits. However, there is a growing perception by the IRS that abuses do exist, and future guidance may rein in some of the more aggressive practices related to donor-advised funds.

Recent changes related to donor-advised funds now state that the sponsoring organization cannot be a war veterans' organization, a fraternal society, or a nonprofit cemetery company. The law also requires the donor to obtain a contemporaneous written acknowledgment from the sponsoring organization of a donor-advised fund that such organization has exclusive legal control over the assets contributed.

The major disadvantage with donor-advised funds relative to private foundations is the degree of control that the donor can exercise. The control primarily relates to control over investment decisions and distribution decisions. With donor-advised funds, the donor is not permitted to retain the same degree of legal control that the founder of a private foundation can retain. In addition, with a private foundation, it may be easier to pass control to family members when the donor dies.

The trade-off between the costs of operating a private foundation and the loss of legal control over funds in a donor-advised fund has to be weighed to make the right choice for each donor.

Other Alternatives

There are numerous other charitable-giving vehicles that you may wish to consider, such as charitable remainder trusts, charitable lead trusts, pooled income funds, and bargain sales. Some of these alternatives (e.g., charitable lead trusts and charitable remainder trusts) are discussed in Chapter 9. For a more complete discussion of charitable giving rules and alternatives, please consult *PricewaterhouseCoopers' Guide to Charitable Giving*.

Year-End Tax Savings Strategies

Chapter 11

Quick Planning Guide

Because most individuals are cash-basis taxpayers (paying tax only on the income they actually receive before year-end and claiming deductions for any deductible amounts they pay before year-end), they probably have more opportunity to implement year-end tax-planning strategies than they previously thought. Before the year closes, taxpayers have an opportunity to take actions that can cut taxes this year. To utilize year-end strategies, a taxpayer should have a good idea of his or her tax picture for this year, as well as a good estimate of what it will likely be in the coming year. Changing tax rules make year-end planning more complex; changes for the coming year, including new rules and inflation adjustments, must be factored into any decisions.

How do you determine which strategies are best for you? The best year-end tax-savings strategies produce the largest overall tax savings, taking 2008 and 2009 into account. There are three basic techniques that, used in combination, can produce sizable tax savings:

1. Tax reduction
2. Tax deferral
3. Income shifting

Tax Reduction

Tax reduction occurs when you take action that results in paying less tax than would otherwise have been due. The savings produced by implementing tax-reduction strategies are permanent savings (they are not timing differences that shift a tax burden to another year). For example, if you switch funds from a taxable investment (e.g., a corporate bond) to a municipal bond that earns tax-free interest or to preferred stock that pays a dividend qualifying for a low tax rate, you will reduce your tax bill. Or you may want to consider contributing to a Roth IRA or Roth 401(k) that can generate tax-free income instead of putting the money into a taxable investment vehicle.

Another option is to shift funds from an investment that produces ordinary income (e.g., a money market account or certificate of deposit) to a stock fund in hopes of earning some lower-taxed dividends and long-term capital gains. By restructuring investments in these ways, you can save enormous tax dollars over time. If you make these changes now, the impact for 2008 may be small because so much of the year has already elapsed, but you will be positioning your affairs to reap more meaningful tax benefits for 2009 and the future.

Observation

When switching investments to obtain tax reduction, such as moving from a corporate bond to a municipal bond, be aware of the after-tax rate of return on each investment. Look at the overall net cash result after tax to determine the true benefit of the strategy.

> **Caution**
>
> When tax planning, do not forget about investment fundamentals. Find a prudent investment balance between risk and reward, taking into account your age, your family situation, and other factors. Taxes are important, but they are far from the only consideration. Work taxes into an overall financial plan, but do not let them be the driving force behind all of your decisions.

Tax Deferral

You achieve tax deferral when you earn income now and pay tax on it in the future. Your retirement plan is an example. Although your retirement investments generate income throughout the years (with some years being unfortunate exceptions), you are generally taxed only when you receive distributions from these retirement plans.

Deferring the receipt of taxable income can save you money, even if it produces little or no tax savings, because you can use your money longer before paying the Internal Revenue Service (IRS). This means greater compounding of earnings for you. However, accelerating income, even if you think you will be in a higher tax bracket in later years, means you will pay the IRS sooner than otherwise might be required. Loss of the use of that money cuts down on the advantage you hoped to achieve.

Another deferral technique is to accelerate deductions from a later year to an earlier year so that you get their benefit sooner. However, when using this technique, you want to ensure that you do not overaccelerate deduction items to defer taxes. To get the deduction sooner, you must usually pay out the dollars that fund the deduction sooner, which means that you lose the use of those dollars. For example, an individual in the 35 percent tax bracket for 2008 and 2009 who accelerates a $5,000 deduction into 2008 defers $1,750 of tax. This may make economic sense if the deduction is shifted from January to December, but it is not beneficial if the deduction could have been postponed for a longer period. The funds you used to generate the deduction could lose more in investment income in five months than the amount you would gain from accelerating the tax deduction at 35 percent for one year.

Those in the lowest two tax brackets generally should not accelerate any deductions that could be paid later than February. If you are in the highest tax bracket, you should not accelerate expenses that could be deferred until May. Further care should be taken because not all expenses can be accelerated without limit. Also, moving up certain deductions, such as state income taxes, could trigger the alternative minimum tax (AMT; see Chapter 14).

> **Caution**
>
> This chapter has been written assuming that income tax rates remain the same. However, with a new president in 2009, there is a possibility that both ordinary and capital gains tax rates could increase (see Chapter 2 for additional discussion on potential tax rate increases). Careful consideration should be given to income deferral opportunities given the possibility of the potential increase of tax rates in future years.

Sometimes a single strategy (see the section on income shifting that follows) can combine tax reduction and tax deferral. By deferring income when tax rates drop from one year to the next, you will not only defer your tax liability to a future year (tax deferral), but you also will owe tax at a lower tax rate (tax reduction), assuming that your financial circumstances are about the same from year to year. Even without a year-to-year tax-rate reduction, you can achieve a similar result by shifting income to a later year if you expect to be in a lower tax bracket in the later year due to a change of circumstances such as divorce or retirement.

Income Shifting

Income shifting generally involves transferring income-producing property to someone who is taxed at a lower tax rate. One example is giving a corporate bond to a family member who is in a lower tax bracket. For example, if you are in the 35 percent tax bracket for 2008, you will pay $350 in taxes on every $1,000 of taxable bond interest you receive. If you give the bond to a child or grandchild in the 10 percent or 15 percent tax bracket, tax on the interest will be cut to $100 or $150 per $1,000. You should note that gift tax consequences should also be considered when making income-shifting decisions.

Another method that combines income shifting and tax deferral is the use of a Section 529 plan. The income on these plans is tax-deferred and, if used for education, are also tax-free. Most of these plans are state sponsored and they allow a tax deduction on the state income tax return for contributions that are made, with limitations. There is no income limitation for the contribution.

> ### *Observation*
> Qualifying dividends are taxed at only a 15 percent tax rate through December 31, 2010. If a dividend-paying stock is transferred to a taxpayer in the 10 percent or 15 percent tax bracket (e.g., a child), the dividends will be taxed at 0 percent through 2010.

> **Caution**
>
> The so-called kiddie tax (i.e., a tax on children's investment income at their parents' tax rate) keeps this family income-shifting strategy from working for children under a certain age. The kiddie tax subjects all but a small amount of the unearned income of a child to tax at his or her parents' marginal tax rate. For 2008, the kiddie tax will apply to children who are under 19 years old or who are full-time students over age 18 but under age 24, if the child's earned income does not exceed one-half of the amount of their support. See Chapter 2 regarding this and other recent tax law changes.

Tax-saving techniques are described in Chapters 12 and 13. Before turning to these chapters, however, it is important to review how capital gains and the AMT affect your tax liability this year, which will help you to determine which year-end tax-savings strategies may work well for you. For more details on accelerating deductions, see Chapter 12. For more on deferring income, see Chapter 13.

Year-End Capital Gains Checkup

Many investors have realized capital losses this year. If you have current capital losses, or unused capital losses carried over from earlier years, you may be able to get some tax advantages from them. You can offset capital gains, even short-term gains, and up to an additional $3,000 of other income with your capital losses. Investors who took profits on long-term gains will get the benefit of favorable capital gains tax rates. Those whose gains are short-term are less fortunate. Their gains are taxed at regular income tax rates.

For example, suppose you have a $10,000 gain on stock in a company that has done well over the year, but that you think is due for a fall. If you sell some other stock at a $10,000 loss, you will be able to sell your profitable stock and fully offset your tax liability with your loss. If you recognized a total of $13,000 of losses during the year, you could offset your $10,000 capital gain and use the extra $3,000 loss to offset $3,000 of other fully taxable ordinary income such as interest or compensation income. If your excess losses total more than $3,000, you must carry them over to future years, when they can again offset capital gains and up to $3,000 of ordinary income. (For more details about capital gains and losses, see Chapter 3.)

You have a great deal of flexibility at year-end to control the timing of investment decisions to maximize your tax savings. As year-end approaches, review your investment results. Calculate recognized gains and losses and compare them with any unrealized gains or losses you currently hold. (See Chapter 3 for more information on netting capital gains and losses.)

For example, if you have capital losses exceeding capital gains realized for the year, and you offset ordinary income to the extent of $3,000—receiving up to a 35 percent tax benefit—then you may benefit from waiting to recognize additional long-term capital gains until 2009, when you will be assured of paying no more than a 15 percent tax rate on them. When making these tax decisions, you must also consider your individual financial and personal situation and the economic viability of particular investments. Taxes are but one factor to consider.

Observation

While capital gains and losses can offset one another without regard to whether the gains or losses are long-term or short-term, for the best tax results you should try to offset short-term capital losses with short-term capital gains rather than offsetting long-term capital gains. Because short-term capital gains are taxed at ordinary income tax rates and long-term capital gains are generally taxed at 15 percent or less, there is a better tax benefit if you offset short-term capital gains first, leaving your long-term capital gains intact to be taxed at the favorable tax rate.

Year-End Alternative Minimum Tax Diagnosis

The AMT is a separate tax system under which certain items of income and deductions receive different—usually less favorable—tax treatment than under the regular income tax system. For example, state and local income taxes and real estate taxes are deductible under the regular system, but are not deductible under the AMT. The standard deduction, personal exemptions, some medical expenses, some interest on home equity loans, and miscellaneous itemized deductions that you can claim for regular tax purposes do not reduce your AMT. Also, the bargain element (the difference between the exercise price and the stock's fair market value at exercise) on incentive stock options (ISOs) that you exercise is *not* subject to regular income tax in the year of exercise, but *is* subject to the AMT. You must calculate taxes under both systems and pay the higher tax bill. (For a more detailed explanation of the AMT, see Chapter 14.)

> ### Observation
> Reduced regular tax rates over the past few years without a corresponding reduction in the AMT tax rates have caused more individuals to become subject to the AMT, particularly individuals who live in high-tax states.

Planning for the AMT can be difficult because many factors can trigger it. If you believe that you are within range of becoming subject to the AMT, year-end strategies may help reduce your tax liability. If you are subject to the AMT, it may be prudent to go a counterintuitive route and implement the opposite of normal year-end tax-planning strategies.

For example, individuals subject to the AMT might benefit from accelerating ordinary income items into 2008 and deferring until

2009 deductions that are not allowed for AMT purposes, such as taxes and miscellaneous itemized deductions.

> **Caution**
> If you choose to defer deductions, such as real estate taxes, into the subsequent tax year, be aware of potential penalties for late payment that could offset the tax benefits achieved.

If your 2008 tax year includes any of the items in the following list, you may need tax planning to avoid or reduce the AMT:

- Exercise of ISOs during 2008 (as opposed to nonqualified stock options) for which the stock is still held on December 31, 2008.
- Large prior-year state or local tax balance paid in April 2008.
- Large fourth-quarter 2007 state or local estimated tax payment that was made in January 2008 rather than in December 2007.
- Expenses that exceed 2 percent of income for investment management or tax-planning services or unreimbursed employee business expenses.
- Tax-exempt municipal bond income from private activity bonds.
- Business interests owned in S corporation or partnership form where these entities own significant amounts of depreciable assets.
- Large amounts of qualified dividends or long-term capital gains.
- Interest on home equity debt up to $100,000 that is deductible for regular income tax purposes, where the borrowed funds were not used to improve the home.
- Passive activity losses that are allowable for regular tax purposes.

After reviewing the three basic tax-planning strategies, we now move on to more sophisticated techniques, starting with accelerating deductions in Chapter 12.

Chapter 12

Accelerating Deductions

Accelerating deductions into an earlier year gives taxpayers their tax benefits sooner. If tax rates are higher in the earlier year, the deduction is more valuable because it offsets income that is taxed at a higher rate. That was the case for deductions that were accelerated from 2003 into 2002. However, because there is a possibility that tax rates could rise from 2008 to 2009 (due to the new agenda of a new president), accelerating deductions at the end of 2008 will most likely only generate earlier—not larger—tax savings. In this instance, it could be prudent to defer deductions until 2009. Nonetheless, those who expect to be in a lower tax bracket in 2009 for other reasons may get both earlier and larger tax benefits from accelerating their deductions into 2008.

Your goal is to use deductions to their full potential, keeping in mind that itemized deductions provide a tax benefit only if their total is more than the standard deduction amount.

Example

The standard deduction for a married couple filing a joint return for 2008 is $10,900. If you accelerate a deduction from 2009 into 2008 and it turns out that your 2008 itemized deductions total less than $10,900, your effort will not have increased the amount of deductions you can claim in 2008. In addition, you will have lost the opportunity to take that deduction in 2009 when it might have reduced your taxes if your total itemized deductions exceed the standard deduction for 2009.

Another important goal of accelerating tax deductions is to maximize other available tax benefits. There are many tax benefits that are phased out if you have an adjusted gross income (AGI) in excess of certain thresholds. For example, the ability to contribute to and take deductions for certain individual retirement account (IRA) contributions, certain credits, and deductions for student loan interest all contain phaseouts based on certain levels of AGI. Accelerating above-the-line deductions that reduce your AGI may allow you to maximize these deductions, credits, or other tax breaks in 2008.

Equally important is something everyone knows but few put into practice: keep track of your deductions as they occur, not six or seven months later. Nothing is more painful than trying to reconstruct documentation of legitimate expenses that are barely remembered. It is much easier to keep expense records current and ready for a running start on accelerating deductions.

If you determine that it pays to itemize deductions for the current year (based on the figures listed later), you can take certain steps to move deductible expenses into 2008. As a general rule, you should pay deductible bills and expenses received this year, rather than waiting until next year to pay them. You should defer the payment of a deductible expense only if there is a clear benefit to the deferral.

If you want to move deductions into this year, you can mail a check for a deductible item postmarked as late as December 31 and still claim it on this year's tax return, even though the check will not be cashed until next year. In the same way, deductible items charged on a credit card by year-end can generally be deducted on the current year's tax return, even if the credit card bill is not paid until the following year.

If your itemized deductions come close to the standard deduction amount (in 2008, $10,900 for joint returns and $5,450 for singles) each year, you may be able to benefit by bunching itemized expenses in alternative years so that you can itemize every other year (and claim the standard deduction in the intervening years). Bunching strategies include timing the payment of larger charitable gifts, making January mortgage payments in December, accelerating or delaying the payment of real estate taxes and state and local income tax payments, and timing elective surgery and other medical expenses prior to year-end (cosmetic surgery is generally not deductible).

Observation

Deduction bunching works best for those who do not have recurring deductible expenses every year in excess of the standard deduction amount. For example, if you pay mortgage interest and state and local taxes each year that are more than your standard deduction amount, bunching may not help you. However, if you have itemized deductions each year that are close to, but under, the standard deduction amount, bunching could work well for you. You might be able to itemize one year and claim the standard deduction the next, increasing your overall deductions and reducing your tax bills.

State and Local Taxes

State and local income taxes are deductible from federal income taxes in the year paid.

If you would benefit from accelerating deductions, consider making December payments of state and local estimated income taxes that are due in January. You also could move up the payment of any balance of state taxes due in April to the previous year-end, but it may be more beneficial to invest those funds for the three-and-a-half-month period, particularly if your marginal tax bracket is below 25 percent.

If you have an unusually large amount of taxable income in 2008 and will have a large balance due on your state or local tax return in April 2009, you should consider prepaying the amount in December 2008 so that you can match the state and local tax deduction with the income that generated it. This technique can help you avoid or minimize the impact of the alternative minimum tax (AMT) on your 2009 tax return. This is particularly so if your 2008 taxable income is expected to be substantially larger than 2009 income (perhaps because of an asset sold in 2008). However, if accelerating the tax payment into 2008 will cause you to be subject to AMT in 2008, then accelerating the deduction is a mistake.

Caution

If you are subject to the AMT, you will lose any tax savings that result from the deduction of state and local taxes, because the deduction is not permitted in calculating the AMT. This means you will receive no tax benefit for an otherwise deductible expense.

Real Estate Property Taxes

State and local real estate property taxes are generally deductible only by the person upon whom they are imposed in the year in which they were paid.

If you would benefit from accelerating deductions, pay your entire property tax bill, including installments due in year 2009, by year-end. As stated in the prior discussion regarding the time value of money, those in the lowest two tax brackets generally should not accelerate deductions that could be paid later than February, and those in the highest tax bracket should not accelerate deductions that could be deferred until May. As with state and local income taxes, real estate property taxes are not permitted in calculating the AMT. Thus, accelerating a real estate tax deduction into 2008 will not produce a tax benefit if you are subject to the AMT.

Interest

You cannot deduct all interest paid on borrowed money. There are six different kinds of interest expense for tax purposes—home mortgage (see Chapter 6), business, investment, passive activity, student loan (see Chapter 7), and personal—and the deductibility of each type is treated differently.

Generally, the way borrowed funds are used determines the category of the interest expense.

Home Mortgage Interest

Homeowners are generally allowed deductions for interest on loans to acquire or substantially improve their principal residence and one additional personal residence. The deduction for home acquisition indebtedness is limited to loan principal of $1 million or less. In addition, homeowners are generally allowed to deduct the interest on home equity loans up to $100,000, regardless of how the borrowed funds are used. For a full discussion of the home mortgage interest rules, see Chapter 6.

> **Observation**
>
> Be conscious of your overall tax picture before deciding whether to borrow funds. The $1 million limit on home mortgage debt for interest deductibility is available only for the original acquisition of the home or for improvements on the home. If you purchase a home with a substantial down payment and later discover you need additional funds, you may be subject to the lower deductibility limits for home equity debt at that point. If you are unsure, you can always secure the larger mortgage loan at closing and then pay it down later if you do not need the funds. It is much harder to create deductible interest later if you let the acquisition mortgage opportunity pass.

Business Interest

If you "materially participate" in the operation and management of a pass-through entity (e.g., a partnership, limited liability company [LLC], or S corporation) or an unincorporated business, generally you may fully deduct interest on business-related borrowings.

> **Caution**
>
> For purposes of determining whether you can deduct interest, managing your investment portfolio is not considered a business. Deductibility of investment interest expense is more limited, as discussed next.

Even if the majority of your personal taxable income is from pass-through entities or unincorporated businesses, the Internal Revenue Service (IRS) and most courts say that interest on a tax deficiency is nondeductible personal interest.

Investment Interest

Interest on money that you borrow to purchase portfolio investments (e.g., stocks, mutual funds, and bonds) that produce dividends, interest, royalties, or annuity income is deductible only to the extent that the portfolio investments produce taxable income. You may carry forward indefinitely any excess investment interest expense and deduct it against your net investment income in later years. To maximize your deductible investment interest, try to match investment income with investment interest expenses. Note that interest is not deductible to the extent that the borrowing was used to purchase or carry investments that produce tax-exempt income (e.g., municipal bonds).

You can also elect to include long-term capital gains and/or qualified dividend income as investment income against which investment interest may be deducted. If you make this election, however, these gains and dividends will be taxed at ordinary income tax rates rather than at the lower 15 percent (or 0 percent) capital gains tax rates. The effect of the election is to save tax currently on your excess investment interest expense at the long-term capital gains tax rate. This election generally makes sense only when you expect to have excess investment interest expense well into the foreseeable future.

Passive Activity Interest

Your share of interest incurred or paid on a passive activity investment is, in most cases, deductible only up to the amount of your income from all passive activities that year. In effect, the interest expense related to a passive investment is treated the same as other expenses or losses associated with passive investments (see the following discussion regarding passive activity losses, including interest expense).

Student Loan Interest

There is an above-the-line deduction (these deductions are subtracted directly from your gross income to calculate AGI)—available even to individuals who do not itemize deductions—for interest paid on a qualified education loan. The 2008 limit is $2,500 for interest paid on qualified education loans. The maximum deduction phases out for single taxpayers with an AGI between $55,000 and $70,000, and for married taxpayers filing jointly with an AGI between $115,000 and $145,000. These thresholds may be adjusted for inflation in coming years (see Chapter 7 for more details).

> **Example**
>
> You finished college with $30,000 in student loan debt that you have arranged to repay over 10 years. Although you were a dependent of your parents while you were a student, you will no longer be claimed on their tax return. You may deduct up to $2,500 of interest for each of the 10 repayment years, subject to the AGI limits.

Qualifying loans generally include only debt incurred solely to pay the higher education expenses for yourself, your spouse, or your children or grandchildren at the time the debt was incurred. Loans from relatives do not qualify. You must be the person legally responsible to repay the loan to deduct the interest. You cannot deduct interest that you may pay, for example, on your child's loan if you are not legally obligated on that loan. Nor can you deduct interest on a revolving credit line not earmarked specifically for higher education expenses. You are also not eligible for the deduction in years when you are claimed as a dependent on someone else's tax return.

Personal Interest

Interest incurred on car loans, credit cards, or IRS adjustments, or any other interest falling outside the other five categories is generally not deductible. If you can obtain a favorable interest rate, you should consider taking out a home equity loan to pay off any of these debts, because the interest on a home equity loan of up to $100,000 can be claimed as an itemized deduction, except in certain situations for purposes of the AMT (see Chapter 6).

Medical Expenses

You can deduct unreimbursed medical expenses (including those of your spouse and dependents) to the extent that they exceed 7.5 percent of your AGI (10 percent for the AMT). Doctors' and dentists' fees, hospital bills, medical supplies, stop-smoking programs, weight-loss programs to treat obesity, and prescription drugs are deductible to the extent not covered by insurance. In addition, your payments for health insurance and certain long-term care insurance (within limits) and long-term care expenses are included as medical expenses.

Do not forget often-overlooked transportation-related medical expenses, including costs of traveling to and from a doctor, dentist, hospital, or pharmacy. Transportation also includes cab, plane, or train fares, or if you use your own car, the standard mileage rate deduction (the 2008 rate is 19 cents per mile), in addition to parking fees and tolls.

If medical expenses seem likely to be close to or exceed the 7.5 percent floor this year, consider accelerating elective treatment or surgery (cosmetic surgery is generally not deductible as a medical expense) and paying for it before year-end. If the floor will not be reached this year but might be reached next year, consider the opposite strategy: delaying payment of medical bills whenever possible.

Other opportunities if you are self-employed include:

- Deducting 100 percent of the annual cost of health insurance for yourself, your spouse, and your dependents. This deduction is not allowed for months during which you are eligible to participate in an employer-provided health insurance plan (including your spouse's plan). Note that this deduction is an adjustment to income rather than an itemized deduction. Therefore, it can be taken even by nonitemizers and is not subject to the 1 percent itemized deduction phaseout (for 2008) on deductions for itemizers at higher income levels.
- Deducting a percentage of the cost of long-term care insurance premiums, as long as you are not eligible for any employer-provided long-term care insurance (including under your spouse's plan).

> ### Observation
> Although cosmetic surgery is not generally deductible, the costs of reconstructive surgery and of radial keratotomy to correct vision without requiring prescription lenses are allowable medical expenses.

Charitable Contributions

Charitable contributions are one of the most flexible deductible expenses, because you can usually control their timing and amount. For example, you could accelerate deductible expenses by making a contribution in December rather than January. A contribution is considered made at the time of delivery (mailing a check constitutes delivery, assuming that it clears in due course). You cannot take a deduction based only on a pledge—you must actually make the contribution.

In general, you can deduct contributions of cash to qualified public charities of up to 50 percent of your AGI. These deductions are also allowed for AMT purposes. Any excess can be carried forward for five years. Contributions to private foundations as well as noncash contributions are subject to lower AGI limitations.

> ### Observation
> Taking advantage of tax cuts may produce more disposable income that could be used to make charitable contributions. Alternatively, tax-rate reductions also remove some of the tax incentive for charitable giving by increasing its after-tax cost. Most charitable givers, however, have more than taxes in mind when they make their contributions.

> ### Observation
> You can establish a donor-advised philanthropic fund as a means to obtain a current deduction and earn a tax-free return until you wish to donate the funds to particular charities (see Chapter 10 for more information). Donor-advised philanthropic funds can be established through community foundations as well as certain mutual fund companies and other financial and charitable organizations. The minimum contribution to establish the fund can be as low as $10,000.

> ### Observation
> Unreimbursed expenses you incur as a volunteer for a charitable organization, including mileage driven in your car, are deductible. The mileage rate for purposes of the charitable deduction is 14 cents per mile for 2008.

Property Donations

Special rules apply to donations of property to charities. If you donate appreciated property, such as securities or land, your deduction is based on the property's current market value rather than on its original cost. Contributions of appreciated long-term capital gain property, however, are generally limited to 30 percent of AGI unless a special election is made to reduce the deductible amount of the contribution.

> **Caution**
>
> Be careful of property donations related to used automobiles. Starting in 2005, strict rules were imposed for deducting motor vehicle contributions to a charity. If the charity sells the vehicle, your contribution deduction is limited to the proceeds received by the charity. If the charity does not sell the vehicle (e.g., it keeps the car and uses it in carrying out its exempt purpose), you cannot deduct more than $500 unless you receive Form 1098-C from the charity acknowledging the fair market value for the car. Additional documentation is required for vehicles with a fair market value exceeding $5,000.

Instead of selling property that has been held for longer than one year and has appreciated in value and then donating the proceeds, consider donating the property itself. If you sold the property and donated the proceeds, you would pay capital gains tax on any appreciation, while receiving a deduction for only the amount of cash that is left to contribute to the charity. If you donate appreciated property directly to a charity, you escape the capital gains tax and receive a deduction for the property's full fair market value.

However, if property that you are considering donating to charity has decreased in value, you should sell it and donate the proceeds. In addition to the charitable deduction, the sale will generate a capital loss that can be used to offset capital gains and up to $3,000 of other income each year. Any excess capital loss can be carried forward indefinitely.

For contributions of appreciated property to a private foundation, the restriction that limited the charitable deduction for gifts of publicly traded stock to your tax cost basis in the stock no longer applies. A full fair market value deduction for contributions of "qualified appreciated stock" is permitted. Such stock must be a long-term capital asset traded on an established securities market. No more than 10 percent of the value of all of a company's outstanding stock may be contributed to a private foundation.

> ### Observation
> The deduction for contributions of long-term capital gain property to a private foundation is generally limited to 20 percent of AGI for any year. Any excess can be carried forward and deducted for five years, subject to the 20 percent limit.

Any charitable contribution of property (other than marketable securities) that is worth more than $5,000 ($10,000 for gifts of closely held stock) must be supported by a qualified appraisal completed by the extended due date of your tax return. The appraiser and a representative of the charitable organization must sign Form 8283 or the deduction will be denied. Additional requirements apply to contributions of art if a deduction of $20,000 or more is claimed. Additional requirements also apply to donations of motor vehicles.

Substantiation Requirements

The general substantiation requirements for a deductible charitable contribution are:

- *Cash contributions under $250:* A canceled check is acceptable as long as no goods or services are received in exchange. Under new substantiation rules, a deduction may be disallowed if you cannot provide a canceled check or a receipt from the charity supporting your contribution.

- *Cash contributions of $250 or more:* These contributions must be acknowledged in writing by the charity. You must obtain this documentation from the charity by the date your tax return is filed or the due date of the return (including any extensions), whichever is earlier. The acknowledgment must state whether the charity provided any goods or services in return for the contribution and, if so, provide the information required for quid pro quo contributions (see the following discussion).

- *Noncash contributions under $250:* The donor should retain a detailed list of the items contributed, including the estimated value of the goods. The Pension Protection Act of 2006 provides that deductions are generally not allowed for items not in good condition or for items of nominal value.

- *Noncash contributions of $250 or more:* The donor must obtain a receipt that describes the donated property (and indicates any goods or services received in exchange). The charity is not required to place a value on the property. For noncash contributions over $500, additional information must be included with the donor's tax return. The substantiation requirements are also more stringent for donations of motor vehicles.

- *Quid pro quo contributions over $75:* A quid pro quo contribution is one that is partly a charitable contribution and partly a payment for goods or services. The charity must provide the donor with a written statement that includes a good-faith estimate of the value of the goods or services provided and must inform the donor that the contribution deduction is limited to the payment in excess of the value of the goods or services. Contributions are fully deductible if goods or services received from the charity are only of nominal value or when only an intangible religious benefit is received.

> **Observation**
>
> A written acknowledgment from a charity is required only if $250 or more is given at one time. For example, if over the course of a year, you make several contributions of $200 to the same charity, the substantiation requirement does not apply.

Deferred Giving

The most common form of charitable contribution is the current gift in which you transfer control of money or property to a charity, and you keep no control over it. In recent years, however, deferred giving has become increasingly popular. This involves an irrevocable transfer to a charity whose ultimate use of the property is deferred to some time in the future. For many, deferred gifts provide the best of all worlds: a current charitable deduction, a retained income stream (or a future interest in the property for your beneficiaries), a charitable contribution to a favorite organization, and a reduction in your taxable estate.

If you make substantial charitable contributions each year, consider establishing a charitable lead trust (CLT) or charitable remainder trust (CRT) to accomplish some of these desirable results. In a CLT, you donate property to a trust that guarantees to pay the charity a fixed amount or a fixed percentage of the fair market value of the trust's assets for a certain number of years. At the end of the term, remaining trust assets revert to you or to a designated beneficiary such as a child or grandchild.

In a CRT, you transfer property to a trust, and the trust guarantees to pay you or a designated noncharitable beneficiary a fixed amount or a fixed percentage of the fair market value of the trust's assets for life or a term of years (not longer than 20 years). At the end of the term, the remaining assets are transferred to the charity.

> **Observation**
>
> The rules for establishing these charitable-giving vehicles are complex. If you are planning to make a large gift, contact your tax advisor to discuss how they work.

> **Caution**
>
> Deductions are not allowed for transfers to charitable organizations involving the use of split-dollar life insurance arrangements if the charity pays any premium for the donor. Employers often use split-dollar life insurance arrangements to provide a substantial amount of insurance coverage for key executives or employees. Split-dollar life insurance is permanent insurance purchased under an arrangement in which the company and the individual share the cost of the policy as well as its benefits and proceeds (see Chapter 5 for more details).

Passive Activity Losses

In general, losses incurred from passive activities may only be deducted against passive activity income. All of your passive activity investments are reviewed on a combined basis to determine if you have net passive income or net passive losses. If the net is a loss, your ability to currently deduct those losses is usually limited.

A passive activity investment is an investment in:

- *An operating business in which you do not materially participate:* Generally, limited partnership investments and other investments where you do not participate in management and day-to-day decisions are considered passive activities.
- *Real estate or another tax shelter:* Generally, these are passive, regardless of your level of involvement; however, renting real estate to yourself or your business will not generate passive income.

Investments in portfolio assets, such as stocks and bonds, are not considered passive activities, and the income from these types of assets is not considered when calculating the passive loss limitations.

You may carry forward indefinitely any excess passive losses and use them to offset passive activity income in future years. Also, you can usually deduct suspended passive losses from a particular passive investment in the year you sell your interest in the particular passive investment. When there is a complete (not a partial) sale or other disposition to an unrelated person of a passive investment in a taxable transaction, net passive losses are applied first against income or gain from other passive investments. Any remaining passive losses from the disposed passive investment are reclassified as nonpassive and can offset nonpassive income, such as compensation income or portfolio income, including interest and dividends.

Example

In the year you sell your ownership interest in a real estate limited partnership, you have $10,000 of passive losses left after offsetting all available passive income for the year, including any gain from the sale of the real estate limited partnership. On your tax return for that year, you may deduct the $10,000 against your nonpassive income.

If your AGI is under $100,000, a special exception permits you to deduct as much as $25,000 of passive rental real estate losses resulting from interest expense and other deductions if you actively participate in the management of the rental real estate. This exception phases out as AGI increases to $150,000. The active participation standard is much easier to satisfy than the material participation standard that generally is applied to determine whether an activity is subject to the passive loss limitations.

> ### Example
> You own a beach house that you rent out for the season each year. You have an agent who handles rentals, but you set the rental terms, approve tenants, make decisions involving maintenance and repairs, and hire contractors to do the work. Your personal use of the property is a very small percentage of the rental time. In this situation, you are an active participant in the rental real estate activity.

There are even more liberal rules for investments in low-income housing and for individuals and closely held corporations that meet the definition of a real estate professional. (See IRS Publication 527, *Residential Rental Property*, for details concerning what it takes to qualify as a real estate professional.)

Tougher rules apply to losses from interests in publicly traded partnerships. Losses from these activities can offset income from the same activity only until you dispose of the ownership interest in the activity.

The passive activity rules are extremely complex. If you think you may be subject to them, you should consult your tax advisor.

Casualty Losses

If you have experienced a natural disaster or another sudden casualty and suffered property damage, a casualty loss deduction is available to help lessen the blow of any unreimbursed losses (casualty losses are deductible to the extent that they exceed any insurance reimbursement). In general, the amount of the loss is the lesser of the decrease in fair market value of the property or your adjusted basis (generally, your cost less depreciation deductions) in the property. Insurance reimbursements reduce the amount of the deductible loss. In addition, the first $100 of each loss is nondeductible. However, if several items are damaged or lost in the course of a single casualty, the $100 floor is applied only once. Finally, only total allowable casualty losses in excess of 10 percent of AGI may be deducted.

Example

Your home was severely damaged by a lightning strike, and your loss, after insurance reimbursement, is $20,000. The first $100 of the loss is not deductible. If your AGI is $70,000, then $7,000 of the remaining $19,900 loss also is nondeductible. Thus, your casualty loss deduction would be $12,900 ($19,900 minus $7,000). If your loss occurs due to a presidentially declared disaster, such as an earthquake or a hurricane, you can claim the loss on your tax return either for the year in which it occurred or on the prior year's return.

Observation

Claiming a casualty loss on the earlier year's tax return (by filing an amended return, if necessary) may get you a refund faster, but the calculations need to be run both ways to see which choice results in the larger tax savings.

Miscellaneous Itemized Deductions

Certain miscellaneous expenses, including job search expenses, unreimbursed employee business expenses, and investment expenses (other than investment-related casualty and theft losses) are deductible only to the extent that they total more than 2 percent of your AGI. For example, if your AGI is $80,000, only

270 Year-End Tax Savings Strategies

miscellaneous itemized deductions totaling more than $1,600 are deductible—and you receive a benefit from these deductions only if your total itemized deductions exceed the standard deduction.

Therefore, it may be desirable to bunch payment of these kinds of expenses to bring the total above the 2 percent floor at least every other year. Similar to medical expenses, these are threshold expenses, or deductible only to the extent they exceed a certain percentage of AGI. By bunching these threshold expenses into one year, there is a better chance to maximize your deduction.

You can generally deduct (subject to the 2 percent floor) unreimbursed payments made in a given year for:

- The cost of unreimbursed job-related education or training.
- Unreimbursed business use of automobiles.
- Subscriptions to business or professional publications (including payment for next year's subscription).
- Membership dues in business or professional associations (including the following year's dues).
- Tax preparation and planning fees.
- Investment expenses (e.g., investment advisory fees or a safe-deposit box).

If you receive tax preparation, investment advice, or certain other financial services under a fixed-fee arrangement, you may be able to take deductions this year for payments covering a period that extends into next year. If you are delaying your deductions, you will want to make these payments after 2008.

> ### Observation
> Miscellaneous itemized deductions are not deductible in the AMT computation. Therefore, the AMT is a consideration when planning any acceleration of these deductions.

> **Observation**
> If you buy and sell securities, you should familiarize yourself with the definitions of *investor* and *trader*. The vast majority of individuals who buy and sell for their own account are investors. Investors deduct their investment expenses as a miscellaneous itemized deduction, subject to the 2 percent floor and the itemized deduction phaseout at higher incomes. Traders, however, may deduct their expenses against their trading income. It is difficult to convince the IRS or the courts that you are a trader unless you regularly do a very large volume of short-term trades.

Moving Expenses

If you relocate because of a new job or business, you may be able to deduct certain moving expenses, including the costs of transporting household goods and traveling to your new residence. For these expenses to be deductible, your new job must be at least 50 miles farther from your former residence than your old job was from your former residence.

Several types of expenses associated with a move are not deductible, including premove house-hunting expenses, temporary living expenses, the cost of meals while traveling or while in temporary quarters, and the costs of selling or settling a lease on the old residence or purchasing or acquiring a lease on a new residence. Employer reimbursements of deductible moving expenses are generally excluded from the employee's gross income, and deductible expenses not reimbursed by the employer are an above-the-line deduction instead of an itemized deduction.

Observation

When an employee is moved for the employer's convenience, employers often reimburse all of their employees' moving costs, including (in many cases) any tax liability for moving expense reimbursements. Some of these reimbursements must be reported as taxable wages.

Above-the-line deductions are subtracted directly from your gross income to calculate AGI. They may be claimed both by itemizers and by those who take the standard deduction.

Depending on your situation, the following idea checklist may provide some help in reducing your tax bill.

Idea Checklist

- ☑ Use flexible spending accounts (FSAs) for medical or dependent care expenses, if your employer offers them. These accounts allow you to pay these types of expenses with pretax dollars, offering real savings. The strategy of using a FSA for medical expenses is particularly appropriate for individuals who are not able to exceed the 7.5 percent floor to receive a tax benefit from claiming medical expenses as itemized deductions.

- ☑ Make deductible contributions to an individual retirement account (IRA).

- ☑ Establish a Keogh retirement plan by December 31 if you have self-employment income and want to deduct your contributions. You can wait until the due date of your tax return (including extensions) to actually fund the plan. Alternatively, you may make deductible contributions to a simplified employee pension (SEP) plan, which can be both established and funded after December 31 (see Chapter 4).

Accelerating Deductions 273

- ☑ Evaluate your form of business entity. Net income from a sole proprietor business, a partnership, or an LLC may be subject to self-employment tax; however, not all income passed through from an S corporation is subject to the self-employment tax.
- ☑ Deduct personal property taxes, such as those required for automobile license plates or tags, if they are *ad valorem* (i.e., based on the value of the property).
- ☑ Remember that business owners can buy office supplies, invest in new equipment, or pay bonuses to their employees to maximize business expense deductions.
- ☑ Remember that business owners can deduct only compensation that is deemed reasonable for services they and their family members provide.
- ☑ Corporate owner-employees should consider the impact of the reduced tax rate on qualified dividends in deciding how much to take out of the corporation as compensation and how much as dividends (see Chapter 13).
- ☑ Review the amount of support that you have provided to dependents this year to ensure that they meet the support test that allows an individual to claim an exemption for the dependents.

This chapter has described many tools and techniques that can help you use tax deductions at the end of 2008 and in future years to lower your tax bills. Chapter 13 sets forth a tax-planning strategy called income deferral that can be an important part of your overall tax-planning program.

Chapter 13

Deferring Income

Deferring income from one year to the next can be a very effective tax-planning strategy, especially for those in high tax-rate brackets, as they will save the most. Many two-income families will find themselves in marginal tax-rate brackets between 28 percent and 35 percent, which makes the tax benefits from deferring income quite meaningful. Almost all individuals report their income and deductions using the cash method of accounting (i.e., income is reported in the year it is actually or constructively received, and expenses are deducted in the year they are paid), which provides quite a bit of flexibility when using tax-deferral strategies.

The key to saving from income deferral is that income is not taxed until it is actually or constructively received. For example, if a taxpayer does work for others, he or she will not be taxed until the year in which payment is received. So deferring billing at year-end results in more income being received and taxed in the following year. Some examples of situations in which income deferral may be useful are discussed later.

Caution

Individuals must be aware of possible alternative minimum tax (AMT) issues if they lower their income too much by using deferral techniques (see Chapter 14 for a discussion of the AMT).

Caution

Individuals should also consider expiring deductions or credits when making deferral decisions. Another item to consider is deductions with an AGI floor, such as medical deductions (deductible only over 7.5 percent of AGI); casualty losses (deductible only over 10 percent of AGI); or miscellaneous deductions (deductible only over 2 percent of AGI). Deferring income from one year to another may result in certain deductions being disallowed in particular years.

Observation

Income deferral is even more valuable when income tax rates are scheduled to drop from one year to the next. Deferring income to a lower-tax year not only delays payment of tax but also lowers the overall tax bill. However, income tax rates could possibly increase between 2008 and 2009, which may cause taxpayers who would typically want to defer income to actually accelerate it. Keep in mind also that income tax rates are currently scheduled to revert to 2001 tax rates starting in 2011, which are higher marginal tax rates than in 2008 and potentially 2009.

Year-End Bonuses

If you expect to receive a year-end bonus or other special type of lump-sum compensation payment, you may want to receive it in 2008 but pay taxes on it in 2009 rather than in 2008. Your employer can probably still deduct the bonus in 2008 if the company is on the accrual method of accounting (which most larger companies are), as long as its obligation to pay you is established before year-end and payment occurs within two and one-half months after year-end (March 15, 2009, for a calendar-year company).

Example

The company where you work uses the accrual accounting method, is on a calendar year, and has an incentive bonus program for which you qualify. In December 2008, the company's directors declare the bonus and set the amount of the payments that will be paid on January 30, 2009. The result is that the company accrues its deduction in 2008 when it becomes liable for payment of the bonuses, but your tax liability is delayed until 2009 when you receive the bonus.

Caution

This strategy of delaying payment of bonuses to the next year does not work for most payments to company owners. The company's deduction for payments to partners, S corporation shareholders, owner-employees of personal-service corporations, or shareholders who own more than 50 percent of a regular corporation is deferred until the year the bonus is actually paid to these owners. The company is unable to accrue its deduction for the year in which the bonus was declared if the bonus is not paid until the following year.

Deferred Compensation

You may want to consider an agreement with your employer so that part of your earnings for this year is paid to you in the future, perhaps over several years. This will delay your tax obligation. If you can wait until you retire to receive the deferred compensation, you may be in a lower tax-rate bracket, further reducing your tax bill on that income. In this type of arrangement, the company often adds interest to your payment to compensate you for the delay in receiving the money. The 2004 Tax Act created strict new rules that must be followed in structuring deferred compensation agreements. In general, these new rules require you to elect to defer income in the year before the income is earned, and restrict your ability to accelerate receipt of the deferred income once a deferral election is made. Failure to follow these requirements will cause the employee to be taxed currently on the deferred compensation (with penalties).

Deferred compensation will not be taxed to you or be deductible by your employer until you actually receive it. Social Security tax and Medicare tax, however, are generally due when the income is earned regardless of when it is actually paid. If you are already over the FICA wage base for the year ($102,000 for 2008, projected to increase for inflation for 2009), you will not owe any additional Social Security tax, but you and your employer will each owe the 1.45 percent Medicare tax on the deferred amount. No additional Social Security or Medicare tax will be owed in the future when you receive the deferred compensation.

Caution

Today's low tax rates on compensation, dividends, and capital gains might cause executives to think twice before deferring salary or bonuses into nonqualified deferred compensation plans. Payments from a deferred

Continued

compensation plan are taxed at ordinary income tax rates, and the executive's tax rate may be higher at the time the payments are received. Thus, executives who elect to defer compensation forgo the opportunity to receive more favorably taxed capital gains and dividends on investments they might have made with after-tax dollars outside of the plan.

Caution

Executives also may question the premise that nonqualified deferred compensation provides an opportunity to shift income to years when they might possibly be subject to a lower marginal tax rate. With marginal income tax rates relatively low from a historic perspective, executives should consider whether tax rates are likely to increase in the future, potentially subjecting their deferred compensation to higher tax rates at the time of distribution.

Example

An employee is considering deferring $10,000 on January 1, 2008. She would elect to receive a lump-sum payout on December 31, 2012. She assumes she will earn 8 percent pretax per year on her investments. She currently has a marginal tax rate of 35 percent for ordinary income. Illustrated are the net after-tax amounts she receives after five years, assuming no deferral with a 28 percent long-term capital gains tax rate, deferral and a payout with a marginal ordinary income tax rate of 35 percent, and deferral and a payout with a marginal ordinary income tax rate of 39.6 percent (no state tax is included):

	No Deferral	35 Percent Tax	39.6 Percent Tax
Amount deferred/invested	$10,000	$10,000	$10,000
2008 tax paid	−3,500	0	0
2008 after-tax investment	$6,500	$10,000	$10,000
Investment at 12/31/12	$9,551	$14,693	$14,693
2012 tax paid	−854	−5,143	−5,818
2012 after-tax investment	$8,696	$9,550	$8,875

Each employee's situation and assumptions will be different, but this does illustrate that it is possible for deferral to be favorable even with rising ordinary income tax rates.

Unlike a qualified retirement plan, which generally must cover a broad range of employees, this nonqualified type of deferred compensation arrangement can usually be made for an individual employee. If you are interested in a deferred compensation plan, you should discuss it with your employer without delay, because such a plan can only cover income you earn in the future, not income you have already earned. As discussed earlier, in most cases you must make your deferred compensation elections before the start of the year. Therefore, you will need to make your 2009 deferred compensation elections before December 31, 2008.

Caution

In general, when you defer compensation, you are treated as a general creditor of your employer, subordinate to all secured creditors. If your employer goes into bankruptcy, you could lose the amounts accumulated as deferred

> *Continued*
>
> compensation. In addition, deferred payouts could be accelerated in situations such as changes in control, your termination, or plan termination. Each plan should be reviewed to understand such possibilities.

Stock Options or Stock Appreciation Rights

If you have nonqualified stock options or stock appreciation rights, in most cases you will have taxable compensation income when you exercise them. Delay exercising them until next year if postponing income would be to your advantage.

> *Caution*
>
> By waiting to exercise their options, employees forgo the opportunity for capital gains on the underlying shares (any increase in the value of stock related to a nonqualified option will be taxed as ordinary income when exercised) and the right to receive dividends, both of which can receive preferential tax treatment. However, option holders receive the leverage effect of being able to participate in the appreciation in the underlying stock without committing capital (the exercise price). Therefore, despite the potential for lower-tax-rate dividends and capital gains, an analysis of exercise timing generally reveals that employees continue to be better off postponing exercise until later years. This may change, however, depending on assumptions regarding future income tax rates and the valuation behavior of the underlying stock.

If you have incentive stock options (ISOs), exercising them does not result in compensation income if the stock you acquire is held for the required periods (at least two years after option grant and one year after the option is exercised). If you meet these requirements, you generally will not owe any tax until you sell the shares acquired through the ISO exercise; your gain is then taxed at more favorable capital gains tax rates rather than ordinary income tax rates related to compensation income. The spread between the option price and the fair market value at the time you exercise the option is added to your income for AMT purposes in the year of exercise. (See Chapter 3 for a discussion of ISOs.)

Caution

If you are a corporate insider as defined under Securities and Exchange Commission rules, you should contact your financial and/or legal advisor. You are subject to special limitations on the sale of your option stock that may impact your ability to participate in income deferral strategies. (See Chapter 3 for more details on stock options.)

Treasury Bills and Bank Certificates

If you invest in short-term securities, you can shift interest income into the next year by buying Treasury bills or certain bank certificates with a term of one year or less that will mature next year. If you buy a bank certificate, you must specify that interest be credited only at maturity.

Dividends

If you have a voice in the management of a company in which you own stock, you may want to take steps to see that dividends are declared and paid in January 2009 rather than in late 2008. This will shift your tax liability on the dividends to 2009 because you will not receive the dividend income until the later year. The extension of the favorable tax rates on qualifying dividends through December 31, 2010, should make this a viable tax-planning strategy for two more years, unless this provision is repealed by a future Congress.

Installment Sales

You generally owe tax on profits from the sale of property in the year in which you receive the sale proceeds. To defer income from a sale of property, consider an installment sale, in which part or all of the proceeds are payable in the following year or later. In that case, tax will be owed as you receive the payments. Part of each installment payment you receive will be a tax-free return of your cost or basis, part will be interest income taxed at regular income tax rates, and part will be capital gain. Make sure that future payments are secured and that the appropriate interest is paid on any unpaid balance.

> **Caution**
>
> If the property being sold has been depreciated, some or all of the gain may be taxed, or recaptured, at ordinary income tax rates. This recapture gain is subject to tax in the year of sale, even if you elect installment tax reporting. That is true even if you do not receive any payment in the sale year. Be sure to get enough up-front cash at least to cover your tax liability on recaptured income.

You need not make the decision of whether you want to report 2008 deferred payment sales on the installment method until you file your 2008 tax return (in 2009). This gives you more time to decide whether to be taxed on profits in 2008 or in 2009 and later years. If you choose not to report on the installment method, you must elect out of it. If you do elect out, you could be liable for tax on income that you will not receive until later years.

> **Caution**
>
> Special rules limit the use of the installment method. For example, inventory items and publicly traded stock do not qualify for installment-sale reporting. Also, installment notes in excess of $5 million may be subject to an interest charge.

U.S. Savings Bonds

Many people are aware that the interest earned on Series EE U.S. savings bonds is tax-deferred for up to 30 years for cash-basis taxpayers. However, many people are not familiar with the newer Series I U.S. savings bonds. Series I bonds provide the same tax-deferral opportunities as Series EE bonds. The major difference between these two bonds is the way the interest is calculated. Series I bonds pay an interest rate that is indexed for inflation.

Both EE and I bonds can be bought at your bank in various denominations. Purchases of these bonds are limited to $5,000 per series, per person, per year in paper form. In addition, individuals can buy up to the same amount of each series in TreasuryDirect online accounts, for a total of $10,000 per series, per person, per year.

> **Observation**
>
> The Series I bonds are one of a very limited number of investments whose return is guaranteed to keep pace with inflation.

Annuities

You can defer current investment income you now earn, such as stock dividends, bond interest, and interest on savings and money market accounts, by transferring the funds into deferred annuities that shelter current earnings from tax. You will not owe tax on a deferred annuity until payouts begin. However, to get this benefit, you generally have to tie up your funds until you are at least 59½. Similar to IRAs, deferred annuities generate a penalty tax on premature withdrawals, subject to certain exceptions.

> **Caution**
> Because earnings from deferred annuities are subject to ordinary income tax when received, they do not benefit from reduced tax rates on dividend and capital gain income. There has traditionally been a school of thought that only long-term periods of deferral would justify the use of deferred annuities (because they can convert lower-tax-rate income into higher-tax-rate income, thereby making short-term deferrals financially unattractive). The reduced tax rate on qualified dividends and long-term capital gains makes variable annuities invested in equities even less attractive.

For portfolios that produce significant short-term capital gains or ordinary income, however, annuities may remain attractive, especially for those far from payout status. Younger taxpayers should continue to consider these investments, because long periods of tax deferral may overcome the disadvantages.

> **Observation**
> The taxation of exchanges of appreciated property for certain private and commercial annuities is complex. Before entering into an annuity contract, you should discuss your fact pattern with your tax advisor.

Individual Retirement Accounts

If you earn compensation or self-employment income, you can establish a traditional individual retirement account (IRA) or a Roth IRA (see Chapter 4 for more information about IRAs). Although your income level may disqualify you from getting the maximum benefits from these savings vehicles, you may still find some limited advantages. For example, even though you may not be able to deduct contributions to a traditional IRA, you may make nondeductible contributions to this type of IRA no matter how high your income is and benefit from tax-deferred earnings until you withdraw your money, usually at retirement.

Caution

Like deferred annuities discussed earlier, the earnings from nondeductible traditional IRA contributions are subject to ordinary income tax when received and, therefore, do not benefit from reduced tax rates on dividend and capital gain income. However, if the scheduled sunset of the lower dividends and capital gains tax rates occurs in 2011, and these tax rates are not made permanent, taxpayers who passed on nondeductible IRAs for several years will not be able to make up those contributions.

Observation

Nondeductible traditional IRAs may be good candidates for conversion to Roth IRAs in 2010, when the income limitations on Roth IRA conversions are scheduled to be lifted. See Chapter 4 for more details.

Regular 401(k) Plans and Roth 401(k) Plans

Both regular 401(k) plans and Roth 401(k) plans are qualified retirement plans established by an employer under which employees can defer up to $15,500 of their compensation income in 2008 (these limits are higher for those age 50 or older). As with an IRA, the earnings are not taxed until they are withdrawn. Contributions to regular 401(k) plans are made on a pretax basis, meaning that you do not currently pay income tax on the amount you contribute. That makes it easier for you to put more money into your account. Contributions to Roth 401(k) plans, like the Roth IRA, are made with after-tax dollars. Social Security taxes are owed on amounts you elect to defer to your regular 401(k) or Roth 401(k) account in the year the income is deferred. In addition, many employers match a portion of employee deferrals. Many 401(k) plans allow you to borrow from your accounts before retirement, if the loan is repaid on a regular schedule. See Chapter 4 for further discussion of 401(k) plans.

Similar benefits are available through 403(b) plans and Roth 403(b) plans to employees of governmental and tax-exempt organizations.

Shifting Income to Family Members

Shifting income to children or other family members in lower tax-rate brackets is an excellent long-term planning strategy for high-income individuals. As a general rule, family income shifting should be done early in the year to get the most tax savings. It is never too early to begin planning for 2009 and later years.

Children age 19 or older as of the end of the year (see *Caution* for exception) are usually taxed at single individual tax rates (10 percent on the first $8,025 of taxable income and 15 percent on higher amounts up to $32,550 in 2008). You can also shift capital gains income from your 15 percent long-term capital gains tax rate into a child's lower capital gains tax rate (see Chapter 3). For 2008 to 2010, a child in the 10 percent or 15 percent tax bracket receives a 0 percent rate on capital gains, so careful planning to take advantage of these tax-free capital gains is encouraged. Note that beginning in 2011, the capital gains tax rate is scheduled to revert to the 2001 rate of 20 percent for all taxpayers if the current legislation is allowed to expire.

Caution

Special care should be considered in 2008 before shifting income to children. Congress has expanded the class of minor children subject to the kiddie tax to children who are over 18 but under 24 as of the end of the year and who are full-time students who do not provide over one-half of their own support.

The issue of who actually controls the funds—you or your child or grandchild—can determine the success of strategies that seek to use a child's lower tax rate. If you keep too much control over the transferred asset, the IRS may argue that you really have not transferred it for tax purposes and will tax you on its income or sale.

The easiest way to effectively shift income is to use a custodial account, either a Uniform Gifts to Minors Act (UGMA) account or a Uniform Transfers to Minors Act (UTMA) account. Keep in mind that state laws typically give the child access to UGMA/UTMA funds at age 18 or 21.

Observation

A few states, such as Alaska, California, and Nevada, allow UGMA and UTMA accounts to continue to age 25 under certain circumstances, as opposed to the cutoffs at age 18 or 21 in most other states. If you want to limit your child's access to the transferred assets beyond what an UGMA/UTMA account permits, consider a trust. But be wary of trust tax-rate brackets. For 2008, the 15 percent tax bracket stops at $2,200 of taxable income, and the top tax bracket starts at taxable income of $10,700. Also, trusts do not qualify for the 10 percent tax rate that applies for individuals. However, the new lower 15 percent tax rate on qualified dividends and long-term capital gains, which applies to trusts as well as individuals, could mitigate most of the negative impact of the compressed tax-rate brackets for trusts.

If you are planning to shift income to children under age 18, keep in mind that a kiddie tax is imposed on their unearned income (e.g., interest, dividends, and capital gains) over $1,800 in 2008. This income is taxable to the child at the highest tax rate of his or her parents. However, there are techniques that you can use to shift income to your children and avoid the kiddie tax.

You can still achieve tax savings by shifting enough assets to a child under the age of 18 to produce up to $1,800 of total 2008 unearned income. The first $900 of that unearned income will be offset by the child's standard deduction, and the next $900 is taxed at the child's 10 percent tax rate.

Example

A six-year-old child has $3,000 of interest income in 2008 and no earned income. His or her 2008 standard deduction of $900 is allocated against his or her unearned income, and the remaining net unearned income is $2,100. The first $900 of the remaining $2,100 is taxed at the child's tax rate. The remaining $1,200 is taxed at the parents' top tax rate:

Unearned income	$3,000
Less: Child's standard deduction	−900
Remaining unearned income	$2,100
Less: Amount taxed at child's rate	−900
Remaining taxed at parents' top tax rate	$1,200

Observation

A transfer of assets that produces $1,800 of income to a child under the age of 18 can save a family in the 35 percent tax-rate bracket $630 per year. When interest rates and investment rates of return are low, transfers of substantial assets can be made without going over the $1,800 unearned income limit. Note that asset transfers should be coordinated with the gift tax rules (see Chapter 9 for a discussion of gift taxes).

Another technique is to transfer assets that generate little or no current taxable income. For example, consider giving a child under the age of 18:

- Growth stocks or growth-stock mutual fund shares.
- Series EE and Series I U.S. savings bonds (the interest on which may be tax-deferred).
- Tax deferral products (e.g., annuities and variable life insurance contracts).
- Closely held stock of a C corporation.

These assets can be converted into investments that produce currently taxable income after the child is age 18 because income and any capital gains recognized on the conversion will be taxable at the child's tax rates—10 percent on the first $8,025 of taxable income in 2008 (see Chapter 16 for 2009 amount) and 0 percent (for years 2008 through 2010) for qualifying dividends and long-term capital gains.

Caution

Savings bonds held in your name may qualify for tax-free treatment when used to pay for your child's college education. If you transfer these bonds to your children, this exclusion will be lost. Because of income limitations on this tax-free treatment of savings bonds, however, it is not available to high-income or many middle-income individuals. Even if loss of the education tax break is not a factor for you, it is still a good idea to purchase new savings bonds for children rather than transferring your own bonds to them.

> *Continued*
>
> That is because you would be taxed on the bond's accrued interest as of the transfer date. Unless the bonds are very new and the accrued interest amount is small, it is better to start with new bonds in the child's name.

Chapter 14 discusses a topic that has recently affected more taxpayers than in prior years: the AMT. Even if you have not already been required to pay the AMT, there is an increasing likelihood that you will be paying the AMT in the near future.

Chapter 14
Alternative Minimum Tax

The alternative minimum tax (AMT) continues to be a widely discussed and hotly debated topic. With an increasing number of unsuspecting taxpayers becoming subject to the AMT each year, the pressure on Congress to provide a permanent solution continues to grow. Enactment of another AMT patch to provide temporary relief for millions of taxpayers for 2008 seems likely, although debate continues in Congress over items such as revenue offsets. Given that only temporary and limited relief seems likely in the near term, taxpayers still need to not only become more educated about the AMT but also actively plan for it.

First instituted in 1969, the AMT was designed to ensure that high-income taxpayers, who had historically benefited from various tax-preference items under the regular tax system, pay at least a minimum amount of tax each year. The AMT is a parallel tax system to the regular income tax system, but generates an alternative tax liability by applying different rules for determining alternative minimum taxable income (AMTI), basically incorporating a flat tax rate, and limiting or eliminating the benefit of certain tax deductions and credits. The AMT system acts on the premise that the taxpayer should pay the higher of the regular tax amount or the minimum tax amount. As a result, the regular income tax rate reductions enacted in past years are not fully realized by taxpayers who find themselves subject to AMT.

To avoid becoming an AMT victim, a taxpayer must first recognize that AMT planning is a complicated task that requires exceptional foresight. For example, typical AMT planning might result in a suggestion that you accelerate your income and defer your deductions, which is in direct contradiction to customary income tax-planning practices.

An inadequate understanding of tax rules and their potential impact on your wealth goals and strategies could jeopardize your assets and long-term plans. Therefore, it is very important to explore and plan for the AMT by running your projected tax calculations under both the regular tax system and the AMT system for the current year and for several years into the future, focusing on the proper management of your overall tax liability for more than simply the current year.

In some instances, an AMT planning strategy may cause an increase in regular tax. Accordingly, a key factor to consider in AMT planning is the break-even point where an individual's regular tax and AMT are approximately equal.

With diligent and thorough planning efforts, the effects of the AMT can often be mitigated.

Understanding the Alternative Minimum Tax

As previously mentioned, the AMT is a separate but parallel tax system to the regular income tax system. It has its own set of tax rates and its own rules for income and deductions that are usually less generous than the regular tax rules. Both systems require a calculation of annual taxes, and the taxpayer must pay the tax under whichever system produces the higher amount.

The AMT system includes, in general, a broader base of income due in large part to a smaller range of allowable deductions. Many favorable tax treatments available under the regular tax system are curtailed for the AMT by a system of adjustments and preferences. If you typically claim deductions or have tax-preference items or other adjustments, you may calculate the numbers under both regular tax and AMT and find that you are required to pay tax under the AMT system. Tax-preference items or adjustments include, but are not limited to:

- State and local income taxes.
- Real estate taxes.
- Miscellaneous itemized deductions such as investment expenses and tax return preparation fees.
- Certain tax-exempt interest income.
- Some depreciation expenses.
- The difference between AMT and regular tax gain on the sale of property.
- Nontaxable income on the exercise of incentive stock options (ISOs).

Planning for the AMT can be difficult because many factors can trigger it. If you believe that you are within the range of the AMT, it may make sense to consider formulating year-end tax-planning strategies geared toward reducing the AMT rather than the regular tax. Again, the factors contributing to both regular tax and AMT must be considered.

As mentioned earlier, the AMT was originally designed to ensure that high-income taxpayers pay at least a minimum amount of tax each year even if their regular tax liability is relatively low because of legitimate tax benefits under the regular tax system.

Why are there exponential projected increases in the number of taxpayers subject to the AMT, short of legislative action? Over the years, inflation has been one of the culprits of expanding AMT liability among taxpayers. The regular tax system—including the personal exemptions, standard deduction, and tax-rate brackets—is adjusted to account for inflation. The AMT tax rates and threshold exemptions have not been indexed for inflation since the Tax Reform Act of 1986. The AMT exemption amount has been increased slightly, but not enough to allow taxpayers subject to the AMT to benefit fully from the reductions in regular income tax rates. As the space between the two tax systems has compressed, it has become correspondingly easier to fall under the AMT.

The failure of Congress to adjust the base level of income that is exempt from the AMT for inflation, together with past tax-rate reductions under the regular tax system, has dramatically increased the number of taxpayers subject to the AMT. Because of the absence of inflation indexing, this trend will continue and more and more taxpayers will have an AMT liability that exceeds their regular tax liability. The reality for many taxpayers is that the AMT is unavoidable, so it is important to run the numbers carefully and plan for the long term.

Alternative Minimum Tax Computation

Under the AMT system, a taxpayer must determine his or her AMTI using the separate AMT rules and then apply the AMT tax rates to the AMTI to determine his or her tentative minimum tax. Generally, if the taxpayer's tentative minimum tax exceeds the taxpayer's regular tax, the excess of the tentative minimum tax over the regular tax becomes the taxpayer's AMT.

The basic formula for calculating the AMT is:
- Start with regular taxable income.
- Add any personal exemption amount claimed.
- Add any disallowed itemized deductions, including medical and dental (note 10 percent adjusted gross income [AGI] limitation

for AMT purposes versus 7.5 percent for regular tax purposes); state and local taxes; certain home equity interest; the bargain element on ISOs that you exercise; and miscellaneous itemized deductions.
- Subtract itemized deductions that cannot be claimed on Schedule A because of certain limits for high-income individuals (i.e., the phaseout amount).
- Subtract refunds for state and local taxes.
- Adjust taxable income for specific tax preferences and other adjustment items to arrive at the AMTI.
- Subtract the AMT exemption amount (i.e., $33,750 for single or head of household, $45,000 for married filing jointly or qualified widower, and $22,500 for married filing separately).
- Multiply the AMTI (excluding long-term capital gain and qualified dividend income) by the AMT rate (i.e., 26 percent up to $175,000, 28 percent thereafter), and add the tax at the reduced rate on long-term capital gain and qualified dividend income.
- Subtract AMT credits.
- Compare the result with the amount of regular tax and pay the AMT to the extent it exceeds regular tax.

This formula should be used only to estimate the amount of your AMT liability. To determine your actual liability, you must calculate the actual AMT liability using Internal Revenue Service (IRS) Form 6251.

The More, the Not-So-Merrier

Taxpayers who are more susceptible to the AMT include those with significant long-term capital gains and dividend income that is subject to preferential low-income tax rates, and/or who have tax-preference or other adjustment items. The AMT can affect retirees, taxpayers with high state tax deductions (e.g., New York, California, and the District of Columbia), corporate executives with large exercised ISO amounts, and business owners with large depreciation deductions or net operating losses, among others. By reducing the regular tax rates, the Jobs and Growth Tax Relief Reconciliation Act of 2003 (2003 Tax Act) increased the likelihood that more and more taxpayers will be subject to the AMT.

While the AMT exemption is not adjusted for inflation, the 2003 Tax Act, the Tax Increase Prevention and Reconciliation Act of 2005, and the Tax Increase Prevention Act of 2007 increased the AMT exemption amounts, which provided AMT relief to middle-income taxpayers through 2007. However, if no additional legislation is passed to the contrary, the lower AMT exemption amounts, noted earlier, that existed prior to the 2003 Tax Act will be effective for 2008. When taxable income reaches a certain level, the benefit of this exemption must be reduced or phased out, creating a greater likelihood that the AMT will apply to many surprised and unhappy taxpayers. The 2007 Tax Act did not alter the income levels at which the AMT exemption begins to phase out. For the 2007 tax year, for married individuals filing jointly or surviving spouses, the phaseout begins at an AMTI of $150,000 and ends at $415,000. For singles or heads of households, the phaseout range is $112,500 to $289,900. For married taxpayers filing separately, the phaseout range is $75,000 to $207,500.

The phaseout of the AMT exemption amount results in $1.25 of additional AMTI for every dollar earned in the phaseout range (see preceding paragraph). In the phaseout range, the marginal AMT rate on ordinary income could be 35 percent, which may be higher than the regular tax rate. Additionally, the marginal AMT rate on capital gains in the phaseout range could be 22 percent, rather than 15 percent. This means that, in some cases, AMT planning for those in the phaseout range can require just the opposite action from those normally subject to AMT. That is, in this phaseout range, effective AMT planning may suggest the deferral of income and acceleration of deductions.

Minimum Tax Credit

All hope is not lost if you are subject to the AMT. The IRS allows a credit for prior year AMT if you meet certain requirements. Two types of adjustments—deferral items and exclusion items—generally trigger AMT. Deferral items generally do not cause a permanent difference in taxable income over time. They are essentially timing differences (i.e., depreciation). Exclusion items do cause a permanent difference (i.e., state taxes, standard deduction). To the extent you are paying AMT due to deferral items, you may claim a minimum tax credit in a subsequent year if you are not subject to AMT in that particular year.

> ### Observation
> Due to stock market declines, many taxpayers have large minimum tax credits that were generated as a result of deferral adjustments related to ISOs. These minimum tax credits are being carried forward from year to year, unable to be used because the taxpayers are subject to AMT in the current year.

Starting with the 2007 tax year, the Tax Relief and Health Care Act of 2006 allows individuals who have unused minimum tax credits to claim a refundable credit equal to 20 percent of the long-term unused minimum tax credits per year (a minimum of $5,000) for the next five years. The AMT credit is phased out for higher-income taxpayers, so you should check with your tax advisor to see if this new provision is applicable to your tax situation.

Top Ten Items That May Cause the AMT

An increasing number of individuals are becoming subject to the AMT. As previously mentioned, reasons for the expected swell in the number of AMT taxpayers include the lack of inflation adjustments to tax-rate brackets and exemption amounts, and the disallowance of deductions for state and local taxes. If your calendar year includes any of the following 10 items, you may need tax planning to avoid or reduce the AMT:

1. ISOs triggering an AMT preference.
2. A transaction that creates significant long-term capital gain income taxed at preferential rates, relative to ordinary income.
3. Investments generating significant qualified dividend income taxed at preferential rates, relative to ordinary income.
4. Paying tax to states with high income taxes and/or property taxes (e.g., New York, California, and the District of Columbia).
5. A significant net operating loss (NOL) from a flow-through entity (e.g., family business owner).
6. Expenses that exceed 2 percent of income for investment management or tax-planning services or unreimbursed employee business expenses.
7. Tax-exempt municipal bond income from private activity bonds.
8. Ownership of businesses operating as S corporations or partnerships that flow through tax attributes to the owner, including AMT adjustments from the business (e.g., depreciation).
9. Passive activity losses that differ for regular tax purposes versus AMT purposes.
10. Interest on home equity debt that is deductible for regular income tax purposes where the loan proceeds were not used to improve the home.

An Unpleasant Surprise for Many

Although the AMT is primarily intended to ensure that wealthy taxpayers pay at least some income tax, it applies to all taxpayers. As mentioned before, the reduction in marginal tax rates and the lack of inflation adjustments to AMT rates have dramatically increased the number of individuals subject to the AMT. Year-end may bring an unpleasant surprise to many unsuspecting individuals. It is now estimated that 30 million taxpayers could be paying AMT by 2010. As a result, the time to start planning is now.

If you believe you may be subject to the AMT this year, you may want to consider a counterintuitive approach and do the opposite of the normal year-end planning strategy. For example, AMT planning frequently focuses on shifting more income to the tax year in which the AMT applies and deferring deductions to the next year. This accelerated income is effectively taxed at the 26 percent or 28 percent AMT rate (rather than the higher regular income tax rates that may apply in a year in which the AMT is not anticipated). Deferring deductions until the next year may result in a 35 percent tax benefit in the next year (compared to no tax benefit at all or a 28 percent tax benefit in the current year to the extent that the AMT applies). However, both of these strategies presume that the AMT will not apply in the succeeding year, which may not be the case. As illustrated next, entirely different tax-planning strategies may need to be considered if the AMT is expected to apply in successive years.

In deciding on the right strategy for you, it is essential to compute both your regular tax and your AMT liabilities. These calculations serve as the basis to manage income and deductions (to the extent that one is able) to lessen the AMT bite in a given year.

Because of the projected increases in AMT taxpayers, it is crucial to start income tax planning as soon as possible.

Since many AMT planning strategies are based on the careful timing of income and deductions, it is important that your plan include multiple-year calculations to disclose the full impact of the reversal of timing differences (i.e., accelerating income or deferring deductions). Perform a year-end diagnosis to see if you may fall prey to the AMT; and if you believe you may be affected, you should discuss your AMT situation with a professional tax advisor.

Alternative Minimum Tax-Planning Strategies

If you believe you are a target for the AMT, consider, preferably under the guidance of a professional tax advisor, the following two lists of the common individual tax-planning items depending on whether you anticipate being subject to the AMT in just the 2008 tax year or you expect to be subject to the AMT in 2008 and beyond.

Taxpayers Subject to the Alternative Minimum Tax for 2008 Only

Taxpayers who may be subject to the AMT should:

- Postpone, as much as possible, the payment of deductions that yield no tax benefit when a taxpayer is subject to the AMT (i.e., state income taxes or real estate taxes).
- Postpone (possibly) the payment of deductions that yield some tax benefit when a taxpayer is subject to the AMT (i.e., charitable contributions).
- Consider strategies to accelerate ordinary income and short-term capital gain in 2008.
- Reevaluate the after-tax returns from investments.
- Ask for prepayments of 2009 salary and bonus income.

- Consider whether any exercised ISOs should be disqualified before year-end to minimize AMT liability if the stock has dropped in value.
- Dispose of investments in private activity tax-exempt bonds.
- Consider intrafamily transactions.

Taxpayers Subject to the Alternative Minimum Tax for 2008 and Beyond

Taxpayers who may be subject to the AMT for the foreseeable future should:

- Recognize capital losses if capital gains are causing the phaseout of the AMT exemption.
- Pay off home equity loans where the borrowed funds were not used to improve the residence.
- Dispose of investments in private activity tax-exempt bonds.
- Consider making shifts in your investment asset allocation.
- Consider individual retirement account (IRA) and/or pension distributions.
- Consider intrafamily transactions.

You may also want to take into account the impact of available annual tax elections that may affect the timing of income or deductions. Additional tax-planning strategies would apply to taxpayers who fall under the regular tax for 2008, but expect to be in the AMT in future years.

These suggested planning items notwithstanding, it is anticipated that the AMT will remain a problematic area for family business owners and corporate executives, as well as many other higher income taxpayers. The inadvertent impact of the AMT on the larger taxpayer population has yet to be fully appreciated and addressed by Congress.

> ### *Legislative Alert*
>
> As of the date this book went to print, the House of Representatives has passed a bill (H.R. 6275) to extend individual AMT relief for 2008. Under this House bill, the AMT exemption amount for 2008 would be $69,950 for married couples filing a joint return and for surviving spouses, $46,200 in the case of other unmarried individuals, and $34,975 for married individuals filing separate returns. This bill would also extend for 2008 the AMT relief that allows certain nonrefundable personal credits to offset both the regular tax liability and the minimum tax liability. The House also passed a bill (H.R. 6049) that would provide for an increase in the AMT refundable credit amount for individuals with long-term unused credits for prior-year minimum tax liability. Debate on both bills continues in Congress over items such as revenue offsets.

Is an AMT solution forthcoming? There have been many proposals put forth in the past several years to reform the AMT system. Until significant changes are made, however, it is best to consult with your tax advisor to fully understand how the AMT may affect your tax situation as well as to discuss planning that can be done to lessen the impact. One barrier to successfully addressing the AMT problem is its technical complexity. The AMT is difficult to comprehend and may arise due to numerous variables. Politicians are hesitant to confront this issue because of a relatively uncertain political outcome and the enormous cost of—and potentially significant budget deficits associated with—changing the AMT. This has started to change, however, as more unsuspecting individual taxpayers, many of whom may not consider themselves high-income earners, become subject to the AMT and begin to exert political pressure on their elected representatives.

■ ■ ■

Chapter 15 goes beyond the personal strategies previously discussed and provides many additional considerations that can generate tax savings for business owners and their companies.

Chapter 15

Year-End Planning for Business Owners

Year-end planning for business owners should incorporate all of the personal strategies previously discussed, but it does not end there. Many additional considerations can generate tax savings for business owners and for their companies.

In a sole proprietorship, business tax savings put more money directly in the hands of the business owner. When a business is operated in a pass-through entity (e.g., S corporation, partnership, or limited liability company [LLC]), year-end tax planning must be addressed at both the entity level and the individual level to enhance and coordinate potential tax benefits. This is because these entities do not generally pay income taxes on their earnings. Instead, the income, deductions, and credits are passed through to the owners and reported on the owners' individual income tax returns. Owners of these types of entities, therefore, need to consider the individual year-end tax-planning ideas outlined in previous chapters, as well as tax planning for the business aimed at benefiting the owner's individual tax position while complementing, or not harming, the business's goals. It is not an easy task, but it is potentially very rewarding: For each

$1,000 of income that a pass-through business defers or each $1,000 of accelerated deductions, an owner in the top federal income tax bracket will save $350 of current federal income tax. Similarly, $100,000 of combined company year-end income/deduction shifting can reduce current income tax by $35,000. There are potential payroll tax and state and local income tax savings as well.

Furthermore, there are often more opportunities for implementing tax-saving ideas at the business entity level than at the individual owner level.

In 2008, effective tax planning may call for the opposite of typical tax-planning strategies. If income tax rates rise in 2009, it could be prudent to accelerate income into the 2008 tax year and defer deductions until 2009.

Individual income tax situations of owners of businesses that are operated as C corporations are not as directly affected by the company's year-end tax strategies as are owners of pass-through businesses. However, taxes saved by a C corporation's successful tax planning result in more capital available for the everyday use of the business, for expansion, or for dividend payments. The 2003 reductions in the long-term capital gain and qualified dividend tax rates, and several more recent changes to the S corporation rules, make it imperative for C corporation owners to reevaluate whether to elect to operate as a S corporation. In many cases, the current tax regime makes it more attractive to elect to be an S corporation by virtually eliminating the prior C corporation federal tax-rate advantage on ordinary income. In addition, S corporations provide a substantial tax-rate advantage for both long-term capital gains and qualified dividends, because C corporations do not enjoy the favorable tax rates on this type of income that apply to individuals. S corporations can pass through capital gains and dividends to shareholders undiminished by entity-level taxation. Many of the factors that should be considered in making the decision to convert to an S corporation are contained in the material that follows.

Increased Section 179 Expense Election

Business owners may elect to treat the cost of qualifying new property as an expense rather than capitalizing and depreciating the cost over the property's depreciable life. For 2008, the maximum amount of Section 179 expense was increased under the Economic Stimulus Act of 2008, effective for tax years beginning in 2008. The new maximum deduction amount is $250,000. The new threshold for the phaseout of the Section 179 expense is $800,000 of new property additions in 2008.

The Section 179 expense is scheduled to decrease in 2009 to the amounts set forth under the Small Business and Work Opportunity Tax Act of 2007. For 2009 and 2010, the maximum amount of Section 179 deduction is $125,000 of new qualifying property and the threshold for the phaseout of the deduction is $500,000. Both the 2009 and 2010 amounts will be indexed for inflation.

Off-the-shelf computer software placed in service before 2011 also qualifies for the Section 179 expensing election.

Businesses may revoke the expensing election on amended tax returns without needing IRS consent. This can enable businesses to retroactively move expensing deductions among tax years for tax-planning purposes to achieve the maximum tax benefit. If tax rates increase in 2009, then businesses may decide to amend their 2008 tax returns to revoke the section 179 expensing election and create more depreciation deductions in 2009 and thereafter. This decision will depend on the size of any tax rate increase and the effective date of the rate increase. Of course, the decision to forgo the expensing election in favor of increased depreciation deductions (at higher marginal tax rates) in the future will have to be weighed against the lost investment earnings produced from receiving an immediate tax benefit if the property is expensed. (See the example in the next section, "Increased Bonus Depreciation.")

While tax considerations are not paramount in a business's decision to purchase equipment, they are a factor and are more important in a year with an increased Section 179 expensing election.

To curb a perceived abuse of the Section 179 expensing election, the American Jobs Creation Act of 2004 limited the expensing of a heavy (more than 6,000 pounds) truck or sports utility vehicle to $25,000 with the balance being depreciated over a five-year recovery period.

Increased Bonus Depreciation

Under the Economic Stimulus Act of 2008, a special 50 percent first-year depreciation allowance, referred to as bonus depreciation, may be claimed for certain property acquired after December 31, 2007, and placed into service before January 1, 2009.

To be eligible to claim bonus depreciation, the property must be one of four types:

1. Eligible for the modified accelerated cost recovery system (MACRS) with a depreciation period of 20 years or less.
2. Water utility property.
3. Off-the-shelf computer software.
4. Qualified leasehold improvement property.

The combination of bonus deprecation, Section 179 expensing, and regular depreciation can enable a small business to deduct all or a significant portion of the cost of new property additions in 2008.

Example

If a business acquires new five-year MACRS property costing $500,000 that qualifies for Section 179 expensing and the 50 percent bonus depreciation allowance, then $250,000 of the cost could be expensed immediately under Section 179, and the remaining $250,000 of adjusted cost basis could be available for the 50 percent bonus depreciation allowance. This would enable an additional $125,000 to be deducted in 2008. The taxpayer is also allowed to take regular depreciation deductions on the remaining $125,000 of adjusted cost basis during the year. In total, the taxpayer could deduct in 2008 a total of $400,000 ($250,000 + $125,000 + $25,000) of the $500,000 cost of new property. The new law also raises the Internal Revenue Code Section 280F limitations on luxury auto depreciation. The first-year limit on depreciation for passenger automobiles placed in service in 2008 is projected to be $2,960 for passenger vehicles and $3,160 for vans and trucks. The new law increases this limit to $8,000 if bonus depreciation is claimed for a qualifying vehicle placed in service in 2008. The maximum first-year depreciation deduction with bonus depreciation cannot exceed $10,960 for passenger vehicles and $11,160 for vans or trucks.

Retirement Plans

If this is the year that a business has decided to start a qualified retirement plan, the plan must be formally established by year-end for contributions to be deductible this year. Contributions (up to the limits spelled out in Chapter 4) are deductible in 2008 if made by the extended tax return due date for the 2008 tax return.

Businesses that miss the year-end deadline can still establish and make deductible contributions to a simplified employee pension (SEP) plan. The SEP is not required to be formed until the extended tax return due date of the year in which the SEP is effective. However, SEPs have stricter coverage requirements than regular qualified plans and generally are not as flexible or customizable. In addition, unlike other retirement plans, SEPs cannot be set up as defined benefit pension plans, so they are less suitable for quickly funding a large retirement benefit for an older owner/employee.

> **Caution**
> Those who plan to set up retirement plans should immediately consult a retirement planning specialist. It takes time and expertise to properly address all of the required formalities.

Bonuses and Deferred Compensation

A business using the accrual, rather than cash, method of accounting can take a current deduction for bonuses that it declares this year, but that are actually paid within the first two and one-half months of the following year. The business gets an accelerated deduction for the bonus that has not been paid as of year-end, and the employee-recipient gets to defer recognizing the income until the following year when the bonus is actually paid. However, this planning opportunity is not available for bonuses paid to majority shareholders or to owners with any interest in an S corporation, a partnership, or a personal service corporation. Compensation that is accrued but not paid for more than two and one-half months after the year-end is subject to different rules. In that case, the business's deduction is delayed until the year that the compensation is paid to the employee. Year-end is usually a good time to consider whether to declare bonuses to key employees before or after December 31. However, if income tax rates increase in 2009, then it may not make sense to generate deductions at a lower tax rate in 2008 and receive income taxed at a higher tax rate in 2009 and thereafter.

Year-end is also a good time to consider whether to establish a deferred compensation plan for key employees. See the discussion of deferred compensation on page 278. The likelihood of higher tax rates in the future must also be considered in evaluating the tax advantages of deferring compensation to later years.

Income Deferral or Acceleration

Generally, a business, like an individual, will want to defer income and accelerate deductions where possible, to reduce current taxes and defer tax liabilities into the following year. For businesses on the accrual method of accounting, this may not be as easy to do as it is for cash-method individuals. However, even for accrual-method businesses, certain recurring items may be currently deducted despite the fact that they will not be paid until the following year. These accelerated tax deductions defer the taxation of income until the following year.

There may be times when it is better for a business to reverse the standard strategy and accelerate income into the current year. That is the case, for example, where the business is in a lower tax bracket in the current year than it expects to be in for the following year. This may be the case for 2008 if the new president and Congress increase income tax rates in 2009. Since taxpayers will know the election results for the next president and Congress in November of 2008, there should be time for calendar-year taxpayers to determine and pursue the appropriate tax strategy after the election.

Taxation of C Corporations

Although corporate income tax rates are graduated, they do not increase in proportion to corporate taxable income. Instead, the first $50,000 is taxed at 15 percent; the next $25,000 is taxed at 25 percent; and the $25,000 after that is taxed at 34 percent. Corporate taxable income between $100,000 and $335,000 is taxed at 39 percent to take back the benefit of the 15 percent and the 25 percent tax brackets. Between $335,000 and $10 million, the marginal tax rate drops back to 34 percent. The effect of this is that C corporations with taxable income between $335,000 and $10 million are taxed at a flat tax rate of 34 percent.

For taxable income between $10 million and $15 million, the corporate tax rate goes up to 35 percent, and there is another bubble tax rate of 38 percent between $15 million and $18.33 million to recover the benefit of the 34 percent tax rate. Corporations with taxable income above $18.33 million are taxed at a flat 35 percent tax rate.

While all of this seems rather complex, it does present year-end tax-planning and tax-saving strategies for C corporations in some situations—especially those that are below either the 39 percent or the 38 percent tax-rate bubbles this year and that expect earnings to increase next year and push them into a higher tax rate. If possible, these companies should try to accelerate enough income or defer enough deductions to take advantage of the lower tax-rate bracket in the current year. One way to achieve this result may be through electing lower tax-depreciation deductions on certain property additions in 2008.

The 2004 Tax Act provided for a phased-in deduction related to domestic production activity (i.e., manufacturing activity). The tax deduction is 3 percent of the lesser of taxable income or the domestic production activity income in years 2005 and 2006;

6 percent in the years 2007, 2008, and 2009; and 9 percent for years thereafter. This deduction was enacted in lieu of lowering the top corporate income tax rate from 35 percent to 32 percent. However, when this deduction is fully phased in after 2009 for a U.S. manufacturer, the effective tax rate will be approximately 32 percent.

Alternative Minimum Tax Planning

Smaller C corporations are generally exempt from the alternative minimum tax (AMT) if their average annual gross receipts for the previous three-year period are $7.5 million or less. New corporations are exempt for their first year, but if they average more than $5 million of annual gross receipts for the first three-year period, they are subject to the AMT after the first year. The AMT is a complicated tax that requires many items to be refigured in a way that often reduces the tax benefit from many tax deductions. If a corporation's average annual gross receipts for the current three-year period are approaching the $7.5 million threshold, it should consider the impact of becoming subject to the AMT. If the current-year increase in gross receipts is an aberration, the company may be better off avoiding AMT liability if possible. If the company is growing rapidly and expects to be subject to the AMT in the future, it still may benefit the company to hold off for another year before crossing the average gross receipts threshold.

For businesses that are operated as flow-through entities (e.g., partnerships and S corporations), the AMT aspects of the business are reported on the personal tax returns of the business owners. This often causes the business owners to be subject to AMT. In these situations, it is important to recognize the AMT impact on the business owners in a timely manner to be able to pursue appropriate tax planning for the owners. It may be advantageous for the business and/or the owner to accelerate income and/or defer deductions in such a situation to take advantage of the lower marginal tax rate under the AMT. These situations clearly require coordination between the tax aspects of the business and the tax aspects of the other items impacting the business owner's personal tax returns.

Accounting Method Changes

An important planning opportunity involves reviewing and possibly changing accounting methods. In addition to a business's overall method of accounting (cash basis versus accrual method), the tax law generally considers the treatment of each individual item of income and deduction recognition as a method of accounting that must be applied consistently. Generally, you cannot change the way you recognize an item of income or deduction without the IRS's permission. However, in recent years, the IRS has announced numerous accounting methods that may be changed automatically by taxpayers (without requiring IRS permission). These automatic method changes provide potent tax-planning opportunities to manipulate taxable income to the taxpayer's advantage.

> ### Observation
> It is widely believed that in the near future the last-in first-out (LIFO) method of accounting for inventories will no longer be permitted for tax purposes. If a taxpayer currently using the LIFO method concludes that 2008 is a good year to accelerate income, then switching from the LIFO method to another method may be advantageous.

Personal Holding Company Tax

To prevent high-bracket individuals from using closely held C corporations to shelter investment income and avoid the shareholder-level tax on dividend income, C corporations were subject to a tax at the top individual tax rate on their undistributed personal holding company (PHC) income. To be subject to this

PHC tax, more than half of a corporation's stock must be owned by five individuals or fewer, and 60 percent of the corporation's income must be PHC income—passive types of income (e.g., rents, royalties, interest, and dividends).

Corporations near the PHC threshold of 60 percent are advised to try to avoid additional PHC income or to increase non-PHC business income to keep the PHC income percentage below 60 percent.

The Jobs and Growth Tax Relief Reconciliation Act of 2003 reduced the PHC tax rate to 15 percent—the same tax rate that applies to qualified dividend income. Corporations potentially subject to the PHC tax can eliminate the tax by declaring a dividend equal to the amount of PHC income while the tax rate on qualified dividends is only 15 percent.

Succession Planning

In addition to income tax planning, year-end is a good time for business owners to contemplate the eventual transfer of their business, whether to family members, other shareholders, key employees, or a third party. Owners must take into account the financial strength of the business; the financial position of a buyer; available sources of financing, collateral, and financial guarantees; tax consequences to both parties; and cash flow issues. The timing of a transfer and the control are also critical considerations. To manage these complex issues, owners should engage advisors who can help them make effective and timely decisions, and give them a detailed understanding of the sale process. Early planning and a sound grasp of objectives are particularly important in family-owned organizations where agreement about family roles contributes to a smooth transition. There are many things to consider, and each closely held business should have a written succession plan that considers alternatives and reflects the forward thinking that increases the likelihood of successful succession.

A business owner who is considering selling the business may want to complete the sale transaction in 2008 to secure the 15 percent capital gains tax rate and the top ordinary tax rate of 35 percent. Since there is a real possibility that tax rates could increase in the near future, the seller's net after-tax proceeds from completing a sale in 2008 could be substantially more than if the deal is delayed into 2009 or a later year.

Buy-Sell Agreements

Every business with more than one owner should consider using a buy-sell agreement to describe the terms and the process for ensuring an orderly transfer of the business ownership interests in the event of an owner's desire to sell, or in case of the disability, retirement, or death of an owner. There are two categories of buy-sell agreements: redemption agreements and cross-purchase agreements. Occasionally, a hybrid of the two types is employed. Under a redemption agreement, the business entity purchases the selling owner's ownership interests using its cash or debt. In a cross-purchase arrangement, the selling owner sells ownership interests to other owners, not the business entity. This gives the buying owner(s) an increase in the tax basis of the purchased ownership interests equal to the purchase price, and this can reduce tax in the future when the ownership interests are subsequently sold. In many cases, there is not enough cash either at the entity level or held by other owners to fund the entire purchase. Often, life insurance that is held individually or by a partnership or trust is used to fund the cross-purchase portion of a buyout, with the balance funded by the business entity through a redemption.

Deferred Compensation Elections

This strategy refers to income that is deferred until a future point in time. Typically, a key employee is offered the opportunity to elect (before compensation is earned) to defer a portion of compensation, and a deferred compensation obligation is established to recognize the fact that this deferred compensation will be paid out at a later date. Paying a retiring owner deferred compensation is advantageous to a buyer of the business because the deferred compensation payments are tax deductible, whereas payments for the retiring owner's stock are not deductible. However, the seller usually prefers payment for his or her stock, the gains from which can be subject to favorable capital gains tax rates. In an environment in which tax rates may be increasing, one has to be cautious about deferring income from a lower-tax year into a higher-tax year.

Covenant Not to Compete

A covenant not to compete is a legal contract that prohibits (for a specific period) a seller from competing with the buyer on the business activities being acquired from the seller. A buyer will frequently offer a portion of the purchase consideration in exchange for the seller signing such a restrictive covenant. This form of consideration is usually deductible to the buyer over a 15-year period, but it is usually taxed as ordinary income to the seller in the year the payments are received.

Earn-Out (Contingent Sale Price)

This element of an acquisition refers to a transaction where the purchase price paid is not fixed, but instead fluctuates based on the future performance of the acquired entity. Typically, the actual price is tied to revenue growth or future profitability over a period ranging from one to five years after the acquisition.

Importance of Early Planning

Often, people find it difficult to discuss issues relating to illness, retirement, or death. Business owners who avoid addressing these eventualities, however, may make succession planning a low priority, putting family members, employees, and others at considerable financial risk. Lack of time is another often-cited factor; but the reality is that a business owner's day-to-day activities are seldom more important than planning for the future success of the business. The importance of early planning cannot be overstated, because it helps owners meet their stated objectives and facilitate the continuity of their businesses, to the benefit of the owners, their families, employees, customers, and vendors.

From a financial perspective, it is often beneficial to transfer some or all of an enterprise that is on the brink of rapid growth in value, and some owners attempt to time their transitions accordingly. Although at this stage a business owner may have no clear picture of the future control and management of the business, this should not deter the owner from acting to save wealth transfer taxes. The practical truth is that there will never be an absolutely clear picture of future control and management. An effective succession plan needs considerable flexibility to deal with changing circumstances and usually involves several different types of trusts or other vehicles to maintain some degree of control for the owner. The important thing is not to delay, but instead to plan as early in the game as possible.

Do Not Wait to Plan

Do not postpone planning; instead consider:

- Early planning produces reduced estate taxes.
- Early planning produces increased value for the next generation.
- Succession plans with longer time horizons are inherently more flexible and usually have better outcomes.
- Conflicting aspirations within a family regarding the details and timing of the business transition may be more easily addressed.

International Financial Reporting Standards

The global economy has created the need for a set of financial reporting rules that are consistently applied throughout the world. As a result, a new set of accounting rules called the International Financial Reporting Standards (IFRS) has been approved by financial accounting rule makers in the United States and many other countries. It is thought that the new IFRS rules will eventually replace the generally accepted accounting principles (GAAP) that currently govern the preparation of financial statements for most companies in the United States. It is not too early for businesses to begin to understand the impact that the conversion from GAAP to IFRS will have on their financial statements.

C Corporation versus S Corporation Comparison

With qualified dividends and long-term capital gains taxed at 15 percent, the decision to conduct business as a C corporation or an S corporation should be reevaluated. In many cases, it may be more advantageous to elect to be taxed as an S corporation.

All income of a C corporation, including qualified dividends and capital gains, is subject to tax at the marginal tax rate of the corporation; there is no preferential tax rate for dividends and capital gains. S corporations provide a substantial tax rate advantage for both long-term capital gains and qualified dividends, because S corporations can pass through the taxation of capital gains and dividends to shareholders. In addition, this income is undiminished by entity-level taxation. Ultimately, the conclusion on whether to convert to S corporation status will be dependent on one or more of these factors:

- *The combined federal and state income tax rates that will be applied to income:* Recent reductions of federal tax rates should cause businesses to reevaluate their choice of business entity, and AMT and state income taxes need to be factored into the analysis.

- *Whether income will be currently distributed:* If the business owners desire significant distributions of income, S corporations have the advantage of avoiding double taxation of the distributed income; however, the 15 percent tax rate on qualified dividends has reduced this advantage.
- *Losses from an S corporation can flow through to the shareholders:* This remains a significant advantage of S corporations over C corporations for businesses experiencing losses.
- *The shareholder ownership restrictions imposed on S corporations (e.g., shareholder limitations, one class of stock):* While S corporations may have tax advantages over C corporations, many businesses are unable to qualify for S corporation status. The 2004 Tax Act increased the maximum number of allowable S corporation shareholders from 75 to 100, and all members of one family (within six generations) may be treated as one shareholder for shareholder counting purposes. Serious consideration should be given to converting to S corporation status (i.e., redeem shares, eliminate multiple classes of stock) before year-end because S corporation elections can be effective only on the first day of a corporation's tax year, and the corporation must be eligible to make the election on that day.
- *The amount of last in, first out (LIFO) recapture from inventories on conversion to S status:* With the relatively low inflation rates recently, recapturing the LIFO reserve on conversion to S corporation status may not be a significant cost. In addition, there is a widely held belief that the LIFO method will be not be permitted for tax purposes in the near future.
- *Whether the business is expected to be sold before the death of the major shareholders:* Generally, buyers prefer to buy business assets as opposed to the stock of an ongoing

business. By operating as an S corporation, the business owners can sell the business assets and distribute the sale proceeds with only one level of tax. The owners of a C corporation generally pay two levels of tax (a corporate tax on the asset sale and a shareholder tax—now reduced to 15 percent—on the distributed sale proceeds). Alternatively, the C corporation owner(s) only want to sell stock to incur a single level of tax. Because the buyer wants to purchase assets, the C corporation seller of stock suffers a reduction in the purchase price that a buyer is willing to pay for the stock.

- *Whether the tax on built-in gains is likely to apply:* When a C corporation converts to S corporation status, the S corporation is subject to a corporate-level tax on any assets sold during its first 10 years as an S corporation. This tax is imposed only on the amount of gain that is present in the sold asset as of the first day as an S corporation. Thus, the post–C corporation appreciation of the assets escapes the built-in gain tax. In evaluating whether to make an S corporation election, it will be important to analyze, and document, the built-in gain at the time of the S election.

S corporations with C corporation earnings and profits generally have the ability under the current tax law to purge themselves of the C corporation earnings and profits at a 15 percent tax cost to the shareholders. This may enable the S corporation to avoid the tax on excess passive income and termination of the S election from excess passive income in three consecutive tax years. This strategy may be appropriate in 2010, right before the reduced tax rates are set to expire under the sunset provision of the current tax law. Alternatively, if tax rates are increased before the tax rates sunset in 2011, this strategy may be appropriate as early as the end of 2008. A 2007 Tax Act change eliminated capital gains from sales or exchanges of stock or securities as an item of passive investment income of an S corporation for purposes of the tax on excess passive investment income.

C corporations with large amounts of dividend and long-term capital gain income will have a significant reason to try to convert to S corporation status if possible. The maximum tax rate differential on this income is considerable (35 percent for C corporations versus 15 percent for S corporations).

■ ■ ■

Chapter 16 moves away from planning suggestions and techniques. It takes a close-up view of basic tax concepts. Understanding these commonly used words and phrases is critical to making the best use of the tax-planning strategies and tools discussed in this book.

A Nuts-and-Bolts Review

Chapter 16

Fundamental Tax Concepts

Tax planning is a difficult, time-consuming activity at best. After reading this book, you have gathered a great deal of information about effective tax planning. To assist you with that task, this chapter provides helpful definitions and illustrations of key tax terms and concepts. These items, which are really a combination of glossary, encyclopedia, and frequently asked questions, constitute an essential reference source for you.

Earlier chapters have described actions you may take at the end of the year to reduce your tax bill. Near the conclusion of this chapter, a checklist of valuable suggestions offers steps you can take in January as part of your tax minimization program.

Gross Income

The Internal Revenue Code casts a very broad net in defining gross income—it consists of basically every type of income you receive, unless Congress has provided a specific exemption excluding that item from gross income.

Common examples of items included in gross income are wages and bonuses, taxable interest, dividends, state tax refunds, alimony, business income, capital gains, traditional individual retirement account (IRA) distributions, taxable pensions and annuities, rental real estate income, partnership and S corporation income, unemployment compensation, taxable Social Security benefits, and net operating loss (NOL) carryovers.

There are some items that are specifically excluded from gross income and are therefore not subject to tax. These include, for example, certain death benefits on life insurance policies, gifts and inheritances received, tax-exempt interest, qualified scholarships, federal tax refunds, and certain fringe benefits.

Adjusted Gross Income

Adjusted gross income (AGI) is your gross income less certain above-the-line deductions (deductions taken above the AGI line of your tax return), including:

- Deductible IRA contributions (see Chapter 4).
- Health savings account contributions.
- Unreimbursed employment-related moving expenses (see Chapter 12).
- One-half of self-employment tax.
- Fully 100 percent of health insurance premiums paid by self-employed individuals (see Chapter 12).
- Keogh and simplified employee pension (SEP) contributions for self-employed individuals (see Chapter 4).
- Penalties on early withdrawals of savings.
- Student loan interest.
- Alimony paid (not child support).

It is important to correctly calculate your AGI, because this amount serves as a threshold to determine numerous limitations on or eligibility for certain deductions and credits. For example, your AGI affects the extent to which you can deduct medical expenses, casualty and theft losses, charitable contributions, and other miscellaneous items. Your ability to benefit from some additional itemized deductions, personal and dependent exemptions, and some credits may be reduced or eliminated as AGI levels increase.

> **Observation**
> Starting in 2006, the phaseouts of itemized deductions and personal and dependent exemptions for high-income taxpayers were reduced. Taxpayers who were subject to these phaseouts now receive more of the benefit of these deductions and exemptions.

Modified Adjusted Gross Income

As the name implies, modified adjusted gross income (MAGI) is simply your AGI modified for certain items of excluded income, or eliminating certain deductions, or both. A number of tax breaks are reduced or eliminated as MAGI exceeds certain levels. These include the adoption credit, the exclusion for employer-provided adoption assistance, the exclusion for interest on savings bonds used for higher education, IRA deductions, Coverdell Education Savings Accounts, Roth IRAs, higher education tax credits, the child credit, and the student loan interest deduction.

Modified AGI is generally higher than AGI because various deductions that normally reduce AGI are disallowed in calculating MAGI.

Itemized or Standard Deductions

To further reduce your tax liability, you will subtract from your AGI either your standard deduction or your itemized deductions, whichever provides the greater benefit.

Your standard deduction is a certain dollar amount based on your filing status.

Your itemized deductions commonly include such things as charitable contributions, real estate property tax, home mortgage interest, investment interest expense, state and local income tax, and certain medical expenses.

> ### Observation
>
> The Tax Relief and Health Care Act of 2006 extended through tax year 2007 the opportunity to deduct actual state and local sales tax paid. Legislation has not yet been passed extending this provision to tax year 2008. However, it is expected that lawmakers will include this in legislation by year-end. Currently, this deduction is available only if sales tax paid exceeds state income tax payments. For those taxpayers residing in a state without an income tax, consider accelerating into 2008 any major purchases that would generate large amounts of sales tax, provided new tax legislation is passed by year-end that mirrors previous law. Keep in mind that sales tax is not deductible for alternative minimum tax (AMT) purposes.

The total of your allowable itemized deductions is reduced if your AGI exceeds a specified dollar amount ($159,950 for 2008 for married individuals filing joint returns, and projected to increase to $166,800 for 2009). For 2008 and 2009, the limitation is 1 percent of your AGI above the applicable threshold, not exceeding 80 percent of your itemized deductions, regardless of your income level. Further, the limitations do not affect certain itemized deductions such as medical expenses, casualty losses, and investment interest expense.

Personal and Dependent Exemptions

From your AGI, you also subtract $3,500 for yourself and each dependent you may claim. As with itemized deductions, the deduction for personal exemptions is reduced if your AGI exceeds a specified dollar amount ($239,950 in 2008 for married individuals filing joint returns).

Marital Status

Your marital status on the last day of the year determines your filing status, which in turn impacts your applicable tax-rate schedule used to compute tax and other tax rules. If you are single for most of the year, but marry on December 31, the tax law treats you as married for the entire year.

Changes in marital status can affect year-end planning. Two individuals with substantial incomes who plan to get married in 2009 might benefit from accelerating income into 2008 to avoid the so-called marriage penalty, which has been reduced, but not eliminated (see pages 338 and 339).

Widows and widowers are allowed to file a joint return with their deceased spouse in the year of the spouse's death and to use joint return tax rates for up to two additional years if they have a qualifying dependent. Surviving spouses who may be eligible to use the more favorable married filing jointly rates in 2008, but not in 2009, could benefit from accelerating income into the earlier year (see Table 16.1).

A Tax Credit or a Deduction

Tax credits are more valuable than tax deductions because they lower your tax liability dollar for dollar. A $100 tax credit reduces your taxes by a full $100. Examples of tax credits are the Helping Outstanding Pupils Educationally (HOPE) scholarship and lifetime learning tax credits, the child credit, the child-care and dependent-care credits, the adoption credit, the minimum tax credit, and the foreign tax credit.

A tax deduction produces less of a tax benefit than a credit because it reduces your taxes by the amount of your deduction *multiplied by your marginal tax rate.* The lower your tax rate, the smaller your tax benefit from a deduction. For example, if you are

Table 16.1 2008 and 2009* Tax Rates

	2008 Taxable Income ($)	2008 Tax ($)	Marginal Tax (%)	2009 Taxable Income ($)	2009 Tax ($)	Marginal Tax (%)	2009 Effective Tax Rate (%)
Single Individuals	0	0	10	0	0	10	0
	8,025	803	15	8,350	835	15	10.0
	32,550	4,481	25	33,950	4,675	25	13.8
	78,850	16,056	28	82,250	16,750	28	20.4
	164,550	40,052	33	171,550	41,754	33	24.3
	Over 357,700	103,792	35	Over 372,950	108,216	35	29.0
Married Filing Jointly	0	0	10	0	0	10	0
	16,050	1,605	15	16,700	1,670	15	10.0
	65,100	8,963	25	67,900	9,350	25	13.8
	131,450	25,551	28	137,050	26,637	28	19.4
	200,300	44,829	33	208,850	46,741	33	22.4
	Over 357,700	96,771	35	Over 372,950	100,894	35	27.0

*2009 numbers are CCH projections for the 2009 tax year and have not been confirmed by the Internal Revenue Service.

332

Fundamental Tax Concepts 333

in the 35 percent marginal tax-rate bracket, a $100 tax deduction lowers your taxes by $35. In the 15 percent tax-rate bracket, that same $100 deduction reduces your taxes by only $15.

> ### *Observation*
>
> It is unwise to pursue tax deductions by spending money on deductible items merely to cut your tax bill. You have to spend more money than you will save in taxes. Keep in mind that a tax deduction is of real value only when the taxes you save reduce the effective cost of an expenditure that you would be inclined to make even if it were not deductible.

> ### *Observation*
>
> There are a number of credits that the environmentally conscious taxpayer can now benefit from.
>
> There are four motor vehicle tax credits that are available to taxpayers both personally and through business operations. Hybrid vehicle tax credits are allowed when purchasing qualified hybrid motor vehicles, advanced lean-burn technology motor vehicles, qualified fuel-cell motor vehicles, and qualified alternative-fuel motor vehicles. The hybrid vehicle credits will be allowed based on the number of hybrids sold during the tax year and the information the auto manufacturer supplies to the IRS.
>
> There are also energy tax credits that are offered to homeowners for energy-efficiency improvements made to their personal residence. Vacation home and rental property improvements do not qualify for these credits. It is important to note that these environmentally friendly credits are often permitted for state income tax purposes and, in some cases, energy-efficiency improvements may result in credits or rebates from the taxpayer's utility company.

Taxable Income

Taxable income is the amount used to determine your tax liability by applying the appropriate tax rate. Taxable income is calculated by adding your income from all sources and subtracting allowable deductions and exemptions:

Taxable Income Computation (for a single taxpayer with one exemption)	
Gross Income	
Wages	$350,000
Interest	26,000
Business income and rental real estate income	5,000
Other income	4,500
Gross income	$385,500
Adjustments to Income	
Moving expenses	(3,500)
Alimony	(60,000)
Total adjustments to income	$(63,500)
Adjusted gross income (AGI)	$322,000
Itemized deductions (after phaseout is applied)	(6,200)
Exemption (after phaseout is applied)	(2,333)
Taxable income	$313,467

Marginal and Effective Tax Rates

Your marginal tax rate is the tax rate imposed on your next dollar of income. By contrast, your effective tax rate is the average tax rate on all of your income. For example, assume that you are married, filing a joint return, and receive

Taxable income	$360,000
Bonus	$ 50,000
Total taxable income	$410,000

Because you are in the 35 percent tax-rate bracket, based on your taxable income before including the bonus payment, the bonus is taxed at 35 percent. You would pay $17,500 ($50,000 × 35 percent) in taxes on that bonus. Therefore, your *marginal* tax rate is 35 percent. For married individuals filing a joint return, the tax on $410,000 of taxable income is $115,075. Therefore, your *effective* tax rate would be 28 percent ($115,075/$410,000).

Caution

Your marginal tax rate might not determine the tax benefit of a deductible expense if your income is above $159,950 for 2008, because at that income level you begin losing some of the benefit of your itemized deductions.

Observation

The Economic Growth and Tax Relief Reconciliation Act of 2001 eliminated the phaseouts of itemized deductions and personal exemptions over time, beginning in 2006. For 2008 and 2009, the phaseouts are only a percentage of what they would have been under the old law. Thus, the phaseout on itemized deductions has declined to 1 percent in 2008 and 2009 for taxpayers above the threshold amount of AGI. Likewise, the phaseout for personal exemptions has been similarly reduced from the prior calculation.

336   A Nuts-and-Bolts Review

Your marginal tax rate may also determine the tax benefit of a deductible expense. For example, if you were in the 28 percent tax-rate bracket and made a $5,000 charitable donation that you claimed as an itemized deduction, you would reduce your taxable income by $5,000, saving $1,400 in tax dollars ($5,000 × 28 percent).

Your actual marginal tax rate can be higher than the 35 percent maximum statutory tax rate due to the itemized deduction and personal exemption phaseout.

2008 Standard Deductions and Personal Exemptions				
Single	Married Filing Jointly	Married Filing Separately	Head of Household
Standard Deductions				
Regular standard deduction				
$5,450	$10,900	$5,450	$8,000
Kiddie tax deduction				
$900	$900	$900	$900
Itemized Deduction Phaseout				
Deductions reduced for AGI exceeding				
$159,950	$159,950	$79,975	$159,950
Personal Exemption				
Each person				
$3,500	$3,500	$3,500	$3,500
Personal Exemption Phaseout				
Exemptions reduced for AGI exceeding				
$159,950	$239,950	$119,975	$199,950

2009 Standard Deductions and Personal Exemptions*

	Single	Married Filing Jointly	Married Filing Separately	Head of Household
Standard Deductions				
Regular standard deduction				
	$5,700	$11,400	$5,700	$8,350
Kiddie tax deduction				
	$950	$950	$950	$950
Itemized Deduction Phaseout				
Deductions reduced for AGI exceeding				
	$166,800	$166,800	$83,400	$166,800
Personal Exemption				
Each person				
	$3,650	$3,650	$3,650	$3,650
Personal Exemption Phaseout				
Exemptions reduced for AGI exceeding				
	$166,800	$250,200	$125,100	$208,500

*Unofficial projections as of September 24, 2007.

Social Security Taxes and Benefits

If you are an employee, depending on your salary level, all or part of your earnings are subject to a 7.65 percent payroll tax (6.2 percent for Social Security and 1.45 percent for Medicare). Your employer also pays the same payroll tax on your earnings to the government. If instead you are self-employed, you pay both halves of this payroll tax—resulting in a 15.3 percent self-employment tax on all or part of your net self-employment earnings (12.4 percent for Social Security and 2.9 percent for Medicare). Self-employed individuals are entitled to deduct one-half of their self-employment tax as an above-the-line deduction. The maximum annual earnings subject to the Social Security portion of the tax is $102,000 for 2008 and is projected to be approximately $106,000 for 2009. There is no limit on the amount of earnings subject to the Medicare portion of the tax.

If you continue to work while collecting Social Security benefits and have not reached your full retirement age (e.g., 65 years and 6 months for those born in 1940), your benefits are reduced by $1 for every $2 that you earn above a specified amount. For 2008, that amount is $13,560 ($1,130 per month) and will increase annually. In the year you reach your full retirement age, you lose $1 of benefits for every $3 of earnings above $36,120 ($3,010 per month) in 2008, but only for months before your full retirement age. Once you have attained your full retirement age, earnings do not cause a reduction in your benefits.

If you work while collecting benefits, you also should consider that your earnings will be subject to income tax and payroll taxes, and these earnings also may cause some of your Social Security benefits to be subject to income tax. Specifically, if your AGI plus half of your Social Security benefits, plus your tax-exempt interest, equals more than $25,000 if you are single, or $32,000 if married filing jointly, half of the excess amount (up to 50 percent of your Social Security benefits) is taxable. If your specially figured income exceeds $34,000 if single, or $44,000 if married filing jointly, up to 85 percent of your Social Security benefits may be subject to income tax.

Marriage Penalty

The marriage penalty describes the additional income tax two individuals will pay under the married individual tax tables over what the combined tax would have been for them under the tax tables for single individuals. This additional tax burden results, in part, because the amount of income subject to higher marginal tax rates is greater for married couples than it is for two single individuals with the same total income. The marriage penalty has been eased somewhat by increasing the size of the 15 percent tax-rate bracket for married taxpayers to double that of singles, and by increasing the standard deduction for married taxpayers to double that of singles. Despite this, the marriage penalty still can be quite substantial for couples in the higher tax-rate brackets.

Some married couples may benefit by filing separately. For example, it may make sense to file separately if one spouse is in a lower tax bracket and has large medical bills. The AGI threshold limiting the deduction of these medical expenses would be lower, allowing a larger deduction.

> ### Observation
> It is important for married couples to analyze both methods (filing jointly or separately) before deciding what to do. Over the years, Congress has added penalty provisions to the tax code to discourage married people from filing separate returns. Therefore, filing separately may seem like a good idea for one reason or another but might result in higher taxes overall than if you file jointly.

Accountable Plan

Business expenses reimbursed by your employer may be included as income on your Form W-2 unless your employer reimburses under an accountable plan. An accountable plan requires documentation of all advances or reimbursed expenses and must require the return of any excess amounts. Expenses reimbursed under a nonaccountable plan must be included in your W-2 income. However, these expenses are deductible, as are unreimbursed employee business expenses, in the miscellaneous itemized deductions category, if you have receipts and other required substantiation.

> **Observation**
>
> A nonaccountable plan is not as good as it may at first sound, because miscellaneous itemized deductions can be claimed only to the extent that they total more than 2 percent of your AGI. For example, if your AGI is $100,000, your first $2,000 of miscellaneous expenses is not deductible. Likewise, this category of deductions is subject to the phaseout of itemized deductions for higher-income taxpayers. Finally, remember you would receive no tax benefit from the deduction of miscellaneous business expenses at all if you are subject to the AMT (see Chapter 14).

Tax Effects of Alimony

Alimony is included in the gross income of the person receiving it and is deductible by the person paying it.

> **Observation**
>
> Alimony is deducted above the line in arriving at AGI. Therefore, it can be claimed whether you itemize your deductions or take the standard deduction.

Payments to an ex-spouse are not treated as alimony for tax purposes if the spouses are still in the same household. It is also important to note that large decreases in the amount of alimony in the second and third years following a divorce trigger IRS concern that property settlement amounts, which are nondeductible, are being treated as alimony. There are guidelines on what payments under a divorce or separation agreement qualify as alimony for tax purposes. For example, making rent or mortgage payments for a spouse or ex-spouse may be deductible alimony, but the value of rent-free accommodations (e.g., allowing a spouse or former spouse to live without paying rent in a house you own) is not deductible. Finally, child support payments are not deductible (nor includable in income).

Social Security Taxes for Domestic Employees

You must withhold and pay Social Security tax for domestic employees earning more than $1,600 during 2008. This figure will be increased for future inflation. You may report this tax liability each year as a balance due on your Form 1040, using Schedule H. Be sure to increase your wage withholding or make quarterly estimated tax payments to pay the tax associated with these employees and avoid an estimated tax underpayment penalty.

You are not *required* to withhold federal income taxes on wages paid to domestic employees. However, you may wish to enter into a voluntary withholding arrangement with your domestic employees to help them manage their cash flow needed to meet their income tax obligations.

State income tax withholding requirements vary by state. You may also be required to pay federal unemployment tax and state unemployment tax contributions related to all or part of wages you pay to domestic employees.

Estimated Tax Payments

The government requires estimated tax payments because it prefers receiving tax payments throughout the year, rather than a lump sum at the end of the year. Individuals with a $1,000 or greater balance due on their tax returns may be subject to an estimated tax underpayment penalty, unless certain standards are met. An interest-based underpayment of estimated tax penalty is charged if no exception applies.

In general, three methods can be used to avoid an underpayment penalty:

1. Estimated tax payments and/or withholding are equal to at least 100 percent of the past year's total tax liability. However, if your AGI for the preceding year exceeded $150,000, your current year's estimated taxes must be 110 percent of your preceding year's total tax liability to fall within this safe harbor.
2. Ninety percent of your current year total tax liability is paid through estimated tax payments and/or withholding.
3. Ninety percent of annualized income tax (determined and paid each quarter based on actual income) is paid through estimated tax payments and/or withholding. This calculation is applied to each quarter using one-fourth of the total annualized amounts.

State governments also require individuals to make estimated tax payments throughout the year. However, estimated tax payment requirements vary from state to state.

Observation

The annualization method is generally best if a large part of your income is received in the latter part of the year. The annualization method rarely helps if a large part of your income is received in the first two quarters of the year.

Dates on Which You Must Pay Your Estimated Taxes	
April 15:	Based on actual income through March 31
June 15:	Based on actual income through May 31
September 15:	Based on actual income through August 31
January 15:	Based on actual income through December 31

Caution

If you use the "90 percent of current year's tax liability" method to calculate your estimated tax payments and recognize a large gain at year-end, you could be saddled with estimated tax penalties from a shortfall in earlier quarterly payments. If you have a choice as to when you recognize the gain, remember to consider estimated tax payment obligations.

Observation

If you fall behind in estimated tax installments at the beginning of a year, you may avoid or reduce an estimated tax penalty by having additional tax withheld from your wages during the latter part of the year. Absent an election to the contrary, wage withholding is treated as occurring evenly over the course of the year, so one-quarter of each dollar withheld is treated as having been withheld in each quarter of the year.

You can make additional payments at any time during the year to reduce or, in some cases, eliminate potential estimated tax underpayments. Be careful not to overpay, though, because the excess payment is essentially an interest-free loan to the government.

Observation

If you do not have wage withholding, you may be able to resolve an estimated tax underpayment by rolling over one IRA to another IRA account (within 60 days) and electing to have tax withheld that will be treated as paid ratably during the year even if the rollover was late in the year. However, if you take this approach, you must have other funds available to contribute to the new IRA account to make up for the tax withheld from the old IRA account. Otherwise, you risk causing unnecessary taxes and potential penalties.

Observation

Use of either the annualization method or the 90 percent of current year's tax liability method is a good idea if your year-over-year income decreases or increases from one year to the next by only a small amount. If you have a sizable increase in income, your prior year's tax (or 110 percent of your prior year's tax) will usually be less than 90 percent of the tax due on your current year's income. The prior-year-tax safe harbor method is also far simpler because you are making payments based on a known amount, not estimates.

January Tax Strategy Idea Checklist

Most tax guides present year-end planning ideas. We have decided to go one step further and suggest strategies that make sense to implement as early in the year as possible. Early adoption of the ideas presented in this list may make sense to maximize your opportunities to defer tax, generate income that is tax-free, and/or shift assets or income out of your estate.

- ☑ Contribute the maximum to an IRA for the previous tax year (see page 75).
- ☑ Contribute to a Coverdell Education Savings Account (see page 162).
- ☑ Contribute to a Section 529 plan, especially if your state allows an income tax deduction for doing so (see page 156).
- ☑ Make a contribution to your Keogh for the previous tax year (see page 70).
- ☑ Consider a Roth IRA conversion (see page 77).
- ☑ Think about making additional gifts if you have not fully used your lifetime gift tax exemption of $1 million (see page 195).
- ☑ Make deductible payments that were due in 2008 that you deferred to 2009 because of the AMT (see page 255).

- ☑ Purchase the annual maximum of Series I bonds (see page 284).
- ☑ Make $13,000 ($26,000 for married couples) annual exclusion gifts to desired beneficiaries (see page 195).
- ☑ Exercise incentive stock options, so that you have a full year to decide whether to sell the stock and be taxed as a nonqualified stock option (see page 51).

Conclusion

Some people enjoy tax planning, and other people would prefer to do almost anything else. What most of us consider a burden need not be a nightmare or a mystery. You can understand your tax options and intelligently choose those options best suited to your needs. This book is intended to be a liberating guide, grounded in our belief that every tax problem has at least one solution, if accurate and accessible information is available.

We have given you much to think about. Chapters 1 and 2 lay out the tax changes that affect taxpayers for 2008 and the changes scheduled to take place in 2010. The rest of the book provides a wide range of information and strategies and covers diverse areas, such as investments, retirement planning, home ownership, education savings, estate planning, and year-end tax planning. It also explains many fundamental tax concepts. The tax laws are incredibly complex. The Internal Revenue Code, along with its regulations and related cases, procedures, and rulings, can fill whole library rooms. As difficult as the law is, specific financial, family, and business situations can complicate things further, making tax planning a highly personal and individualized undertaking.

This book offers you a foundation—information and strategies that will make most individuals aware of ideas that may work for them and help them avoid costly tax mistakes. You should supplement this new foundation in taxes by considering how your personal situation plays into tax decisions. Tax planning never occurs in a vacuum, but is just a part, albeit an important part, of an overall financial planning process.

The tax strategies described in this book have been developed from the combined experience of many PricewaterhouseCoopers professionals. However, because every individual has unique circumstances, you should consult a tax professional before implementing the tax strategies described in this book or elsewhere.

ABOUT THE AUTHORS

Richard Kohan is a Personal Financial Services Partner in PricewaterhouseCoopers' Private Company Services practice in Boston. Rich's responsibilities include serving as the national strategic leader of the PCS focus on high-net-worth individual (HNWI) clients, as the tax leader of the Boston PCS tax practice, and as a trusted advisor to HNWI clients. He is the client engagement partner on several high-net-worth individual client relationships. As their personal trusted advisor, Rich addresses many tax, wealth management, and transfer matters for them and their families. In addition, Rich speaks on leading-edge financial planning topics such as executive wealth transfer techniques, investment strategies, employee benefits, stock options, and retirement planning. He leads seminars on various aspects of financial planning for PricewaterhouseCoopers professionals, as well as top executives in a number of Fortune 1000 companies. Rich received a BS in political science from Syracuse University, a JD from Western New England School of Law, and an LLM in tax from Boston University School of Law. Rich is a member of both the American and Connecticut bar associations.

About the Authors

Mark T. Nash is a Personal Financial Services Partner in PricewaterhouseCoopers' Private Company Services practice in Dallas. He has over 20 years of experience in the areas of individual, estate, gift, and trust tax compliance and planning. His professional practice deals extensively with high-net-worth individuals and family groups, closely held businesses, and corporate executives. His clients have included C-level executives at Fortune 500 companies as well as several individuals on the *Forbes* list of wealthiest Americans. Mark holds a BS in commerce from the University of Virginia, and master's degrees from Southwestern Baptist Theological Seminary and Oxford University. He is a member of the American Institute of Certified Public Accountants, the Texas Society of CPAs, and the Dallas Estate Planning Council. Mark is also a Certified Financial Planner and holds the AICPA Personal Financial Planning Specialist designation.

Brittney B. Saks is a Personal Financial Services Partner in PricewaterhouseCoopers' Private Company Services practice in Chicago. Brittney has provided income, trust and estate tax consulting and compliance services, which include compensation, investment, business succession, charitable giving, and retirement planning strategies, to business owners, corporate executives, and wealthy families for the past 17 years. Most of Brittney's time is spent working with high-net-worth family tax and financial planning issues, both from a consulting and from a compliance perspective. She is the lead engagement partner on some of the largest and most complex family office clients in Chicago. Brittney has received the Personal Financial Specialist designation and is a certified public accountant. She has a BS in accounting from the University of Illinois at Urbana–Champaign, where she graduated with highest honors, and a master's in taxation from DePaul University, where she received special distinction. She is a member of the AICPA (Tax and Personal Financial Planning Division) and the Illinois CPA Society. Brittney is currently serving a three-year term on the AICPA Executive Personal Financial Planning committee.

INDEX

A

Above-the-line deductions, 258, 272
Accountable plan, 339–340
Account-based health-care arrangements, 177–182
Accounting methods, 316
Accrual accounting, 316
Acquisition indebtedness, 136, 137
Adjusted gross income (AGI), 276, 328–329
 and charitable contributions, 230
 and miscellaneous deductions, 269–270
Adoption credit, 331
ADRs (American depositary receipts), 33
AGI (adjusted gross income), 276, 328–329
Aircraft, 223–224

Alimony, 340–341
Alternative minimum tax (AMT). See AMT (alternative minimum tax)
American depositary receipts (ADRs), 33
American Jobs Creation Act of 2004, 310
AMT (alternative minimum tax), 6–7, 46, 293–305
 computation, 296–297
 exemption for 2008, 304
 exemption phaseout, 12, 298
 and income deferral, 276
 income from long-term capital gains and qualified dividends, 34
 investments in private activity bonds, 47
 and ISOs, 50, 51
 and miscellaneous deductions, 37, 270

350 *Index*

AMT (alternative minimum tax) (*continued*)
  and ordinary income, 52
  planning for business owners, 315–316
  projected increases, 301
  and real estate taxes, 255
  and retirement planning, 60
  and state and local taxes, 254
  taxpayers subject to, 302–305
  tax-planning strategies, 302–305
  top ten causes of, 300
  understanding, 294–296
  year-end diagnosis, 248–249
Annualization method, 342
Annual renewal term life insurance, 94
Annuities, 284–285. *See also* specific types, i.e. Charitable remainder trust
  deferred, 285
  life, 103
  tax-deferred, 82–83
Antiques, 222
Appraisals, 222, 223, 225–227
Artwork, 222, 225
Asset replacement trusts, 119
Asset transfer, 287–291
At-risk rules, 43–44

B

Bank certificates, 282
Basis price, 37
Beneficiaries, 110–111
  of life insurance, 106–111
  and retirement plans, 88–89
Boats, 223–224
Bond premium, 47–48
Bonds, 45–46, 219–220
Bonus, year-end, 277, 312–313
Bonus depreciation, 310–311

Breadwinner insurance, 99–102
Bunching strategies, 253, 270
Business:
  closely held, 220
  home offices, 140–143
  interest deductions, 256–257
  and life insurance, 120–124
  property, 13–14
  year-end planning for owners, 307–324
Buy-sell agreements, 121–122, 318

C

Call option, 31
Capital gains, 22–24
  calculating income, 27
  on home sales, 147
  and income shifting, 170–171
  within IRAs, 74
  and retirement planning, 60
  shifting to family members, 287
  year-end checkup, 246–247
Capital losses, 28–30, 246–247, 263
Carryover basis, 17
Cars, used, 223–224, 262, 263
Cash basis accounting, 316
Cashless exercise, 52
Casualty losses, 268–269, 276
Catch-up contributions, 65, 66
C corporation, 308, 316–317
  compared with S corporation, 321–324
  stock, 32
  taxes, 314–315
Charitable contributions, 213–237
  deductions, 213–214, 230–233, 260–266
  and life insurance, 118–119, 266
  making, 214–216

quick guide to deductible and
non-deductible, 215–216
reduction of amount, 228–230
valuation of, 217–224
Charitable lead annuity trust
(CLAT), 204–205
Charitable lead trust (CLT),
204–205, 265
Charitable lead unitrust (CLUT),
204–205
Charitable remainder trust (CRT),
31, 82, 119, 203–204,
265–266
Children:
and Coverdell Education
Savings Account, 163–164
giving IRAs to, 80, 209
as owners of life insurance, 107
shifting capital gains income to,
25, 287
and U.S. savings bonds, 290
Child tax credit, 13, 331
Closed-end funds, 39
Closely held businesses, 220, 225
Clothing, used, 224
Collateral assignments, 125
Collectibles, 26, 224
Community foundations, 235
Community property, 114, 193
Company-owned life insurance
(COLI), 123
Compensation:
deferred, 243, 278–281,
312–313, 318–319
equity-based, 53–55
lump-sum, 277
Compounding, tax-deferred, 80
Contingent marital deduction, 113
Contingent sale price, 319
Corporate insider, 282
Corporation:
as owner of life insurance, 110

Cosmetic surgery, 260
Covenant not to compete, 319
Coverdell Education Savings
Accounts, 156, 162–164
Credit shelter, 193–194, 199–200
Cross-purchase agreements,
122–123, 318
CRT (charitable remainder trust),
31, 82
Crummey powers, 112
Custodial accounts, 288

D

Death benefit, 95
Death taxes, 194–195
Deductions:
accelerating, 243–244, 251–273
bunching, 253
deferring, 249
defining charitable, 213–214
goal of accelerating, 252
for interest paid on borrowed
money, 255–259
limitations on charitable
contributions, 230–233
standard, 253, 329–330,
336–337
student loan interest, 169
versus tax credit, 331, 333
Deductions, itemized. *See*
Itemized deductions
Deferral items, 299
Deferred compensation, 243,
278–281, 312–313, 318–319
Deferred giving, 265–266
Defined benefit pension plans,
67–69
Defined contribution plans, 62–67
Dependency deductions, 167
Dependent-care credits, 331

Depreciation, 146, 310–311
Disclaimers, 191
Discount, 47–48
Discounting, 220
Diversification, 55–56
Dividends, 282–283. *See also*
    Qualified dividends
  effect of reduced tax rates on, 207–208
  within IRAs, 74
  and life insurance, 96–97
  and short sales, 35–36
  taxes on, 33–38
Domestic employees, 341
Domestic production activity, 314–315
Donation value, 217–224
Donor-advised funds, 235–237, 261
Dynasty trust, 203

E

Earn-out, 319
Economic benefit regime, 126
Economic Growth and Tax Relief Reconciliation Act of 2001, 4, 8, 183–185, 335
Economic Stimulus Act of 2008, 5, 309, 310
Education:
  funding with Roth IRAs, 165
  loans, 169–170
  maximizing savings for, 155–176
  tax breaks for, 173–174, 290
  using life insurance to fund expenses, 116
Effective tax rates, 334–337
83(b) election, 54, 55
Employee split-dollar arrangement, 126

Employers:
  education assistance, 172–173
  retirement plans, 61–69, 84
Endorsement arrangement, 125
Energy tax credits, 333
Equity-based compensation, 53–55
Estate planning, 183–211
Estate tax, 8
  changes in 2010, 16–17
  exemptions, 185–186, 200
  and irrevocable life insurance trust, 111
  and life insurance, 103–106, 121
  maximizing savings, 199
  phaseout of, 24
  planning for phasedown and repeal, 190–192
  and qualified tuition programs, 162
  rates, 187–190
Exchange-traded funds (ETFs), 40–41
Exclusion items, 299
Exclusive-use requirement, 141
Exemptions, 12
  dependent, 330
  estate taxes, 200
  personal, 330, 336–337
  phaseout in 2010, 12, 23
Exercise and hold strategy, 48–49, 52
Exercise and sell transactions, 52
Expenses:
  allocation of trust expenses, 208–209
  deductible, 336
  interest, 36–38
  investment-related, 36–38
  moving, 271–272
  reimbursed, 339–340

tax-free qualified tuition plans, 158–162
unreimbursed, 261
Extraordinary dividends, 35

F

Fair market value, 187–188, 217, 218–219
Fair rental value, 140
Family trust, 193–194, 199–200
15 percent rate, 24–25
50 percent limitation, 232
Financial aid, federal, 171
First-time homebuyers tax credit, 5, 151–152
$500,000 exclusion, 145
529 tuition plans, 156–162, 196, 245
Flexible spending accounts, 181–182
Foreign tax credit, 36, 331
Foundations, private. *See* Private foundations
401(k) plans, 64–67, 286–287

G

Gems, 223
Generally accepted accounting principles (GAAP), 321
Generation-skipping tax, 16–17, 18, 113–114, 203
Gift tax, 143, 171, 184, 195–197
 changes in 2010, 17–18
 exemptions, 185–186
 paying now, 209–210
 and qualified tuition programs, 162
 rates, 187–190

Grandchildren:
 and Coverdell Education Savings Account, 163–164
 giving IRAs to, 80, 209
 as owners of life insurance, 107
 transferring assets to, 25
Grantor retained annuity trusts (GRATs), 105, 201–202
Gross income, 327–328
Group term insurance, 101

H

Health care. *See* Account-based health-care arrangements
Health reimbursement arrangements (HRAs), 180–181
Health savings account (HSA), 76, 177–180
HEART (Heroes Earnings Assistance and Relief Tax) Act, 5
Hedge fund life insurance, 115–116
Hedge funds, 42–43
Hedging strategies, 31
High-deductible health plan (HDHP), 177–180
High-income individuals, 60, 68, 167
Hobby collections, 224
Home equity loans, 137–138, 169
Home office, 141–143
Home ownership, 135–153
Home purchases, 148–152
Home sales, 144–148
HOPE (Helping Outstanding Pupils Educationally) scholarships, 160, 163, 166–167, 331
Household goods, 224
Housing Assistance Tax Act of 2008, 5–6, 136, 146, 149, 151

HSA (health savings account), 76, 177–180
Hybrid vehicle tax credits, 333

I

IFRS (International Financial Reporting Standards), 321
ILIT. *See* Irrevocable life insurance trust (ILIT)
Imputed income, 126, 127
Incentive stock options (ISOs), 49–52, 249, 281–282
  and AMT, 51, 248, 299
Income:
  acceleration, 313
  and AMT, 276
  deferring, 243, 244–245, 275–291, 313
  gross, 327–328
  imputed, 126, 127
  from interest, 47
  ordinary, 52
  retirement, 59–60
  shifting, 170–171, 245–246
  taxable, 334
Income tax, 330
  changes in 2010, 11–16
  and life insurance, 128–130
  marginal rates, 279
  rates, 12
Index funds, 40
Individual retirement accounts. *See* IRAs
Insider, corporate, 282
Installment sales, 283–284
Intentionally defective trust, 206
Interest:
  deductions for, 255
  earned on bonds, 45
  expense, 36–38
  expense on life insurance policy loans, 130
  on home equity loans, 137, 138
  income, 47
  on loans, 38
  mortgage, 136–137
  student loans, 169
  from U.S. savings bonds, 168
International Financial Reporting Standards (IFRS), 321
Investments, 21–58
  interest, 37–38, 257
  life insurance, 114–118
  passive activity, 267
  related expenses, 36–38, 257
  tax issues, 22–26
Investment vehicles, 38–55
Investor, 271
IRAs, 69, 72, 75–76. *See also* Coverdell Education Savings Accounts; Roth IRAs
  and capital gains, 74
  and deferred income, 286
  and education funding, 165–166
  maximum annual contribution, 73–75
  required minimum distributions, 88
Irrevocable life insurance trust (ILIT), 108–109, 111–114, 200–201
ISOs. *See* Incentive stock options (ISOs)
Itemized deductions, 329–330, 336
  miscellaneous, 36, 37
  phaseout in 2010, 12, 23

J

Jewelry and gems, 223
Jobs and Growth Tax Relief Reconciliation Act of 2003, 4, 298, 317

Joint life insurance. *See* Second-to-die insurance

K

Keogh plans, 69, 70–71
Key person life insurance, 120
Kiddie tax, 25, 170, 246, 288, 289

L

Last-in first-out (LIFO) accounting method, 316, 322
Level premium term life insurance, 94–95, 101
Life annuity, 103
Life cycle funds, 40
Life insurance, 93–134. *See also* specific types, i.e. Universal variable life insurance
  beneficiaries, 110–111
  for breadwinners, 99–102
  for businesses and owners, 120–124
  buy-sell agreements, 121–122
  and charitable bequests, 118–119
  and cross-purchase agreements, 122–123
  diversification among carriers, 106
  and dividends, 96–97
  and education expenses, 116
  foreign, 131
  how long to have, 101
  how much to buy, 100
  illustrations, 132–133
  and income taxes, 128–130
  as investment, 114–118
  needs worksheet, 102
  owners, 106–107
  and pension funding, 117–118
  policy selection and servicing, 133
  terminology, 131–132
  trustees and trustee power, 113
  types of, 93–99
  using for estate tax liquidity, 103–106
  valuation of for charitable contribution, 221
  what kind to buy, 105
Lifetime learning credits, 160, 163, 166–167, 331
LIFO (last-in first-out) accounting method, 316, 322
Limited liability company (LLC), 110, 307
Loan regime, 125–126
Loans. *See* specific type, i.e. Home equity loans
Long-term capital gains:
  appreciated property, 262
  changes in 2010, 13
  and charitable donations, 228
  and dividend income, 257
  and income shifting, 170–171
  minimum holding period, 26–27
  on sale of principal residence, 136
  taxes on, 34
Losses, 29, 45. *See also* specific losses, i.e. Passive activity losses
Low-income housing credit, 6
Lump-sum compensation, 277

M

MAGI (modified adjusted gross income), 84, 329
Margin accounts, 36

Marginal income tax rates, 279, 334–337
Margin interest, 137
Marital status, 331
Market value, 224
Marriage penalty, 331, 338–339
Matching contributions, employer, 64
MECs (modified endowment contracts), 129
Medical expenses, 259, 276, 339. *See also* Account-based health-care arrangements
Medicare Prescription Drug, Improvement, and Modernization Act, 177
Military personnel, 5
Minimum depositing, 132
Minimum distributions, 86–90
Minimum tax credits, 50, 299, 331
Miscellaneous deductions, 36, 37, 269–271, 276
Mixed whole-life and term insurance, 97
Modified adjusted gross income. *See* MAGI (modified adjusted gross income)
Modified endowment contracts (MECs), 129
Mortgage insurance, 138
Mortgage insurance/decreasing term, 94
Mortgage points, 149–151
Mortgages:
  foreclosure forgiveness, 14
  interest deductions, 255–256
  interest on, 136–137
  reverse, 152
Motor vehicle tax credits, 333
Moving expenses, 271–272
Muni bonds, 45
Mutual funds, 33, 38–40

N

Net asset value (NAV), 39
Netting rules, 27–28
Net worth, 192
Nongrantor CLT, 205
Nonoperating foundations, 234
Nonqualified deferred compensation plans, 68–69, 123–134
Nonqualified stock options, 48–49
Nonrecourse debt, 43
Notes, 221

O

OID (original issue discount), 47–48
Open-end funds, 39
Operating foundations, 234
Ordinary income, 52
Ordinary life insurance. *See* Whole-life insurance
Original issue discount (OID), 47–48

P

Paintings, 222
Partial exclusion, 145, 146
Partnerships:
  as owner of life insurance, 110
  publicly traded, 42–43, 268
Passive activity:
  interest deductions, 257–258
  investment, 267
  losses, 44–45, 266–268
Pass-through entity, 256–257, 307
Pass-through private foundations, 234

Pension Benefit Guaranty
    Corporation (PBGC), 67
Pension max technique, 102–103
Pension plans. See Defined benefit
    pension plans
Pension Protection Act of 2006,
    65, 81, 157, 264
Pensions, retirement, 102–103,
    117–118
Performance stock, 54
Personal holding company (PHC),
    316–317
Personal interest, 259
Personal residence trust, 143–144
PMI (private mortgage
    insurance), 14
Points. See Mortgage points
Portfolio management, 36, 55–56
Postdeath distribution deferral, 89
Preferred stocks, 41–42
Premiums, life insurance, 131–132
Prepaid tuition plans, 156–158
Principal place of business, 142
Principal residence, 148
Principal residence gains
    exclusion, 144
Private activity bonds, 46, 47
Private equity funds, 42–43
Private foundations, 233–235
    alternatives to, 235–237
    donations of appreciated
        property to, 263
Private mortgage insurance
    (PMI), 14
Private pension, 117
Private placement variable life
    insurance, 115
Private split-dollar
    arrangement, 127
Profit-sharing plans, 64
Property:
    appreciated, 262–263
    business, 13–14
    sale of, 283
Publicly traded partnerships,
    42–43, 45, 268
Put options, 30–31

Q

Qualified appreciated stock,
    230, 263
Qualified dividends, 13, 34, 41
Qualified domestic trust (QDOT),
    206–207
Qualified personal residence
    trust, 202
Qualified retirement plans, 61–68,
    108
Qualified small business stock
    (QSBS), 26, 32
Qualified terminable interest
    property (QTIP) trust, 189
Qualified tuition programs, 196
Quick pay premiums, 131–132
Quid pro quo contributions,
    264–265

R

Real estate:
    depreciated, 26
    property taxes, 255
    rental (See Rental real estate)
    taxes, 148–149
    valuation of for charitable
        contribution, 221–222
Real estate investment trusts
    (REITs), 6, 41
Recapture rules, 228–229
Record keeping, 32–33
Redemption, 122, 318

358 Index

REITS (real estate investment trusts), 6, 41
Rental real estate, 44, 140–141, 268
Restricted stock compensation, 53–55
Restricted stock units (RSUs), 54
Retail property valuation, 218
Retirement assets, 190
Retirement pensions, 102–103, 117–118
Retirement planning, 59–92
   benefits of deductible plans, 70
   and employers, 84
   and self-employment, 69
   tax credit for saving, 81
Retirement plans:
   beneficiaries, 89
   required distributions, 86–90
   year-end planning for business owners, 311–312
Revenue offsets, 304
Reverse mortgages, 152
Risk minimization, 55–56
Roth 401(k), 73
Roth IRAs, 72–73
   changes in 2010, 14–16
   contributions to, 76
   conversions to, 77–81
   and deferred income, 286–287
   distributions, 86, 90
   and education funding, 165
   gifts to, 209
RSUs (restricted stock units), 54

S

Sales price, 37
Sales tax, 330
Savings, education, 155–176
Savings bonds, U.S., 48, 167–168, 284, 290
Savings Incentive Match Plan for Employees. *See* SIMPLE (Savings Incentive Match Plan for Employees)
S corporations, 307, 308, 321–324
Second-to-die insurance, 98–99, 104, 105, 121
Section 501(c)3 organizations, 214–215, 233
Section 529 programs. *See* 529 tuition plans
Section 179 expenses, 309–310
Securities, 32–33, 271
Self-employment:
   deductions, 260
   home office, 140–143
   retirement plans, 69
   taxes, 338
SEPs (Simplified Employee Pension plans), 69, 71–72, 311–312
September 13, 2003, 127–128
SERP (supplemental executive retirement plan), 123
Shareholder split-dollar plan, 126–127
Short sales, 30, 35–36
Short-term capital gains, 247
SIMPLE (Savings Incentive Match Plan for Employees), 62, 67
Simplified Employee Pension plans. *See* SEPs (Simplified Employee Pension plans)
Small Business Act, 25
Small Business and Work Opportunity Tax Act, 50, 309
Social Security, 60, 84–86, 337–338, 341
Sole proprietorship, 307
Split-dollar insurance plans, 124–128, 266

Spouse:
  non-U.S. citizen, 206, 207
  as owner of life insurance, 107
  tax basis step-up, 189
Statement of Value, 222
Stay-at-home caregiver, 100
Step-up allowance, 17, 24, 184, 188, 189, 190
Stock appreciation rights, 54, 281–282
Stock-based compensation, 53–55
Stock options, 38–55, 281–282
  exercise methods, 52–53
  nonqualified, 48–49
  trust, 207
Stocks:
  donation of, 263
  preferred, 41–42
  protecting and postponing gains, 30–31
  restricted, 54
  valuation of, 219–220
Student loans, 169–170, 258
Substantiation, 225–227, 264–265
Succession planning, 317–320
Supplemental executive retirement plan (SERP), 123
Supporting organizations, 235
Surrender of policy, 130
Survivor pension, 102
Survivorship insurance. *See* Second-to-die insurance

T

Taxable bonds, 45–46
Taxable OID bonds, 47
Taxable tax-exempt bonds, 46–47
Tax Act of 2004, 278, 314

Tax credits, 331, 333. *See also* specific type, i.e. Lifetime learning credits
  for first-time homebuyers, 151–152
  for retirement saving, 81
Tax-deferred accounts, 56
Tax-deferred annuities, 82–83
Taxes. *See also* specific taxes, i.e. Estate tax
  advantages of home ownership, 135–153
  breaks for education, 173–174
  deferring, 243–245
  and dividends, 207–208
  and efficient portfolio management, 55–56
  estimated payments, 341–344
  fundamental concepts, 327–346
  individual rates, 7
  looking at the year ahead, 3–9
  marginal and effective rates, 334–337
  preparing for 2010, 11–19
  rates for 2008, 2009, 332
  real estate, 148–149, 255
  recent legislation, 4–6
  reduction strategies, 242–243, 245
  and Section 529 tuition plans, 159
  state and local, 254
  year-end savings strategies, 239–324
Tax-exempt bonds, 45–46, 47
Tax Increase Prevention Act of 2007, 298
Tax Increase Prevention and Reconciliation Act of 2005, 77, 298
Tax Reform Act of 1986, 296
Tax Relief and Health Care Act of 2006, 299, 330

Term life insurance, 94–95
30 percent limitation, 232–233
Three-year rule, 110, 200
Trader, 271
Trading fees, 37
Treasury bills, 282
Trustees:
   investment decisions, 207–208
   and life insurance, 113
Trustee-to-trustee transfer, 69, 78
Trusts, 199–207, 288. *See also* specific type, i.e. Family trust
Tuition payments, 196
Tuition programs, 156–162
20 percent limitation, 233

U

Uniform Gifts To Minors Acts (UGMA), 288
Uniform Transfers to Minors Act (UTMA), 288
Unincorporated business, 256–257
Universal life insurance, 95–96, 105
Universal variable life insurance, 83–84
Unlimited marital deduction, 106
U.S. savings bonds, 48, 167–168, 284, 290

V

Vacation homes, 138–140, 148
Valuation:
   of charitable contributions, 217–224
   discounts, 197–199
   penalties for overstating, 227–228
Vanishing premiums, 131–132
Variable life insurance, 98, 115
Vehicles, used, 223–224, 262, 263
Volunteering expenses, 261

W

Wash sale rule, 29–30
Whole-life and term insurance, 97
Whole-life insurance, 96–97
Wills, 191, 192–193
Withdrawal right, 112

Y

Year-end bonus, 277